CONTENTS

PREFACE

As a teacher–educator, dancer, choreographer, and woman (who is approaching yet another passage of life—reaching "middle-age"), I have begun to do that which dancers are asked not to do: "Think! Don't just do it!" I remember sitting in the office of my dissertation advisor and pondering the question, "How do you think about your body in dance?" I quickly replied, "We don't think about our bodies other than how they perform." Yet, I left his office troubled by the question and even more troubled by my response. Why do we not think about the body in dance in terms other than as an object or instrument of performance? Furthermore, why are we not encouraged to engage in dance in ways other than those reduced to a matter of simple skill development? The limitations of (and sometimes simplistic thinking in) dance have promoted a field that has not considered seriously the cultural and aesthetic assumptions implicit in the ways we think about dance; nor has the field considered how such assumptions affect our teaching and research. This is especially troublesome given that these assumptions are Eurocentric and patriarchal as well as racist and classist. Only recently, for example, have we begun to ask questions concerning the image of the female ballet dancer as Caucasian, fragile, ethereal, virginal, and submissive. Indeed one can argue that much of dance in the professional world has been dominated by such images.

I have come to struggle with such questions in my work as a dance educator in a small, southern, private liberal arts college for women. In my work as an educator, researcher, and choreographer, I question the dominant Western paradigm for teaching dance, which is all too often accepted as the norm. I am not alone in this. Throughout the international dance community, many are beginning to question major assumptions that underlie how we think about, teach, research, create, and appreciate dance. These questions are directed not only toward how dance is taught, researched, and critiqued but also with regard to the cultural and existential purpose of dance as well as the aims of dance education. Simply put, what exactly is the purpose of our teaching, and what are the inherent values that our students are learning?

This book came about through conversations with other dance educators—all of us struggling with what we saw as the too limited discourse of dance education. I met with some of the authors of this book at the international conference of daCi (dance and the Child international). For many of us this was not our first meeting. Yet, over early breakfasts, children's performances, tea breaks, meetings, and formal presentations we heard each other sharing similar concerns about the need for developing a new, more expansive discourse. Such a discourse would need to explore questions of democracy, justice, community, and identity. In addition some of us wanted to try to capture more authentically some of the experiences of *being* a dancer. In our work we found ourselves borrowing critical, social, and cultural theories from other disciplines so that we might go beyond the narrow confine of the limited language of dance. It is out of this struggle that this book was created. I hope that it points the way to a richer, more critical way of understanding the power of dance in the lives of our students.

It goes without saying that this book would not have been possible without the enthusiasm and cooperation of the authors. I thank them for their patience and commitment to this project. I hope that they share the same sense of satisfaction as I do in seeing this work come to fruition. I also would like to acknowledge the contributions of the dance, education, and critical–intellectual communities that have nurtured the ideas and experiences that are embodied in this book. I also want to thank my colleagues and students at Meredith College who have provided me with an environment in which to develop my ideas and practices; Meredith also provided me with a sabbatical leave that enabled me to complete much of the work on this manuscript.

In particular, I am indebted to Sue Stinson who has helped pioneer a vision of dance education that addresses issues of caring and meaning in the world. Sue recognized my questions before I was able to articulate them clearly, and she encouraged me to pursue what I have come to call a critical pedagogy of dance. And to my husband and colleague, Svi Shapiro, who sits with me for hours discussing everyday concerns in relationship to their social and philosophical underpinnings, who changes the bed sheets, critiques my work, and struggles with me to live the ethics that we teach, I thank you.

PRELUDE

Dance education as a discipline and curricular subject cannot forego a critical reflection upon issues of its historical, social, and cultural construction. The contributors to this collection raise just such issues. We believe that a significant number of professionals in the field of dance education, scholarship, and research are ready to "deconstruct" many of the ongoing traditions of dance, yet they have been isolated from one another. This collection is meant to lessen that isolation, and, it is hoped, promote a dialogue for "re-construction." Most important, the dance educators who have contributed to this book hope to provide a powerful new discourse that connects dance and education to critical, social, and cultural concerns. The authors not only provide an understanding of the political and moral influences that shape the aesthetic of dance, but they also provide us with ways in which we can begin to reenvision dance as a practice of hope and possibility in a postmodern world. In a sense, this is a book that opens a dialogue toward transforming our understanding of dance and its connections to the broader questions of human existence.

This book is written for those who are teaching in the field of dance, whether their focus is philosophy, research, pedagogy, choreography, technique, history, or appreciation. Readers involved in cultural and feminist studies can see how cultural values are "embodied"—a process well described by many of the authors in this volume. In particular, the authors articulate how the image of the dancer and the institution of Dance represents western European hierarchical values and traditions. This book also is intended for other arts educators, classroom teachers, and community educators, as questions are raised concerning the place of the body in transformative forms of education as well as the relationship of other art disciplines to dance performance and the larger community.

This collection gives particular attention to the feminist critique of dance and reflects upon the present, "what is," and the possibilities of the future, "what should be." The chapters are written by practicing dance educators from the United States, England, Canada, New Zealand, and Brazil. Their work reflects the influences of the broader development of critical and postmodern theories and draws upon neo-Marxist perspectives, feminist theory, and Paulo Freire's work in critical pedagogy. The book includes autobiographical reflections in curriculum and research, consideration of issues of power and values in teaching, cultural diversity, and the place of dance in interdisciplinary education. The strength and unity of the collection is in the nature of the authors speaking from their considerable experience as teachers, researchers, and dancers.

At the center of this work is a questioning of traditional practices in the pedagogy and curriculum of dance and a concern with dance as liberating possibility, bridging critical questioning to creative empowerment. This collection of essays grew out of a desire to recreate dance so that it responds to questions of global healing and social transformation and enhances the possibilities for dance to participate in cultural communication and dialogue. The end of each chapter includes the sections "Critical Reflections" and "Take a Moment to Reflect." I have sought, here, to create a place for dialogue to begin in relationship to the ideas presented in each chapter. As such the questions asked are meant to encourage the interweaving of thoughtful reflection, intellectual inquiry, and personal narrative.

Many of the contributors use somatics as a starting point for further inquiry. Somatics, which generally includes several body-mind and mind-body practices, acknowledges the complex interdependence among the mind, the physical body, and social and behavioral expectations of both the mind and body. Such consideration can inform dance education and dance theory given, on the one hand, the dominance of masculine, authoritative figures in mainstream formal dance education and theory, and, on the other hand, the significant (and increasing) participation of those who are neither masculine nor authoritative—women, children, indigenous cultures, the elderly—in all aspects of dance and dance education. This is particularly striking in dance education for the nonprofessional dancer (see especially chapters 4 and 7). Acknowledging the importance—or even very existence—of the body also forms the basis for the feminist and critical perspectives in this book.

The book is divided into three sections. Part I, *Foundations*, introduces the reader to foundational questions concerning curriculum, pedagogy, and research. In the first two chapters, the authors integrate questions of power, identity, gender, and cultural difference in dance pedagogy. In chapter 1 the nature of dance itself is "problematized." Here, influenced by feminist and postmodern theories, a discourse for an "embodied" pedagogy is offered, that is, one that taps into the emotional mapping of the lives we live within a social context. My attempt, as author, is to provide ways of understanding how this deeper reality of feeling can be used to develop a critical understanding of the relationships between self and culture. Drawing on Marxist aesthetics I connect philosophy and practice and the cementing of purpose and action. I contextualize this through a brief retelling of how I struggled to develop a curriculum program for dancers in my college that speaks to a philosophy of education concerned with not simply understanding the world but changing it.

Sue Stinson continues this dialogue in chapter 2. She takes the reader through an autobiographical journey of her own deeper questions concerning myths perpetuated in creative dance, which all too often presents "images of bright and happy children, running and skipping joyfully, seemingly untouched by poverty, hunger, homelessness, or any other realities with which so many children live." She questions who the children and adults that participate in dance will become, and she reflects upon the relationship between what we believe and the consequences of the choices we make as individuals and as educators.

In chapter 3 Sylvie Fortin presents findings from a series of in-depth case studies of three women modern dance teachers who have an extensive background in somatics and dance science. Central to this chapter is the question of the empowerment of teachers and the deleterious effects of hierarchical authority. The pedagogic practices of traditional dance classes are challenged, which reinforce a conception of human beings as world "receivers" rather than "creators." This study follows the story of these three women and how their teaching practices exemplify a break from these traditions.

While part I sets out to ask broad questions concerning the philosophy of pedagogy in dance, part II, *Telling Stories*, presents personal stories that place these broader questions in the context of specific situations. In chapter 4 Jan Bolwell discusses issues facing dance educators in the context of her own country, New Zealand, where they are involved with the inclusion of the Maori culture into the standard curriculum. Bolwell argues for a model that expands our vision for dance education by connecting the inclusion of the native culture with the need for interdisciplinary institutional and curricular structures. Her voice joins others who recognize that separate subject areas and fragmented curriculum models maintain an education that treats and values knowledge as disparate and unconnected. She argues for the necessity to research curriculum models that prepare performing arts educators through interdisciplinary study, where some generic basis exists across performing arts disciplines. This sort of training, she asserts, will enrich the teaching of the individual disciplines of music, dance, and drama and strengthen the position of dance by decreasing its isolation from the other arts.

Chapter 5 tells a personal story of what it means to "live out" one's life as a southern female with a history of childhood abuse who is a wife, mother, educator, and dancer. Sondra Sluder tells a story of courage and of "remembering of the body"; of the women in our lives; and of the potential of dance to bridge communities, destroy ignorance, and eliminate prejudice. She addresses the power of dance as an art form that can bring a sense of wholeness through the mind–body connection, resulting in a process that is at once healing, educational, and empowering.

In chapter 6, the focus is on authority and power. In this interpretive research work, Clyde Smith deconstructs the dance technique class by examining abuse of authority by the teacher and questioning how students are complicit in this process of abuse by their own submission. He analyzes the relationship between the dance class and Michel Foucault's notions of social coercion and surveillance directed in and through the body/subject, and he finds similarities between the behaviors in a dance class and Arthur

Deikman's identification of cult behavior characteristics. Noting that certainly not all dance classes and dance instructors are the same as those discussed here, Smith suggests nonetheless that many teachers are unknowingly complicit.

Part III, *Writing New Stories*, discusses the role of dance within the broader political and social arena. Through project descriptions this section focuses on the traditions of dance aesthetics and master-narratives. In chapter 7 Christine Lomas takes up the question of the aesthetic value given to Dance Art. Her essay is based on her involvement with the work of "Jabadeo," a community-based dance company in West Yorkshire, England, which prioritizes disenfranchised groups such as the elderly, people with mental and physical disabilities, and those isolated in their homes or in residential care. Lomas questions established aesthetic codes and ponders why community-based dance work such as Jabadeo's is admired and supported and yet simultaneously devalued by those who uphold the notion of Dance Art. She challenges the way in which we have been "culturally structured" to appreciate dance, and she suggests another vision that values intent and context as well as content and form.

Isabel Marques, in the final chapter, delves into questions concerning the relationship between dance and dance education in Western postmodern society. She looks at the field of dance education and considers how the master-narratives concerning the education of a dancer isolate the dancer from making connections between dance and society. Marques proposes a different approach to dance education and questions those who have been her own "masters": Rudolph Laban and Paulo Freire.

The authors in part III bring to our attention the possibility for an aesthetic language that goes beyond the language of dance to one of human concern and civic responsibility. I hope that the essays in this book stimulate us all to begin to redefine our own visions of the power and potential of dance.

PART I

FOUNDATIONS

TOWARD TRANSFORMATIVE TEACHERS: CRITICAL AND FEMINIST PERSPECTIVES IN DANCE EDUCATION

SHERRY B. SHAPIRO

Professor of Dance and Education, Meredith College

The author reflects on the development of a curriculum and pedagogy for dance education that incorporate concerns for issues of power, identity, gender, and cultural differences. The ideas presented here arose from her work as coordinator of the dance education program at a private, southern, liberal arts college for women. The author weaves together her own struggles to make problematic (i.e., call into question) the nature of dance itself as well as the purpose of dance as an educational experience. Central to this discussion are issues of imagination, creativity, and an attention to "body memories" that can lead women to a more critical understanding of their lives in dance and in their culture.

Collective sharing of experience is the source of knowledge.
—(*Weiler 1991, 467*)

I recall this statement in relationship to an experience shared with me by one of my students, who was substitute teaching at an area high school. Angie's story goes like this: "Dr. Shapiro, you won't believe what happened yesterday at the high school. I was walking down the hall toward the Home Economics classroom I was substituting in, and all these students came running toward me. They were screaming, panicked. Then I saw a student at the end of the hall waving a gun around. I got the students into the classroom, and we began to talk about what they had experienced, what was happening, how they felt about it, and why. I remembered why it was important to do this."

This dance education student's recognition of the need to open the space for her students' struggle to understand, that is, to make sense of, their own lives and experiences is profoundly connected to both critical and feminist pedagogical perspectives (Greene 1988, 120). It is through the critical process of reflecting upon "lived experiences" that students can interpret the individual and social relationships in which they interact and can begin to understand their own power to reshape and recreate those relationships, hence, their own lived world. Instead of sitting her students down to a textbook, Angie encouraged the students to examine what had just happened in order to illuminate the social processes, events, and ideology that shape an event and our experience of it (Weiler 1991, 466). The individual experience is also a collective experience. Angie, my student, had been able to translate her understanding of a critical and feminist pedagogy of dance to the situation at hand.

We are living in a time of educational, epistemological, and pedagogical turmoil. Through the process of "problematizing" (calling into question) authority, power, and identity and examining issues of gender, class, race, sexual preference, and cultural difference, certainties about reality and truth are being challenged. A vision that validates difference, denies universal claims to truth, and seeks to empower people for social transformation is emerging out of this challenge to the Western epistemological dominance in our educational institutions. Central to this critique is a renewed attention to the body.

This recent shift has not gone unnoticed in dance education. As a white Southern feminist writing and teaching in the traditions of both critical and feminist theory, I have been in the process of developing a curriculum and pedagogy for dance education that has arisen out of my own struggles to name, or make problematic, the nature of dance itself as well as the purpose of dance as an educational experience. All of this work has been inspired by Paulo Freire (1988) and other critical pedagogues who have called upon educators to redefine the purpose and practices of education in all of its concerns. They demand an education that is focused on human praxis—the thoughtful and conscious struggle to reshape our world into one that is more just and compassionate. This notion is joined to a feminist pedagogy that insists that education must start from the lived experiences of our students' lives. As Sue Middleton (1994) expresses it, a feminist pedagogy requires us as teachers to explore with our students our individual biographies, historical events, and the power relations that have shaped and constrained our lives. Out of these critical and feminist perspectives, my work concerns itself with a number of questions: What kind of human and social vision impels our educational work? How can we understand through our *embodied knowledge* what it might mean to live freer and more empowered lives? How can we redefine aesthetic education so that it becomes relevant to the struggle for a more just and loving existence? This chapter explores these questions from the perspective of my own experiences in developing a pedagogy for dance education, K-12, at a private Southern liberal arts college for women where I am the Coordinator for Teacher Certification in Dance.

BREAKING THE MOLD

Let me begin with a story. As I shared in the preface, I was sitting in the office of one of my doctoral professors one day having a discussion about the meaning of dance when he asked me, "How do you think about your body [as a dancer]?" My immediate response was "I don't think about my body." After reflecting a bit I continued, "Well, you know in dance the body is really only thought about in technical terms, that is, how well you do something technically." It was only later in my studies that I realized the truth of what I had said, stated from my own lived experience of dance. The body for the dancer was a tool, an instrument objectified for the benefit of the dance. I have developed this more fully in Taylor [Shapiro] 1991a.

What I did not understand at the time of my conversation with my professor was the possibility for the body to be understood as subject—that is, that which holds the memory of one's life, a body that defines one's racial identity, one's gender existence, one's historical and cultural grounding, indeed the very materiality of one's existence. This body that I had treated as an object to perfect both visually and technically can be a rich source of knowledge. As Susan Bordo states, "the body is seen instead as the vehicle of the human making and remaking of the world, constantly shifting location, capable of revealing endlessly new `points of view' on things" (1990, 144). Taking issue with the objectification of the body in dance led me deeper into reflection on the purpose of dance in education and the role of dance in society.

One of the important dimensions in feminist research is the salience of the lived experiences of women. The subjects of feminist study, women's ideas and concerns, are taken seriously. The subjects speak in their own voice and interpret experiences through their own knowledge. They are understood as knowing subjects (Thomas 1993, 75). Why mention research at this point? Because the aim of such a methodology is to examine critically the social and cultural forces and discourses of power that construct our being in the world. Feminist research reflects the earlier intentions of feminism to "raise consciousness" for the purpose of understanding and making change possible. In pedagogy it translates into a student-centered approach where personal experience is validated and provides a core from which students can reflect critically on their experiences in relationship to the world in which they find themselves. The second major point of this methodology is the revelation of the researcher as an active agent in what comes to be known. In contrast to positivistic research, the feminist researcher's own concerns and experiences are taken into account. Clearly my own dance and teaching experiences shape the reflective questions I ask my students. Furthermore, I understand the limitations of my experiences, or as Sue Middleton calls it my "life history" (1994, 140). This recognition of how one's personal experiences shape one's critical thinking is directly linked to issues of cultural diversity. With the discovery of voice and relational and situational knowing, a realization also is made of the multiplicity and plurality of human experience. How can we have both equality and distinction? How can one find one's own voice and create a self in the midst of other selves? How, asks Maxine Greene, "in educating for freedom can we create and maintain a common world?" (1988, 116). How does the purpose of dance education connect to issues of human freedom and a common world?

EMBODIMENT OF THE IDEOLOGY

I had never before questioned the relationship I had to my own body, the objectification of my body, or the abstraction of my own life experiences in dance until I began to question the traditionally held notions of the body as an object in dance. I had never considered how the body is inscribed through power relations in the way Michel Foucault (1993) describes (as cited in Ramazonogle), or how, as Sondra Fraleigh (1987) ponders, the lived body is experienced in dance. From these reflections I began to redefine the purpose of dance, moving from a technical language to one concerned with human liberation. My guidelines came from my own experiences and those of critical and feminist scholars.

By resisting the objectification of the body I began to understand the body as a site for critical reflection on one's life. My intention became to relate movement vocabulary to the students' experiences whether in preschool or senior grade levels. Building on the work of Sue Stinson (1988), I sought ways to connect the movement curriculum to students' lives, utilizing dance as a vehicle for self- and social understanding. Yet, as a dancer and choreographer, I also understood the importance of nurturing the imaginative and creative components of dance. But here, unlike in much artistic discussion and writing that narrowly defines imagination and creativity in terms of artistic ability, these human capacities are understood in a much broader sense. They are revealed as the underlying power to reenvision and recreate the world in which we live. I have written elsewhere about my development of a choreographic process that addresses my critical and feminist pedagogic concerns (Shapiro and Shapiro 1995). Such a critical and feminist pedagogic perspective demands that a much greater value be placed on the development of the imagination and creative powers. They can now be understood as powers that are no longer bound to the stage, the canvas, or the stone but as powers released into the world as expressions of who we are *and* who we want to become. My belief in the valuing of childhood imagination and creativity became a major component of my philosophical commitments. I began to know the power of dance, not as a form of entertainment, not for self-esteem or even self-actualization, and not as a grooming tool, but for its possibilities for enriching students' critical, creative, and moral capacities. Through becoming a feminist, I began to develop a program for certification in dance education (Bartky 1990). Following is a brief description of some of the premises of feminist and critical philosophies that I used to structure my program of study.

INTEGRATING KNOWLEDGE: SELF, DANCE, AND TEACHING

> All knowledge is constructed, and the knower is an intimate part of the
> known.   (Belenky et al. 1986, 137)

The act of coming to know is a passionate one. Belenky et al. (1986) write about the act of making the unconscious conscious; consulting and listening to the self; voicing the unsaid; listening to others; staying alert to all the currents and undercurrents of life; and imagining what could or should be, in terms of self, other, or world. All become an integrated force that enters the knower into a union with that which is to be known. Such a union implies an act of responding with sensitivity to situations and the contextualizing of thoughts, feelings, and ideas. In the act of responding one also takes responsibility for one's opinions. An opinion is more than an exercise of intellect; it is a commitment, something to live by (149). Implied is a moral response. The nature of the act of knowing can be understood as one that involves the heart and the mind situated in the realm of morality.

In feminist education, the traditional "mind training" pedagogy that relies on abstract knowledge and the regurgitation of memory must be challenged. To impart a feminist pedagogy, body knowledge as understood in the sense of "body memories" must be included. Body memories are indeed that which hold life experiences; to remember my father is to remember the stature and power he presented as he returned home at five o'clock each day in his dark suit, pressed white shirt, and tie just as my mother finished setting the dinner table with the evening meal, always scheduled exactly to meet his arrival and awaiting his placement at the head of the table. To define a leap is to express a bodily feeling expressing contradictory modes of being—that of being grounded and that of being free—representing our desires to have both. To recall the smell of school cafeteria food is to remember myself as a child in training: to be on time, stay in a straight line, sit still, eat quickly, refrain from doodling or daydreaming. I was in training to be a "good girl" who knows how to follow the rules, makes no waves, and views my body as something to be managed. To live with, in, and through my female body is to do so in relationship to objectified images of women found in fashion magazines, on the street, and imaged on our television sets.

Our bodies provide an emotional mapping of who we are and how we have been shaped by the dominant society. The exploration of body memories or feelings, as Audre Lorde suggests, can lead us to both analysis and action (Weiler 1991, 464). Lorde insists that the deeper reality of feeling is closer in touch with what it means to be human. She questions the depth of critical understanding that depends upon the rational or abstract methods of knowing. Like Freire, Lorde retains a faith in the possibility that human beings can create new ways of being in the world out of our collective struggle and a human capacity to feel (464). Kathleen Weiler states that "this validation of feeling can be used to develop powerful sources of politically focused feminist education" (465). Women need to examine what they have lived in concrete ways in their own bodies.

I am reminded of a recent incident when a dance educator who was taking a summer course I teach, called "Bodies of Knowledge: Narrative of the Self," asked rhetorically, "What am I supposed to do with these students on the last days of classes? I can't get them to do anything. They are so wild." I responded by suggesting that she have them create movements about their feelings on school ending, about leaving their fifth grade (10 to 11 years old) class, and about how this experience of ending or finality is also reflected in other "out of the classroom" experiences. Her frustration at trying to "get them to learn" the stated curriculum out of context (i.e., apart from their everyday lives) is often the tradition in education and in dance. When looked at critically we begin to understand that our educational systems do little in the ways of relational knowing, in connecting students' lives to the curriculum, in valuing students' voices, in processing self- and social understanding in relationship to the dominant ideology, or in assisting in their development as critical and creative human beings concerned with broader social issues. These questions helped formulate my vision of a dance education program that is concerned with empowering students within a liberatory pedagogy.

STRUCTURING THE PROGRAM: THREE CONCERNS

In structuring my program, I began with a premise taken from creative dance that focuses on the child as a creator. Pulling from my knowledge of critical and feminist perspectives, three areas of concern needed to be addressed. The first of these concerns entails a vision for dance education. Such a vision draws from my own experiences of dance as a process of liberation. As a woman I felt freed, powerful, and in control of my own body when dancing. Yet when understood in "real-life" situations, dancing did nothing to change my life or the social or political world in which I lived. I began to question, "How can dance become a liberatory pedagogy?"

TOWARD A CRITICAL VISION FOR DANCE

Taking from critical pedagogy I began to connect the Laban Movement Framework (a movement vocabulary mandated by the North Carolina Public School System as the curriculum base for dance education in public schools) with students' experiences, both in feeling and action. Weaving together the movement vocabulary with students' concerns, experiences, fears, and dreams in the real world, students were able to explore self, other, and the world through movement. For example, in exploring the movement concept of time, a lesson plan may be developed to teach qualities of quick and slow. Students are directed through warm-ups, combinations, and explorations, which have them experience quick and slow movements; and they are asked to describe "what happens in the body" when moving quickly and slowly. Connecting to how students experience time depends of course on their age, but imagine for a moment that you are working with high school students. You might encourage them to think reflectively about their own lives and the social construction of time by asking them to articulate (as you write what they say on the board) phrases we all use to denote time (e.g., "killing time," "saving time," "time on my hands," "spending time," "time limits," "out of time," "all the time," "being on time"). From these phrases, they explore two or three examples, "set" their improvisations, and share them as informal compositions. Pedagogically, the important part of the lesson is to follow the compositions with a discussion that helps students to think critically about the issue of time and make connections to their own experiences. Several issues could be chosen as the focus. I have taught this lesson choosing to discuss the relationship between language and life, or how we can come to understand our cultural values through the metaphors we use. In this discussion we examined how we experience time as a commodity and then further explored notions of "having" and "being" in a consumption-driven culture.

A liberatory pedagogy demands self-exploration by the teacher as well as by the students. This process of self-exploration, or *currere*, as William Pinar (1978) names it, is a model for curriculum that involves both the teacher and the student in remembering their experiences with as little editing as possible (Taylor [Shapiro] 1991b, 144). It is both personal, in that it turns inward for reflection, and social, as this affective insight is reconnected to being in the world. The quest is not to surrender to the subjective; instead the project is to formalize the life–world. The attempt is to constitute a human being who is educated in the process of critical reflection for the purpose of self-understanding, who is therefore capable of conscious choice. When connected to the notion of a liberatory education, self-exploration becomes a means of respeaking with the heart's core in a voice that speaks from lived experience.

What many critical educators have helped us to understand is no teaching is value-free. We must therefore seek to understand the "hidden curriculum"—that is, *all* the things that are learned within a teaching–learning situation, from whose history is told in our textbooks to what gender, class, or ethnicity is most valued in the classroom or dance studio. All education involves the teaching of a moral and political point of view. So the search begins with the self: What do I believe in? What kind of world should this be? What do I value in human existence? In my own vision, the purpose of education is *not simply to understand the world but to change it*. It is the radicalization of reason that includes the aesthetic as a contributor to the possibility of human transformation.

THE IMPORTANCE OF EMBODIED KNOWING

The second area of concern in structuring a dance education program is the body. Terry Eagleton writes that "there is something in the body which can revolt against power which inscribes it" (1990, 28). Paradoxically dance is about the body and not about the body. Dance education is about body movement in relationship to a movement framework, yet it has not taken seriously the connection between body movement in relationship to the child's life. As mentioned earlier, the body in feminist and postmodern

theorizing comes to be seen as the personal material on which inscriptions or particular discourses of the culture have become embedded. To read the body in dance education is to see the values of the culture from whence it comes. In Western traditions, the body in dance is discussed in terms of size, shape, technique, flexibility, and life (that is of the body). It is a biological and physiological object.

Contrary to Western traditions, I see the body first as a subject inscribed by the cultural meanings and values of our time. The body is a vehicle for understanding oppression, resistance, and liberation. This shift from dis-embodied knowing to embodied knowing calls into question traditional dance pedagogy. The question of knowledge changes the relationship between the teacher and the student. The intent of the learning experience moves from one of learning movement vocabulary for the sake of creating dance to gaining an understanding of the self, others, and the larger world for the possibility of change.

As a teacher–educator I am concerned with teaching my dance education students how to address issues of difference with sensitivity. I share with them the book, *People*, by Peter Spier. This book is filled with pages of different images of human beings, from the shape of their eyes, noses, and hair styles to their chosen dress, religious beliefs, and architecture. The message in the book is a simple but important one for young children: Difference is better; sameness is boring. Children must learn to show respect for diversity. After looking through the book we engage in a dialogue about how they, as dance educators, can develop a lesson plan using this book with young children to discuss and create movements attending to issues of difference and furthermore how we create the notion of people whom we consider to be "other." I encourage my students to think about what kind of experiences their dance students might have had, what are the important cultural messages they want their students to consider, and what is appropriate for their students developmentally.

One of the lesson plans created by my students used the movement concept of shape and the body concept of noses. Children gave descriptive words for noses, such as long, short, broad, and thin. Next, the teacher directed them in exploring shapes using their words. "Runny noses" was used to develop locomotor movements that could represent either "slow, runny noses" or "oozing, runny noses" (not too appetizing for adults, yet very fun for young children). The final dance phrase was shape, move, shape, move, and ending shape. Bringing the class to closure was a return to both the movement concept of shape and the cultural concept of diversity.

For high school young women (ages 14 through 18), a generative theme is one of body image. My dance education students and I discussed images of women in magazines and what cultural values those images reflect. I asked them to design a lesson plan for an improvisation with high school students that was based on images of women's bodies and provided an opportunity for critical dialogue revealing the harmful effects of those images. They were to include a written body reflection in which the high school students would be asked to see their bodies in their minds and write a description of the body part on which they focused the most in that mental image. From these reflections, the high school students used their descriptions to explore movement qualities and create compositions. Again, the class ended with the students voicing their thoughts and feelings through a dialogue directed by the teacher, which helped to make the students more aware of issues of anorexia and bulimia and to question why we live in a culture that values this particular image of women as thin. Remember that the discussion is always directed by the particular issues brought up by the students themselves. The teacher then draws their attention through thoughtful reflection to a broader class analysis of the relationship of their experiences to the broader culture. The issues of cliques, competition, violence, and machismo are examples of relevant themes from which I have developed curriculum for fifth grade students.

A dance educator was taking my Theory and Methods of Teaching Dance class. One night in class she said, "Wow! This opens up a whole new world of curriculum." Students' lives become the core of the curriculum; the content of study becomes the vehicle for critical reflection and understanding. Yes, *it is* a whole new world of curriculum concerned with "poetic justice" and a radical act of love needed to express human solidarity and bring mutual relationship to life. It is, as Sharon Welch (1985) terms it, "a poetics of revolution," speaking our souls, our desires for wholeness, mutuality, and self-transcendence.

Life is a principle, not a thing. The body is not life; it is a manifestation of life. In touching and being touched the body stores memories of human connection. Loving touch bears with it the hope for sisterhood and brotherhood. With love we affirm and are affirmed. In the sociopolitical struggle against death from hunger, disease, exploitation, war, destruction of the earth, and hopelessness a great and growing need exists for our capacity to become "body-full" with love (Taylor [Shapiro] 1991b).

"A recovery of the importance of the body has been one of the most precious achievements of recent radical thought." (Eagleton 1990, 7)

EDUCATING FOR WHAT PURPOSE?

The third concern in my program is to address the question: What are we teaching for? What kind of human action is implied by the way in which we teach dance to young children? In critical educational scholarship a thorough distinction has been made between "schooling" and education. In education the question of being—or how one lives in the world—is central. The shift from epistemologically oriented knowing to ontological knowing reasserts the connection between education and the reality one lives. Again it is the reality we experience that education must address and redress. Like changing clothes, education must look into the social mirror and recognize the relationship between what our social values are and what we are teaching. And it must do so with the notion of cleaning out the closet; attending to what we choose to replace it with; and considering what effects this cleansing has on us, others, and the larger world. In a poignant song sung by Sweet Honey In the Rock, they question the buying of clothes produced in third-world countries in factories where children, young people, and women are exploited. We, too, must ask ourselves, "Are our hands clean?"

I have touched briefly thus far on aspects of both critical and feminist pedagogy. Together they share a belief in each person's ability to understand and critique her or his own experiences and social reality, and that is what any project of pedagogical and social transformation rests upon (Weiler 1988, 23). What is significant is the belief in the capacity of individuals to act upon and react to the social world they inhabit. From this perspective, education is viewed as praxis, as an emancipatory act that answers my third concern. Maxine Greene reiterates this concept, stating, "I have been concerned with finding ways of arousing students from submergence, awakening them to critical consciousness and to the possibility of 'praxis' in a world they share" (1981, 303).

Freedom is a way of living—a praxis as the possibility of giving meaning to one's life through a process of making connections. Praxis, in the critical sense, is a bonding between the two faces of thinking and being—a "moral cementing" as thinking and feeling combine in an impassioned understanding of human concern. David Purpel provides insight into the critical, creative, and moral aspects of education:

> Indeed, the essence of education can be seen as critical, in that its purpose is to help us see, hear, and experience the world more clearly, completely, and with more understanding.... Another vital aspect of the educational process is the development of creativity and imagination, which enables us not only to understand but to build, make, create, and re-create our world.... We are talking about a vision that can illuminate what we are doing and what we might achieve.... The questions of what our vision is and should be are in fact the most crucial and basic questions that we face. (1988, 26-27)

CONCLUSION

And so I end where I began. Arts education can be a place where students make connections between the personal and the social; develop their perceptual, imaginative, and sensual abilities; find their own voices; validate their feelings and capacity for compassion; and become empowered through affirmation of their ability to be co-creators of their world. As I come to understand the power of dance education to be a transformative experience, I become more convinced that dance educators have been given a unique gift. We have the opportunity to work with young children in ways that affirm their identities; challenge their taken-for-granted assumptions (Greene 1978); and impart a way of being in the world that is compassionate, critical, creative, and bound to a vision for social justice. This is an aesthetic rooted in a transformative sensibility (Marcuse 1969). And the beautiful is an essential quality of freedom where "the form of freedom is not merely self-determination and self-realization, but rather the determination and realizations of goals which enhance, protect, and unite life on earth" (Marcuse 1969, 46). And the beautiful, here, leaves behind a notion of abstract ethereal beauty and replaces it with one that belongs in the realm of sensuous liberation. Arts education, then, becomes revolutionary as it shows us reality—the "what is" of our lives—in ways that heighten our perception of reality and present images to us of "what should be."

Throughout the courses I teach, from Dance Appreciation, Dance Technique, Choreography, and Theory and Methods of Dance to Social Foundations of American Education and Curriculum Development, a common thread can be found that weaves together the critical, creative, and moral dimensions of feminist and critical pedagogy as a process for human liberation with concern for all living things. What I have experienced in working with women pursuing teacher certification in dance has been meaningful and transformative for them and for me. My work has produced a constant dialogue traveling in and out of our lives together, our wounds and diseases, as well as our hopes and dreams. As I finished working with my last choreographic project, "Eating," which focused on women's relationship to food, I was reminded that dancing is a process of liberation, a constant struggle for freedom that holds together the possibility to break with a reified notion of dance. Through dance, the body can move with passionate commitment to one's life and responsibility to others and the larger world.

Critical Reflections

This chapter raised several important questions concerning the philosophy and pedagogy of dance education. Beginning with a critique of the European paradigm usually implicit in dance education, the text made connections between how we structure what the dance experience is to be and what it is that students learn. We must give greater attention to the underlying vision or philosophy that shapes dance education. In particular, we must look more carefully at how we think of and value "the body" in dance. Do we see it merely as an object for perfection? Perhaps we have come to a necessary juncture in dance where we must engage in our own re-search to discover the true nature of dance and its role in the wider culture. We must question our values and how our beliefs are transmitted to our students. Are students learning to simply regurgitate what the teacher knows or teaches? What is the role of dance in society? Does dance, as an institution, have any responsibility to the dancers or the dance?

Whether you accept or reject ideas presented in this chapter, it is important that you evaluate the philosophy or purpose by which you teach, dance, create, write, or research.

Take a Moment to Reflect

Read the following questions keeping in mind your own work and experience in the field of dance. Write freely as you record your responses. It may be helpful to focus on one experience as you reflect on your responses to these questions.

1. Why do you dance (or why is dance important to you)?
2. From your experience in dance, what messages have you received that affected your understanding of the human body?

3. Does dance need to have an underlying vision? If so, should this vision be an ethical or social one?

4. Considering your role as a teacher, what cultural values (if any) should you impart to your students?

5. In your dance experience, what have been the implicit messages about masculine and feminine roles?

6. Do teachers of dance, or of the arts in general, have any particular responsibilities toward their students?

In chapter 2, Sue Stinson elaborates on some of the issues raised in this chapter. Her story concerns her struggles with the limitations of and possibilities for children's dance within the context of feminist theories.

REFERENCES

Bartky, S. 1990. *Femininity and Domination*. New York: Routledge, Chapman, and Hall.

Belenky, M., B. Clinchy, N. Goldberg, and J. Tarule. 1986. *Women's Ways of Knowing*. New York: Basic Books.

Bordo, S. 1990. "Feminism, Postmodernism, and Gender-Skepticism." In *Feminism/ Postmodernism*, L. Nicholson (ed.). New York: Routledge, Chapman, and Hall.

Eagleton, T. 1990. *The Ideology of the Aesthetic*. Cambridge, MA: Blackwell.

Fraleigh, S. 1987. *Dance and the Lived Body*. Pittsburgh: University of Pittsburgh Press.

Freire, P. 1988. *Pedagogy of the Oppressed*. New York: Continuum.

Greene, M. 1978. *Landscapes of Learning*. New York: Teachers College Press.

———. 1981. "The Humanities and Emancipatory Possibility." *Journal of Education*, 163(4): 287-305.

———. 1988. *The Dialectic of Freedom*. New York: Teachers College Press.

Marcuse, H. 1969. *An Essay on Liberation*. Boston: Beacon Press.

Middleton, S. 1994. *Educating Feminists*. New York: Teachers College Press.

Pinar, W. 1978. "Currere: Towards Reconceptualization." In *Curriculum and Introduction to the Field*, I. Gress, Jr. and D.E. Purpel (eds.). Berkeley, CA: McCutchan.

Purpel, D. 1988. *The Moral and Spiritual Crisis in Education*. Granby, MA: Bergin & Garvey.

Ramazanogle, C., (ed.) 1993. *Up Against Foucault*. London: Routledge & Kegan Paul.

Shapiro, S. and Shapiro, S. 1995. "Silent Voices, Bodies of Knowledge: Towards a Critical Pedagogy of the Body." *Journal for Curriculum Theorizing* 11 (1): 49-72.

Spier, P. 1980. *People*. New York: Doubleday.

Stinson, S. 1988. *Dance for Young Children*. Reston, VA: Alliance for Health, Recreation and Dance.

Taylor [Shapiro], S. 1991a. "Dance in a Time of Social Crisis: Towards a Transformational View of Dance Education." In *Proceedings of the 1991 Conference of Dance and the Child International*, S. Stinson (ed.). Salt Lake City: University of Utah.

———. 1991b. "Reclaiming Our Bodies: Towards a Sentient Pedagogy of Liberation." Ph.D. dissertation, University of North Carolina-Greensboro.

Thomas, H. 1993. *Dance, Gender and Culture*. New York: St. Martin's Press.

Weiler, K. 1988. *Women Teaching for Change*. Granby, MA: Bergin & Garvey.

———. 1991. "A Feminist Pedagogy of Difference." *Harvard Educational Review* 61 (4): 449-474.

Welch, S. 1985. *Communities of Solidarity and Resistance*. New York: Orbis Books.

CHAPTER 2

SEEKING A FEMINIST PEDAGOGY FOR CHILDREN'S DANCE

SUSAN W. STINSON

Department of Dance, University of North Carolina at Greensboro

This chapter documents an autobiographical journey as well as a theoretical framework for a feminist pedagogy for children's dance. Using lenses of feminist and critical theory, the author offers a critique of both traditional dance pedagogy and creative dance pedagogy as well as a feminist critique of critical pedagogy. Stinson concludes with some suggestions for incorporating feminist values into teaching dance to children and adolescents, as well as some unresolved issues. An earlier version of this paper was published in 1993 (Stinson 1993a).

I cannot remember when I first heard the truism, "What we teach is who we are." Our shared sociocultural experiences and our unique personal experiences construct the selves that we become and that we share in teaching. Some educational theorists (Greene 1973, 1978; Pinar 1988) have noted the importance of reflection upon how our experience has shaped what we believe and why and how we both participate in and resist the shaping of our beliefs. Similarly, some feminist educators (e.g., Grumet 1988) advocate revealing our own subjectivity in our work, bringing the personal (often considered "feminine") into public discourse (often considered more "masculine").

It is in this spirit that I share my own story of becoming—and continuing to become—a dance educator and a feminist. I do not think that this is my story alone because I know that the forces that have affected my own experience and thinking have also affected those of other dance educators, regardless of whether they have come to the same conclusions. In other words, the *I* that makes this my own experience is an *I* shaped by sociocultural influences.

PERSONAL AND THEORETICAL CONTEXT

Except for one year of ballet as a child, I began my dance studies at the relatively late age of 16. When I entered college I alternated modern dance classes with other highly physical activities, primarily as a form of release from academic pressures. I studied dance more regularly but still avocationally during my last two years of college while I pursued a major in sociology. I abandoned my intentions of becoming a social worker at the end of my senior year. As a white middle class woman in 1968, I felt incapable of making a difference in the urban areas of the United States where riots were a regular weekend event. I decided to be a teacher instead of a social worker, and the only subject I loved enough to teach was dance. This led me to graduate school in dance, a modest amount of performing, and teaching children; eventually I was hired for a position in teacher preparation in dance at the university level.

I thus entered dance education out of a sense of powerlessness to change the larger world. When I danced I could escape that world temporarily and even feel some sense of personal power within the safe space of the studio. When I taught creative dance to children, I felt I was making a small contribution to the world without having to deal with the difficult problems outside my own small corner of it. Dance and dance education offered me a safe home, and it never occurred to me to be critical of home. I would have felt inadequate to criticize anyway because I had not reached the "pinnacle" of the field—professional performance.

Much later, during my doctoral program in cultural studies, I started to re-examine my experiences in learning and teaching dance, and I became aware of what else students may be learning besides dance skills and knowledge—what curriculum theorists refer to as the "hidden curriculum." I also encountered two questions posed by curriculum theorist James B. Macdonald (1977), which he names as the essential questions for educators: What does it mean to be human? How shall we live together? With these influences I started asking questions not only about which pedagogical methods have the best chance of making good dancers but also about the kind of people, the kind of art, and the kind of world produced in the process.

At the same time that I was questioning dance pedagogy, I was also asking questions about what it meant to be a woman in the world. Betty Friedan's *The Feminine Mystique* was published in 1963; the same year I decided not to become a social worker, she was a guest speaker at the small women's college where I was a senior. I graduated feeling free to make many choices that had not been available to my own mother, yet most of mine were traditionally female ones anyway, including a conventional marriage that produced a daughter and a son. Although I took my career seriously, one could hardly pick a more traditionally feminine choice than being a dance teacher. My beliefs, however, were less traditional than my choices. As a charter subscriber to *Ms.* magazine and a self-declared feminist, I attempted to figure out how to be a woman and a mother, as well as a dance teacher, in a changing world.

One of my most helpful realizations was that the term "feminism" was an oversimplification, hiding the diversity in points of view that developed to such an extent that "feminisms" became a more appropriate descriptor. Allison Jaggar's (1983) definitions of different feminist perspectives are helpful in clarifying this diversity.

The best known feminism, which Jaggar defines as liberal feminism, focuses on opportunities that are systematically denied to women because they are women and on the imposed barriers that keep women from competing on an equal footing with men. The goal is equal opportunity for women to enter the power structure within society and move up its hierarchy based on their abilities. Such feminists tend to deny any basic differences between men and women other than those that are created (unfairly) by society, leaving women at a disadvantage in a competitive world. This was the kind of feminism that I first encountered in the 1960s.

Other visions of feminism, instead of denying differences between men and women, emphasize them. They point out that certain qualities and characteristics are found more often in men or women; there is often controversy regarding whether these differences are biologically or culturally determined, although it is generally agreed that they do not apply to *all* women or *all* men. Regardless of the source of the differences, such feminists note that the qualities identified as feminine—and the tasks that capitalize on them, usually known as "women's work"—are not valued as highly in our patriarchal society as those identified as masculine. They point out that structures of society, institutions such as religion and education as well as corporate capitalism, were created by men and embody masculine values. Such values include individualism; competition; objectivity; abstraction; rationality; and a valuing of mind over body, culture over nature. Masculinist institutions are problematic not just because women have been denied access to power within them but because they have collectively created a world that is "not healthy for children and other living things," to quote a popular t-shirt slogan reflecting this feminism. The goal is not only to allow women to compete in a man's world but also to change that world.

Some feminists, labeled by Jaggar (1983) as "radical feminists," believe that this different world should replace masculine values and institutions with feminine ones. Others, called "socialist feminists" by Jaggar, believe we must create new structures, new forms that deal with oppression due to race and class as well as gender, to have the best chance for providing a humane life for all human beings.

This brief discussion does not exhaust the list of feminisms, either in Jaggar's book or other sources. It is relevant to reveal, however, that I position myself in the category of socialist feminism. I have chosen this stance because I do not think that a world dominated by women would necessarily be any better than one dominated by men. Furthermore, I dream of a world that liberates my son as well as my daughter from narrow perceptions of gender roles, a world that responds to similar wishes by mothers of color and those who live in poverty.

Deciding on basic positions of belief and value, however, does not necessarily determine how we will live our lives. Most of us have a great deal of inconsistency between what we say we believe and what we do, a conflict we are able to maintain only by not thinking about it too much. Engaging in a reflective process brings these conflicts to the forefront, the painful process that is necessary to generate growth. I try in this chapter to highlight my own engagement in this process as I have tried to figure out how to be a feminist dance educator and what that means to me. In the following sections, I examine critically several approaches to teaching dance and their relationship to a feminist pedagogy.

TRADITIONAL DANCE PEDAGOGY

Education has traditionally been a way to acculturate the young, to socialize them into the larger community and thus perpetuate it; this is the reproductive function of education. Traditional methods for teaching dance technique fulfill this function. The traditional technique class is the primary kind of dance class most students take, and it is ordinarily the only kind to which both teachers and students refer as a "dance class." (Other kinds are known by other names, such as choreography class and dance history class.) Like most dance students I spent many hours in technique classes, finding satisfaction in my growing strength, flexibility, control, and skill. The traditional technique class was the first kind of class I taught, and it is the first kind of class I critiqued.

In most dance technique classes, the teacher is the authority and the only recognized source of knowledge. All students face the teacher and a mirror, and the teacher often faces the mirror as well, seeing her students only as reflections. Interaction among students is frowned upon. The teacher's voice is expected to be the only one heard, except in the case of a well-focused question. The teacher tells and shows the students what to do and, in some classes, how to do it. Students attempt to duplicate the movement done by the teacher. Then the teacher gives verbal corrections, the students usually repeat the movement, and the teacher continues giving corrections until it is time to move on to the next sequence. Some teachers give directions and corrections that refer to internal sensation and artistic qualities, not just to the mechanics of the movement. But in reality, most dance training consists of learning how to follow directions and how to follow them well. The model for traditional dance pedagogy seems to be the authoritarian father in an individualistic world of "every man for himself."

A field study carried out by Judith Alter (1986) reveals evidence of masculinist values in dance. In an advanced modern dance class in a private studio setting, Alter discovered a number of strong but unspoken rules of behavior among dance students, including the following: "Students never talk to each other during class . . . students rarely commiserate with each other even nonverbally. . . . never show how bad or good you feel about yourself, your dancing, or the teacher" (69-70). Alter found a sense of hierarchy among students, with "old-timers" (the most skillful dancers who were usually members of the dance company associated with the studio) having priority in choice of space and the amount of space claimed. Old-timers were allowed to take exception to the unspoken rules of the class. Furthermore, Alter found that "the entire emotional/physical atmosphere was . . . full of . . . tension and . . . most students felt unable to dance or dance their best" (49). Although this was a class for adults, similar pedagogy prevails in most professional preparation classes in dance, which may begin for children as young as age eight.

Stinson, Blumenfeld-Jones, and Van Dyke (1990) further illuminate this model through interpretations of dance pedagogy by 16- to 18-year-old women who studied a variety of forms of dance in studio and conservatory settings. The young women made it clear that the focus of the dance (technique) class is doing the movement as given by the teacher and getting it right. For example, one respondent described her thoughts in class as "I gotta get it. Oh God, I did that wrong. I gotta do this right" (17). Another characteristic of the dance class was competition, with most students regarding it as constructive. As one respondent said, feeling competitive "is good in a way because it makes you strive for more" (18).

Even though authoritarian pedagogy for dance technique is used in classes populated by both men and women, I believe that it affects men and women differently. Most women begin dance training as little girls, usually between the ages of three and eight. Dance training teaches them to be silent and do as they are told, reinforcing cultural expectations for both young children and women. In their landmark work, *Women's Ways of Knowing* (1986), Mary Belenky and her colleagues point out that adult women are silenced much more often than men. Their analysis reveals that "finding one's voice" is a metaphor that appears frequently when women describe their own journeys from silence to critical thinking; for women, learning to think means learning to speak with one's own voice. Traditional dance pedagogy, with its emphasis on silent conformity, does not facilitate such a journey. Dancers typically learn to reproduce what they receive, not to critique or create.

In contrast, most males in our society begin dance training later, at late adolescence or even early adulthood, when they have developed some sense of individual identity and "voice." In addition, limits for males seem made to be broken, and dance is likely no exception. To a young man, dance training may seem comparable to military training in that the necessary obedience is a rite of passage but not a permanent state. Once he is good enough, he will then have the power to tell others what to do, to reconceptualize what he has learned, to create art and not just reproduce it. This differential impact of dance training may contribute to the differences that are observed in leadership within the dance field. Although men are a minority among dancers, they are overrepresented in positions of power and influence and as recipients of grants (particularly the largest grants) and national awards (Van Dyke 1992).

In addition to reinforcing the idea of the silent, passive woman (or the "good little girl"), dance training also intensifies cultural expectations in relation to female body image. The current dance aesthetic demands a long, thin body, carried to the extreme in ballet; many choreographers and directors, usually male, encourage and even demand the "anorexic look."

(See Brady 1982; Gordon 1983; Innes 1988; Kirkland 1986; Vincent 1979.) The same is increasingly true in modern dance, with many professional modern dancers now regarding the ballet class as their basic form of training and many modern dance choreographers setting their work on ballet companies. Even among young women in nonprofessional classes, criticizing one's body is part of the expected behavior. Alter (1986) noted that weight occurred as a topic in 18 of the 31 classes she studied. In the Stinson, Blumenfeld-Jones, and Van Dyke study (1990), the young respondents made comments about their bodies such as, "I don't like my body, the way it looks"; "Lots of time I think I'm too much of a brute to be a dancer"; and "If my legs matched my body then I'd be perfectly happy" (17). Surely such feelings about the body are enhanced by a pedagogy in which the goal is an unattainable ideal and every attempt is met with corrections—indications of how one does not measure up—all the while dressed in clothing that reveals every flaw and looking in a mirror. In traditional dance classes the body often seems to be regarded as an enemy to be overcome or an object to be judged. Dance training merely intensifies the values of the larger social world, however, to which both dance and women belong. In our society, being overweight is dreaded by all and the body is regarded as an enemy by both men and women who exercise compulsively and obsessively; women's bodies, however, are more often identified as objects to be looked at and judged.

Traditional dance pedagogy in many ways embraces the values of a male-dominated society, such as separation and competition, despite the preponderance of women in the art. The goal is individual achievement—being on top—with little emphasis on community and caring, values more often regarded as feminine (Gilligan 1982). Another example of masculine values in dance classes is the way the natural human body is denied in favor of a reshaped and highly trained body reflecting the cultural aesthetic. A number of feminist theorists have pointed out that the human body and Nature (as in Mother Nature and Mother Earth) are more closely connected with women, whereas the mind and culture are regarded as the province of men (see Jaggar 1983). Furthermore, in most dance technique classes, emotional feeling (again, regarded as feminine) is repressed, as students are required to leave any personal concerns outside the studio door. In some classes, even physical feeling is to be ignored ("no pain, no gain").

CRITICAL PEDAGOGY

In contrast to its reproductive role, education has also been used as a way to challenge the status quo by helping students question and proposing alternatives to "the way things are"; this is the critical or emancipatory function of education. Critical pedagogy has developed as one alternative to traditional authoritarian pedagogy. Such pedagogy has its roots in critical social theory, which calls for social and economic justice as well as fundamental changes in how we view the worth of individuals. Elizabeth Ellsworth (1992) states that critical pedagogy "supported classroom analysis and the rejection of oppression, injustice, inequality, silencing of marginalized voices, and authoritarian social structures. . . . The goal of critical pedagogy was a critical democracy, individual freedom, social justice, and social change" (92). Critical pedagogues most often cite the work of Paolo Freire (1983; Freire and Macedo 1987) as an example of this approach. I first resonated with Freire's critique of what he calls the "banking concept" of education because in it I recognized traditional dance pedagogy:

a) the teacher teaches and the students are taught;

b) the teacher knows everything and the students know nothing;

c) the teacher thinks and the students are thought about;

d) the teacher talks and the students listen—meekly;

e) the teacher disciplines and the students are disciplined;

f) the teacher chooses and enforces his choice, and the students comply;

g) the teacher acts and the students have the illusion of acting through the action of the teacher;

h) the teacher chooses the program content, and the students (who were not consulted) adapt to it;

i) the teacher confuses the authority of knowledge with his own professional authority, which he sets in opposition to the freedom of the students;

j) the teacher is the subject of the learning process, while the pupils are mere objects. (Freire 1983, 59)

Freire's work as a critical educator with illiterate Brazilian peasants sought to supplant banking education with a different approach, one that was designed to promote democratic change in the society as a whole. The literacy program Freire designed (Freire and Macedo 1987) taught his adult students not only to read in the literal sense but also to name their own oppression and to recognize their capacity to remake society.

Whereas Freire focused on class oppression and did not discuss gender, some critical theorists (Apple 1984; Giroux 1991) have included women as another example of an oppressed group, and many feminist educators have adopted critical pedagogy as a model for feminist pedagogy (Maher 1987). Carolyn Shrewsbury, in a 1987 article in *Women's Studies Quarterly*, defines the vision of the feminist classroom as

a liberatory environment in which we, teacher–student and student–teacher, act as subjects, not objects. Feminist pedagogy is engaged . . . with others in a struggle to get beyond our sexism and racism and homophobia and other destructive hatreds and to work together ... with the community, with traditional organizations, and with movements for social change. (6)

Shrewsbury notes three concepts that are central to feminist pedagogy: empowerment, community, and leadership. In some cases, however, these terms may be defined in a way different from common usage.

Leadership, for example, is defined by Shrewsbury as "the embodiment of our ability and our willingness to act on our beliefs" (10). A feminist classroom, according to Shrewsbury, develops students' leadership skills such as planning, negotiating, and evaluating; understanding and articulating one's own needs and their relationship to the needs of others; and analyzing problems and finding alternative solutions.

Shrewsbury writes that feminists focus on power not as domination but as creative potential and see power as "the glue holding a community together" (8). She lists six strategies for achieving power in a feminist classroom, which include ways to move students toward greater autonomy / responsibility for their own learning, rather than dependence on the instructor. At the same time, students are encouraged to connect with others in the class in mutually productive ways and to recognize "the responsibility of all members of the class for the learning of all" (9). In addition, a successful feminist pedagogy "expand[s] the students' understanding of the subject matter of the course and of the joy and difficulty of intense intellectual activity as they actively consider learning goals and sequences" (9).

Shrewsbury asserts that community is important in a feminist pedagogy because "women seek to build connections" and to "maintain connections that have been built" (10). In a feminist classroom community, decisions are made not just according to formal rules but also according to consensus.

On the surface it is difficult to argue with any of these points. Indeed, a reviewer for an earlier version of this chapter questioned whether Shrewsbury's three principles can be claimed exclusively by feminist pedagogues. What educator would admit to disagreement with the goal of helping students become independent learners who can work with others or helping them learn to solve problems? It is very easy for the strategies Shrewsbury outlines to become co-opted by those without the more radical agenda of critical pedagogy, which is to change society by helping students recognize their power to become agents of change.

When I first encountered critical pedagogy, it sounded to me like a noble endeavor not only for Brazil but in this country as well. I knew I wanted to teach prospective dance educators to critique their own educational experiences in dance and in schooling, and I wanted them to recognize that they had the capacity to imagine and create a world that might be different. Within the fairly traditional boundaries of my dance education theory courses, I thought I was doing this to some extent. I also knew other educators attempting to integrate dance practice with ideas of critical theory.

Isabel Marques, a Brazilian dance educator, has applied the Freirian vision in a project to help classroom teachers (with little or no dance background) learn to use dance and movement with their young students (Marques 1995). She describes informing teachers how to use "generative themes," ones in which dance structures can be learned in the context of questioning and transforming social reality. The teachers with whom she worked, primarily kindergarten teachers, reported great difficulty in working with the idea of generative themes and in bringing up social content in class. Although that particular project ended due to a political change in the country, Marques has continued to develop her work into an approach that she calls "context-based dance education," with promising outcomes (Marques 1997; see also chapter 8).

Sherry Shapiro (1996) practices critical pedagogy by integrating development of a choreographic work with helping students to become conscious of their relationship to a particular theme. Shapiro selects a generative theme, such as eating, for example, and encourages student dancers to keep a journal about their feelings and experiences concerning the theme while she asks provocative questions that encourage them to challenge this relationship. The students' words as well as their movement suggestions are selected and formed by Shapiro to become a piece of choreography. Because her students are all women, Shapiro's choices of themes have been ones of particular importance to women.

I find the model of critical pedagogy useful in helping us recognize women as an oppressed group in solidarity with other oppressed groups and in empowering women to create change. I have not found it difficult in my own teaching to encourage prospective dance educators to be critical of educational structures and practices and to want to change them. A fair number of my students have also made the connection between oppressive educational practices and the larger social structures that schooling is designed to support. For example, they can recognize that schooling as it currently exists helps perpetuate inequalities among people; they also can see that it is a myth that all children have an equal chance for success in school. They can even recognize that our system needs some people to fail in school as a way to justify the unequal distribution of goods and services in our society. They have a harder time, however, in taking the next step: to imagine how things might be different than they are. This step either produces fears of socialism or leads to the resignation that utopias are impossibilities.

I, too, have a harder time finding answers than I do asking questions at this step in the process of critical pedagogy. At an earlier stage in my life, I could easily imagine a world in which people would live together in small communities where everyone's contributions were equally valued, everyone shared in the responsibility for the community as a whole, and decisions were made by consensus. At this point, however, I am all too aware that communities frequently end up in conflict when people have different visions of their community's purpose, or when some do not do their share of the work of the community and others become resentful. Would these kinds of conflicts still happen if everyone were educated through a feminist critical pedagogy? Is human nature such that self-interests take priority over community? Even if all members of a particular community agree, will they inevitably have conflict with other communities? These are large questions with which I still am struggling.

I also have some questions about outcomes of critical pedagogy with students in public schools, especially if it is used successfully. I was an undergraduate student in 1968 when students took over administration buildings and closed a number of college campuses in making demands for change. What are the implications of inciting younger students to revolution in institutions where they have even less power to make changes than they did in the 1960s? Karen Anijar (1992) reported a middle school student's problems with the administration following her consciousness-raising in a dance project with emancipatory intent. Furthermore, when I talk with prospective teachers about serving as change agents in the organizations they will enter, I sometimes worry whether I am trying to take the easy way out, trying to get others to be on the front lines of the revolution while I take the ivory tower role of the professorial advisor, safe in my own tenured chair. Although I work to make modest and incremental change in my own institution and community, I do so within the given power structures. I still use words more than actions to try to accomplish social change, knowing that others need to take more direct action that may put them more at risk. Clearly we need to make sure our students are aware of the risks of becoming change agents so that they are able to make informed choices; we also need to reflect on the morality of encouraging others to take risks we are not willing to assume ourselves.

Of course, many themes with prosocial content can be introduced to public school age students, ones that seem relatively risk-free. We can have students make dances about recycling or appreciating differences and feel that we are doing good without taking chances. To have this kind of student work become critical pedagogy, however, I think that we have to go further. In going further, students may want to do more than dance about an issue. They may decide, for example, to take on local industries that discharge pollutants or local groups campaigning against gay rights—actions of which many administrators are likely to disapprove. Clearly, critical pedagogy is not for the faint-hearted.

I also believe that pragmatic limitations exist in using methods of critical pedagogy with younger students, particularly preadolescents. The discourse of critical pedagogy as described by Freire and Shrewsbury demands the capacity for rational and even abstract thought, which are capacities that develop only with age (Stinson 1985).

Some other limitations to critical pedagogy are also persuasive, having to do with its emphasis on rational dialogue in which all voices may be heard. Elizabeth Ellsworth, in an article discussing the "repressive myths of critical pedagogy" (1992, 90) notes that critical pedagogy's demand for rational dialogue can be problematic even for adults. This is because our narratives—the stories we tell in making sense of our lives—are partial and contradictory and are grounded in our immediate social, emotional, and psychic experiences, which are not always rational. Furthermore, she points out, in most situations all voices cannot be heard equally; therefore, a demand to speak can be just as oppressive as a demand for silence. As Patti Lather reminds us, "We must be willing to learn from those who don't speak up in words. What are their silences telling us?" (Lather, cited in Orner 1992, 81).

My concerns about critical pedagogy do not mean that I am willing to give it up completely, any more than I am willing to give up pliés because they are often taught through an oppressive pedagogy. But I take my concerns with me in my continuing construction of my own pedagogy.

GENDER MODELS FOR PEDAGOGY: CREATIVE DANCE

A number of feminists have taken the image of the mother and used it as the basis for feminist pedagogy. Nel Noddings (1984, 1992) discusses caring, which she defines as receptivity, relatedness, and responsiveness, as an essential aspect of pedagogy. She believes that caring derives from the "language of the mother" (1984), a feeling-level responsiveness of mother to infant. Gilligan (1982) also notes the particular importance of caring in the lives of women; she found that an "ethic of care" underlies the moral thinking of women, as contrasted with the ethic of individual rights that predominates among men. In my study of public school dance students on the high school level, student respondents told me that perceiving that the teacher cared about them was one of the most important factors in their engagement and learning in all subjects (Stinson 1992, 1993b). It is true that the concept of caring can easily be sentimentalized and can provide an excuse for making students overly dependent and denying them the opportunity to set and meet challenges. Certainly part of caring is encouraging students to ask for help when they need it and to help others when they can, but another part is encouraging them to find and develop their own capabilities. Like many women, I find it challenging to avoid being seduced into attempting the role of self-sacrificing surrogate mother to my students. I find the same conflict in teaching as in parenting, a struggle to figure out when to help and when to back off and allow my students or my children to discover that they can handle the difficulty they face on their own.

In addition to Noddings, other feminists have derived models for pedagogy based not on women's oppression but on "those aspects of female identity that come from their roles as mothers of children and their occupancy of the so-called private sphere of life" (Maher 1987, 95). Maher refers to these as gender models for pedagogy, which not only offer a critique of critical pedagogy but also emphasize "the subjective roots of our thinking processes, on the relation of personal experiences, emotions, and values to what we know" (96).

Mary Belenky appears to support a gender pedagogy in *Women's Ways of Knowing* (Belenky et al. 1986), which describes the difference between separate knowing and connected knowing. Belenky explains that separate knowing, found most often among men, begins with doubting one's own beliefs and those of others, then continues to the development of new beliefs through rational abstract thought; while authoritarian pedagogy values separate knowing, so does critical pedagogy, at least in its prefeminist state. Connected knowing, found most often among women, involves listening to the voices of self and others, trying to perceive the world through a variety of lenses. While either of these routes culminates in the realization that Truth is relative and depends on the perspective from which one looks, the two are not equally valued in education. Because men have held primary power in academia, separate knowing has been more valued there. Belenky states that an emphasis on relationship is essential in teaching girls and women.

The kind of educational approach advocated by Belenky makes so much sense to me as a woman that I have had to question why it has not been followed at least at the K-12 level, where women, many of whom are mothers, have predominated in the classroom for decades. Why do women teachers participate in what Madeline Grumet calls "delivering children to patriarchy," establishing classrooms that "cannot sustain human relationships of sufficient intimacy to support the risks, the trust, and the expression that learning requires" (1988, 56)? Grumet offers an explanation through a historical look at women and teaching, in which she describes how women became teachers as a way to leave the hearth and gain access to at least some of the power and prerogatives of men denied to them in the home. No wonder that these women, educational pioneers in a man's world, resisted a definition in the role of teacher that replicated the nurturant role of the mother. Today, several generations removed from these women pioneers, I see a similar explanation for why so many women teachers accept a pedagogy that denies their personal values: When one is trying to find power and influence, one often emulates those who already hold it. Women in the professional dance world, where men occupy more positions of power and influence, emulate those men by embodying masculinist values.

In contrast, I found myself attracted to what I see as a gender pedagogy for dance, one in which women are not only the primary occupants but also the ones with the most influence; this approach is known as creative dance for children. Indeed, this was where my own first attempt to find an alternative to traditional dance pedagogy led me. I felt at home when I read the words of Virginia Tanner, who was featured in the first International Conference of Dance and the Child held in Alberta, Canada, in 1979:

> [The child's] world is filled with fantasy, which is frequently dimmed when parents, teachers, and friends turn down the lights in his [sic] treasure house of imagination. A child quickly recognizes whether or not you offer warmth, understanding, and interest. Only when rapport is established will he unlock the facets of his heart and allow you to share your treasures with him and his with you. (Tanner 1981, 30-31)

Tanner shared with pride a review of her students in performance by dance critic Walter Terry:

> From the first there was beauty. But more important . . . was the vital innocence of the dancers themselves. . . . the children danced as if they had faith in themselves, had love for those who were seeing them, actively believed in their God, and rejoiced in all these. (Terry, cited in Tanner 1981, 39)

Ruth Murray, regarded as one of the primary influences in the development of creative dance in the United States, wrote about self-expression in "A Statement of Belief" for a 1981 publication produced by a national-level Task Force on Children's Dance:

> Dance provides a primary medium for expression. . . . Dance and the movement that produces it is "me," and as such, is the most intimate of expressive media. A child's self-concept, his [sic] own identity and self-esteem are improved in relation to such use of his body's movement. (5)

Murray described problem solving as the preferred methodology in teaching children's dance because a "creative process can only be realized by a teaching method that is, in itself, creative" (7). Tanner, Murray, and other practitioners of creative dance reflected the philosophy of Margaret H'Doubler, regarded by many as the "Grandmother of Dance Education" in the United States for her success in establishing the first dance program in higher education and for teaching generations of dance educators. H'Doubler wrote about her vision of education in words first published in 1940:

Education should be a building toward the integration of human capacities and powers resulting in well-adjusted, useful, balanced individuals. The desire to find peace within ourselves and to bring about an adequate adjustment to life around us is the basis for all mental and physical activity. (H'Doubler 1977, 60)

H'Doubler stated the beliefs of practically every creative dance teacher when she noted that every child has a right to dance just "as every child has a right to a box of crayons" (66).

Creative dance at first seemed to me to embody all the good things I hoped to do for children. The methodology encourages self-expression and teaches problem solving, not passivity. It is non-elitist because everyone can dance. It is about education rather than training, and it uses "natural" movement rather than stylistically contrived forms. The teacher is expected to be accepting and nurturing instead of demanding because "there are no wrong answers" in creative dance. The model for such a pedagogue is the loving mother within a supportive family.

Certainly it had been difficult for me to speak critically of traditional dance pedagogy, which had helped me develop the physical power and skill I treasured. It has been even more difficult to speak critically of creative dance, a realm in which I have found love and acceptance among children and those who care for them. Using the lens of critical pedagogy, however, I eventually started to see that the myth perpetuated by creative dance is populated by images of only bright and happy children, running and skipping joyfully, seemingly untouched by poverty, hunger, homelessness, or any of the other realities with which so many children live. The poster for a 1991 international conference on dance for children exemplified this by showing children with smiling faces and open arms, dressed like fairies, cavorting across a wooded background; all the children except one in the corner of the poster were Euro-American.

Creative dance all too often tries to create a make-believe world for the child, fostering escapism. Certainly mental escape from problems that cannot be changed may be an appropriate pursuit, and children easily create their own make-believe worlds without any assistance from adults. I admit that I treasure the times I get invited into them. Yet, despite my concerns about critical pedagogy, I still assert that eventually children need to grow into adults empowered to change those things in the world that should not be tolerated. Virginia Tanner thought that creative dance could help change the world, stating, "If our children could have their creative selves always fed, their destructive selves would gradually starve" (1981, 38). I began to question, however, whether creative dance pedagogy went far enough.

Other problems, too, are embedded within the pedagogy of creative dance, which derives from the progressive values of Dewey (1970), Pestalozzi (1970), and Froebel (1970). Although progressive pedagogical methods avoid the coercion of authoritarian styles, their goals are similar: producing docile, well-disciplined individuals who will fit into the way things are rather than attempt to change them. H'Doubler's language about adjusting to the world around us as a goal of education reflects this. Walkerdine (1992) notes that progressive education established the schoolroom (and, one might add, the children's dance studio) as

> a laboratory, where development could be watched, monitored, and set along the right path. There was therefore no need for . . . discipline of the overt kind. . . . The classroom became the facilitating space for each individual, under the watchful and total gaze of the teacher, who was held responsible for the development of each individual. . . . [In such a classroom] the children are only allowed happy sentiments and happy words. . . . There is a denial of pain, oppression. . . . There is also a denial of power, as though the helpful teacher didn't wield any. (17-20)

Thus, Walkerdine explains, when the nurturing mother figure replaced the authoritarian father figure in the classroom, both oppression and the powerlessness of the oppressed simply became invisible. Walkerdine suggests that the cost of the fantasy of liberation found in progressivism, "is borne by the teacher, as it is borne by the mother. . . . She is the servant of the omnipotent child, whose needs she must meet at all times. . . . The servicing labor of women makes the child, the natural child, possible" (21).

In recognizing that creative dance, too, was problematic, I felt much like Eve must have felt upon leaving the Garden of Eden. Creative dance offers a chance to live in a beautiful, loving, and joyful world. The world outside is difficult and often ugly, and at times I wish I had never eaten the fruit from the tree of consciousness that made me recognize what was missing. Perhaps this is why I have looked for another model that preserves the image of the caring mother, yet expands it to fit the kind of mother and the kind of teacher that I want to be.

A FEMINIST'S PEDAGOGY FOR CHILDREN'S DANCE: IN PROCESS

Maher (1987) asserts the need for a synthesis between critical or liberatory pedagogy and gender pedagogy in order to have an adequate theory of feminist pedagogy. This may describe my current approach to teaching dance. My vision of feminist pedagogy is concerned with both individuals and relationships, both liberation and caring. It is a vision that is still evolving, reflecting the partiality of my own experience and my attempts to expand it. It reflects my own concerns about dance, about education, about girls and women, and about the world; but it also contains the contradictions within my own values as well as questions that remain for now

© Jack Vartoogian

unanswered. I believe it best reflects the complexity and paradoxes of trying to make a new world when all that we are has been shaped by the old one. The vision I share here describes what I do and encourage other teachers to do, what I try to be doing, and what I see others doing that I wish I were.

FINDING ONE'S OWN VOICE AND INNER AUTHORITY

I encourage even very young children not to look to me as their only source of knowledge but to find their own inner teacher and inner dancer: "Be your own teacher. Tell yourself when to change shapes." Instead of focusing on a mirror or on me as the teacher, I suggest that each student listen to his or her own body. With young children, this involves such activities as listening to their breathing and learning how to energize or calm themselves. With older students, activities extend to monitoring their own level of readiness for strenuous movement and recognizing how gently or vigorously to do a movement. I use language such as, "Notice how you are using your feet" or "Find the tempo at which the movement feels most fulfilled on *your* body."

Internal awareness requires silence, an active silence, in which one listens to the inner self. It is essential, however, that students have opportunities to speak, to find their own voice in words as well as movement, and to share that with others. Despite the limited possibility for all voices to be heard equally, I believe in classtime discussion and personal reflection during which students may identify the sources of their own visions. To ease the pressure to speak, I have created opportunities in my university-level classes for written participation, an option appreciated by students who need more time to think about what they want to say; I can then share these written ideas in a later class.

I also encourage students to suggest images for movement and to create their own movement. Although some dance teachers believe that this kind of activity is only appropriate in choreography classes, I believe that movement awareness, technical skills, improvisation, and composition/ choreography can all be integrated into a *dance* class.

CULTIVATING AWARENESS OF RELATIONSHIP

Because I see the world as a "web of relations" (Gilligan 1982), I look for ways to help students perceive relationships on several levels. One level comprises the relationships between and among students. As dance students discover their own skills and create their own knowledge, I encourage them to share these with peers as well as with me. When possible, students can help each other by serving as another set of eyes and offering suggestions; this kind of partnering is easily incorporated into a dance class, enhancing the formation of supportive student relationships. As the class members learn to see and respond to others, they become better prepared to become teachers or choreographers themselves.

Emphasizing relationship can also enhance performance skills. It has always interested me that, although most performance opportunities require ensemble work, dance technique classes rarely cultivate the skills necessary to dance *with* another. Small-group work is common in creative dance classes for children; but even in technique class students' facings can be adjusted to facilitate relationship. For example, when travelling across the floor, students can be divided into two groups that move toward each other. When small groups of students do a combination, teachers can ask students to sense each other, to dance *together*. Such an approach helps dance class become not just preparation for dancing but dancing itself.

Developing relationship in dance also includes reminding students of connections to their own bodies. In addition to facilitating more ease in movement and fewer injuries, such a relationship may have deeper implications. As noted previously, our bodies are a manifestation of nature, and nature is personified as female (Mother Nature); some feminists have noted that a connection exists between domination of nature and domination of women (see Jaggar 1983). While I am wary of some of the "back to nature" trends that I see among ecofeminists, I encourage dance students to care for and to cherish the body as a lovable and sensuous part of themselves instead of a beast to be brought under control, a machine to be well-tuned, or an aesthetic object to be judged (Moore 1985).

A third kind of relationship I try to cultivate is that between what goes on in the studio and what happens outside it. Like traditional creative dance teachers, I structure many lessons for young children on themes from nature or other aspects of the child's world, in hopes that students will recognize their relationship with other life forms. As students get older, however, teachers can also connect issues faced within the dance class itself (such as sexism, homophobia, and fat phobia) to the same issues as they are manifested in society by posing questions for discussion or having students keep journals. We can question why most dance studios are populated primarily by white middle-class students. We might explore why dance is a stereotypically female activity, and what girls have learned through dance about being female. When students study dance history, criticism, and aesthetics, they might reflect on such issues as why some forms of dance are considered art and others are considered recreation or entertainment, and who makes such decisions.

RESPONSIBILITY AND POWER FOR CHANGE

Exploring the issues just mentioned and many others can raise critical consciousness, which Kenway and Modra describe as enhancing "analysis of the context of problem situations for the purpose of enabling people together to transform their reality, rather than merely understand it or adapt to it with less discomfort" (1992, 156). Some choreographers are able to use this kind of discussion as a springboard for socially conscious art, in which dancers' words and movement in relation to a particular issue are incorporated into the choreography. It may well be that socially conscious art, by presenting audiences with different images of society, may facilitate change. I am also aware, however, that recognizing a problem does not necessarily lead to a commitment to solve it. We must also recognize a responsibility for others and our own power to create change.

Martin Buber (1955), in describing *I–Thou* relationships, helps me understand how relationships can lead to taking responsibility to care for that with which we are related. Buber speaks of "feeling from the other side," or feeling the results of our actions simultaneously with experiencing ourselves as causing them. He gives two examples, one of a man who strikes another and "suddenly receives in his soul the blow which he strikes" (96). The second example involves a caress by a man who "feels the contact from two sides—with the palm of his hand still, and also with the woman's skin" (96). If we truly feel the pain we cause others, we are less likely to cause it, and if we experience the pleasure we cause others we are likely to increase it. To recognize relationship with another is to recognize the responsibility to care for the other as we care for ourselves. As Buber states, "love is the responsibility of an *I* for a *Thou*" (1958, 15). I hope that emphasizing relationships in dance class and extending class activity into discussion can be a small part of urging students to feel a sense of responsibility for themselves and others.

Power, skill, and courage are other essential ingredients for change. I know the sense of physical power that I have felt in dance, a sense that evaporates as soon as I leave the security of the studio. I know the skills I have developed in dance, which have not seemed to translate into life skills. I developed courage to express my own ideas in dance and to share them in public, courage that does not necessarily transfer to other situations. Can there be transfer from art to life, from studio or stage to the places we live our lives? I hope that, as we help students to find their own authority and voice, they will recognize that they can speak and act for more than dance. Shrewsbury's (1987) ideas for helping students develop power and leadership skills, presented earlier in this chapter, are part of the answer. Yet I still have more questions than answers about how to construct the bridge from dance to the rest of the world and about how great an impact dance can have in it.

SOME FURTHER QUESTIONS

My vision of a feminist pedagogy for dance is very clearly culturally bound, which concerns me as I educate dance teachers in an increasingly global society. At this point I am comfortable applying it only to teaching Western dance forms. Many non-Western forms are also taught using a pedagogy in which the teacher is master, and silent students receive knowledge. Yet I am uncomfortable critiquing a cultural tradition I can understand only as an outsider. I acknowledge my limitations in this regard, and I hope that feminists within non-Western traditions may provide insight into applying a feminist approach to teaching dance forms from their cultures.

Another conflict I face even in critiquing Western dance pedagogy is my continuing ambivalence over the issue of professional training. I wonder if the whole concept of the "professional" reflects male-dominated, hierarchic thinking, leaving no room for a feminist pedagogy. But if I question hierarchy in dance and argue that all of us are dancers as a virtue of being human, I have to extend similar questioning to my role as a professional educator. How can I deny hierarchy in dance performance if I am one of those who possesses position and prestige in dance education?

CONCLUSION

Changes in dance pedagogy will change the art, perhaps in very significant ways. We do not really know what changes a feminist pedagogy might stimulate. I imagine that it would create greater diversity and more room in the field for individual visions. I can also imagine less technical virtuosity, more variety in shapes and sizes of dancers, and probably more "bad dance" (self-indulgent, poorly crafted, and all of the other negatives pointed out by critics) as well as more "good dance." Perhaps we would have less interest in judging dance as good or bad and might see it less as an object and more as shared experience. Perhaps there would be more women in leadership positions in dance and even new definitions of leadership. As someone who is an educator first and a dance educator second, I admit that I am concerned more for young people and the adults they will become than for maintaining the art form in its current state.

As I continue to recognize ways that dance mirrors the larger culture, I find myself focused less on dance education specifically. Instead I am concerned more with structures both inside and outside dance that keep us from being the people we wish to be and responding to the relationships that connect us with each other and the world we share. For me, dance education has become less an escape from the world than a laboratory for understanding it and understanding myself.

It is clear to me that traditional dance pedagogy, and even creative dance pedagogy, contribute to maintaining not just the dance world but the larger world as it is. It is less clear whether we can change the larger world through any changes we might make in dance. I cannot help but think of the words my mother wrote in a book of remembrances for my daughter, when she described me as someone who, when I was an adolescent, "wanted to change the world," and then noted that I "became a dance teacher instead."

Even if our pedagogy does not lead to changes in the world, reflecting on it does change those doing the reflecting. My own thinking about dance curriculum and pedagogy and their relationship to my values has clearly changed my consciousness. My goal, however, is not to persuade my students or others to teach as I do but for each of us to engage in ongoing reflection about what we believe and why and about the consequences of the choices we make as persons and as educators.

Critical Reflections

Nostalgically we recall the sweet and joyous images of children dancing—eyes dancing, cheeks blushed with movement and laughter, exuding life. These images remind us of our dreams for all children. Yet when examining these images critically we must ask ourselves the following: Who are these children? Do they represent *all* children? Do these images tell the stories of many of our children? The answer to these questions unfortunately is no. Describing herself as a socialist feminist, Sue Stinson drew our attention to her own reflective process in answering these kinds of questions. She discussed how and why traditional dance pedagogy reproduces education that values "the authoritarian father," creates a "silent majority," and requires a notion of "every man for himself." Citing the work of Paulo Freire within the context of feminist theories, Stinson considered what it might mean to synthesize this kind of liberatory or critical pedagogy with a gendered one. Such a pedagogy for children's dance would then try to bring together "masculine" and "feminine" values and, more specifically, point to a process concerned with the cultivation of students' voices, relational understanding, helping students cherish their bodies, and urging a sense of responsibility for themselves and others.

Take a Moment to Reflect

Within our work as educators, whether male or female, as discussed in chapter 1, we always hold some premise that has an impact on how and what we teach. Feminist theorists have offered us questions that help to reveal some of the problems with basic (and often accepted without question) pedagogic principles. Take your time in answering the following questions. Try to be honest with yourself and open to questioning your own work.

1. What is a "good" teacher? What defines a "good teacher" in dance?
2. In what ways do dance classes mirror traditional types of classrooms, such as in the relationship between teacher and student? In what ways are dance classes different?
3. What changes might a feminist-oriented pedagogy for dance stimulate?
4. What values or skills do you choose to instill in your students?

Critical and feminist questions are not only being asked in terms of pedagogy but also in dance research. In the following chapter, Sylvie Fortin analyzes positivistic research within the context of critical and feminist work. Of particular significance is the process of empowerment in the act of researching three dance teachers who have a background in somatics.

REFERENCES

Alter, J. 1986. "A Field Study of an Advanced Dance Class in a Private Studio Setting." *Dance Studies* 10: 49-97.

Anijar, K. 1992. *Listening in Liberty*. Paper presented to the International Human Science Research Conference, Oakland, MI.

Apple, M.W. 1984. "Teaching and 'Women's Work': A Comparative Historical and Ideological Analysis." In *Expressions of Power in Education: Studies of Class, Gender and Race*, E.B. Gumbert (ed.). Atlanta: Center for Cross-Cultural Education, Georgia State University.

Belenky, M.F., B.M. Clinchy, N.R. Goldberg, and J.M. Tarule. 1986. *Women's Ways of Knowing: The Development of Self, Voice, and Mind*. New York: Basic Books.

Brady, J. 1982. *The Unmaking of a Dancer: An Unconventional Life*. New York: Harper & Row.

Buber, M. 1955. *Between Man and Man*. Translated by M. Friedman. New York: Harper & Row.

———. 1958. *I and Thou*. 2d ed. Translated by R.G. Smith. New York: Scribner's.

Dewey, J. 1970. "Experience and Education: Traditional vs. Progressive Education." In *Foundations of Education in America: An Anthology of Major Thoughts and Significant Actions*, J.W. Noll and S.P. Kelly (eds.). New York: Harper & Row.

Ellsworth, E. 1992. "Why Doesn't This Feel Empowering? Working Through the Repressive Myths of Critical Pedagogy." In *Feminisms and Critical Pedagogy*, C. Luke and J. Gore (eds.). New York: Routledge.

Freire, P. 1983. *Pedagogy of the Oppressed*. Translated by M.B. Ramos. New York: Continuum.

Freire, P., and D. Macedo. 1987. *Literacy: Reading the Word and the World*. South Hadley, MA: Bergin & Garvey.

Friedan, B. 1963. *The Feminine Mystique*. New York: Norton.

Froebel, F. 1970. "The Education of Man: The Law of Self Activity." In *Foundations of Education in America: An Anthology of Major Thoughts and Significant Actions*, J.W. Noll and S.P. Kelly (eds.). New York: Harper & Row.

Gilligan, C. 1982. *In a Different Voice: Psychological Theory and Women's Development*. Cambridge, MA: Harvard University Press.

Giroux, H. 1991. "Modernism, Postmodernism, and Feminism: Rethinking the Boundaries of Educational Discourse." In *Postmodernism, Feminism and Cultural Politics: Redrawing Educational Boundaries*, H. Giroux (ed.). Albany, NY: State University of New York Press.

Gordon, S. 1983. *Off-Balance: The Real World of Ballet*. New York: Pantheon.

Greene, M. 1973. *Teacher as Stranger*. Belmont, CA: Wadsworth.

———. 1978. *Landscapes of Learning*. New York: Teachers College Press.

Grumet, M.R. 1988. *Bitter Milk: Women and Teaching*. Amherst, MA: University of Massachusetts Press.

H'Doubler, M.N. 1977. *Dance: A Creative Art Experience*. Madison, WI: University of Wisconsin Press.

Innes, S. 1988. "The Teaching of Ballet." *Writings on Dance* 3 (Winter): 37-47.

Jaggar, A.M. 1983. *Feminist Politics and Human Nature*. Totowa, NJ: Rowman & Allanheld.

Kenway, J., and H. Modra. 1992. "Feminist Pedagogy and Emancipatory Possibilities." In *Feminisms and Critical Pedagogy*, C. Luke and J. Gore (eds.). New York: Routledge.

Kirkland, G., and G. Lawrence. 1986. *Dancing On My Grave*. New York: Doubleday.

Macdonald, J.B. 1977. "Value Bases and Issues for Curriculum." In *Curriculum Theory: Selected Papers from the Milwaukee Curriculum Theory Conference held at the University of Wisconsin, November 11-14, 1976.* (Monograph), A. Molnar and J. Zahorek (eds.). Washington D.C.: Association for Supervision and Curriculum Development.

Maher, F.A. 1987. "Toward a Richer Theory of Feminist Pedagogy: A Comparison of 'Liberation' and 'Gender' Models for Teaching and Learning." *Journal of Education* 169 (3): 91-100.

Marques, I.A. 1995. "A Partnership Toward Art in Education: Approaching a Relationship between Theory and Practice." *Impulse: The International Journal of Dance Science, Medicine, and Education* 3 (2): 86-101.

———. 1997. "Context-Based Dance Education." In *The 7ᵗʰ International Dance and the Child Conference Proceedings*, E. Anttila. (ed.) Kuopio, Finland: daCi.

Moore, C.L. 1985. "Body Metaphors and Dance Instruction." Paper presented at the Annual Conference of the American Alliance for Health, Physical Education, Recreation & Dance, April, Cincinnati.

Murray, R.A. 1981. "A Statement of Belief." In *Children's Dance*, G. Fleming (ed.). Reston, VA: American Alliance for Health, Physical Education, Recreation & Dance.

Noddings, N. 1984. *Caring: A Feminine Approach to Ethics and Moral Education*. Berkeley, CA: University of California Press.

———. 1992. *The Challenge to Care in Schools: An Alternative Approach to Education*. New York: Teachers College Press.

Orner, M. 1992. "Interrupting the Calls for the Student Voice in 'Liberatory' Education: A Feminist Poststructuralist Perspective." In *Feminisms and Critical Pedagogy*, C. Luke and J. Gore (eds.). New York: Routledge.

Pestalozzi, J.H. 1970. "How Gertrude Teaches Her Children and the Method." In *Foundations of Education in America: An Anthology of Major Thoughts and Significant Actions*, J.W. Noll and S.P. Kelly (eds.). New York: Harper & Row.

Pinar, W. 1988. "'Whole, Bright, Deep with Understanding': Issues in Qualitative Research and Autobiographical Method." In *Contemporary Curriculum Discourses*, W. Pinar (ed.). Scottsdale, AZ: Gorsuch Scarisbrick.

Shapiro, S.B. 1996. "Toward Transformative Teachers: Critical and Feminist Perspectives in Dance Education." *Impulse: The International Journal of Dance Science, Medicine, and Education* 4 (1): 37-47.

Shrewsbury, C. 1987. "What Is Feminist Pedagogy?" *Women's Studies Quarterly* XV (3&4): 7-13.

Stinson, S.W. 1985. "Piaget for Dance Educators: A Theoretical Study." *Dance Research Journal* 17 (1): 9-16.

———. 1992. "Reflections on Student Experience in Dance Education." *Design for Arts in Education* 93 (5): 21-27.

———. 1993a. "Journey toward a Feminist Pedagogy for Dance." *Women & Performance* 6 (1): 131-146.

———. 1993b. "Meaning and Value: Reflecting on What Students Say About School." *Journal of Curriculum and Supervision* 8 (3): 216-238.

Stinson, S.W., D. Blumenfeld-Jones, and J. Van Dyke. 1990. "Voices of Young Women Dance Students: An Interpretive Study of Meaning in Dance." *Dance Research Journal* 22 (2): 13-22.

Tanner, V. 1981. "Thoughts on the Creative Process." In *Children and Drama*, 2d ed., N. McCaslin (ed.). New York: Longman.

Van Dyke, J.E. 1992. *Modern Dance in a Postmodern World*. Reston, VA: American Alliance for Health, Physical Education, Recreation & Dance.

Vincent, L.M. 1979. *Competing with the Sylph: Dancers and the Pursuit of the Ideal Body Form*. Kansas City, MS: Andrews & McMeel.

Walkerdine, V. 1992. "Progressive Pedagogy and Political Struggle." In *Feminisms and Critical Pedagogy*, C. Luke and J. Gore (eds.). New York: Routledge.

CHAPTER 3

SOMATICS: A TOOL FOR EMPOWERING MODERN DANCE TEACHERS

SYLVIE FORTIN, PHD
Université du Québec à Montréal

This chapter presents three in-depth case studies conducted with three women who are experienced modern dance technique teachers with extensive background in somatic studies. In each of the independent case studies, the author applied ethnographically oriented tools of interviewing, participant observations, and examinations of a variety of documents. Inductive analysis of the different data sources produced three case narratives. Speaking through their narratives, these teachers explain how, as a result of their background in somatics, they began to distance themselves from their "apprenticeship of observation," question their role as a teacher, and develop a more generic dance technique. The implications of this process are discussed in terms of building a class that empowers teachers and students, as opposed to the often hierarchical and disempowering structure found in many dance technique classes.

A growing number of dance educators claim that somatics[1] has begun to influence the teaching of dance (Dunn 1990; Wilson 1990). Little concrete empirical evidence is available, however, to substantiate how that is happening. Over the last few years, I have attempted to fill in part of this gap. I have focused my research on the impact of somatics on the teaching of modern dance technique through a series of in-depth case studies of women, each with an extensive background in somatics (Beaulieu and Fortin 1996; Fortin 1990, 1994; Fortin and Siedentop 1995).

After finishing the individual case studies, I realized that each woman had brought up an issue that I had not initially considered: empowerment. I decided to re-examine the raw data from the individual case studies in order to conduct a cross-case analysis with the concept of empowerment in mind. This concept was still vague to me at that point, although it is familiar in the literature on feminist pedagogy. Until then, I had not thought of my work in relationship to feminist pedagogy, but I was comfortable with this new situation as a researcher. I felt confident that the concept of empowerment would become clarified by the data and that I would eventually be able to relate it to a review of literature, as often happens in postpositivist research. Emerging design is after all a trademark of postpositivist research methodology.

METHODOLOGICAL ASSUMPTIONS

Within the postpositivist paradigm, a case study represents a researcher's attempt to give meaning to a complex reality. In fact, postpositivist researchers claim the existence of multiple realities constructed by each individual's encounter with the world. This contrasts with the positivist research method that aims to verify facts and causal relationships in order to develop theories that reflect reality and that may be generalized as applying to large popula-

---

[1] Somatics, body therapies, and body-mind practices are interchangeable terms referring to idiosyncratic practices developed by individuals such as Alexander (1985), Bartenieff and Lewis (1980), Bainbridge Cohen (1983), Feldenkrais (1949), and Sweigard (1974). For an introduction to somatic practices, see Hanna (1983, 1986), Mangione (1993), Myers (1980, 1989), and Johnson (1995).

tions. Both positivist and postpositivist paradigms call attention to a tension between that which is generic and that which is unique to each teacher's practice. While we conduct a case study, we acknowledge the uniqueness of a single person, working in a particular context, at a given time. This being said, a number of case studies may be looked at in order to find patterns across individual cases. Without making claims for generalization, we can look at those aspects that appear to extend beyond the scope of one particular case. Cross-case analysis often reveals generic qualities. Such was the hunch I had at the end of the individual studies. As I said, I felt that somatics had been a vehicle for empowering the dance teachers I had observed.

DESIGN

To compare and contrast each case study, I needed to delineate my sampling and work with a manageable amount of data. Thus, I selected among my series of studies the individual cases of three American women: Glenna Bateson, Martha Eddy, and Mary Williford.[2] I learned a tremendous amount from each of them, and I warmly thank them for their generosity. These three women are all experienced freelance dance teachers who were then in their early forties, who have had extensive training in one or several of the following somatic practices: Alexander, Feldenkrais, Ideokinesis, Bartenieff Fundamentals, Laban Movement Analysis, and Body-Mind Centering. All have studied anatomy. Glenna has a degree in physical therapy, Martha has a master's degree in exercise physiology, and Mary is a recognized professional dancer. Although Glenna and Martha have performed publicly, their professional reputations rely more on their contribution as dance and somatic educators. All three women have taught in academic as well as studio settings.

My task, when conducting the individual case studies, was to collect as much information as possible in order to understand each woman's teaching approach in its multiple facets. In each case study the data consisted of expanded field notes from classroom observations that were audio- or videotaped, transcribed interviews, and a variety of documents such as planning sheets and publicity pamphlets. I observed each teacher's classroom for a minimum of 30 hours and a maximum of 55, and I spent between 6 and 12 hours interviewing each individual. I conducted the interviews and classroom observations during dance festivals in the summers of 1991 through 1994.

---

[2] In the other case studies I completed, I looked at the teaching of women from Canada and Europe. For the cross-case analysis, I decided to limit my sampling to women from the United States. Interestingly, I did not purposely decide to study only women. Nevertheless, I have only women in my sampling. Is this a result of the fact that dance teachers are mostly women or that somatics "speaks" to women?

I analyzed the data by sorting out, from the raw material, all vignettes that could be linked to the notion of empowerment; I then grouped them to allow various categories to emerge. The process of cross-case analysis flowed back and forth between the data and the literature. Beginning with a vague notion of the meaning of empowerment, I eventually identified specific ways in which somatics contributed to empowering the three women and transforming their pedagogy.

RESULTS

Analyzing the case studies revealed that, due to their experience with somatics, these three women began to (1) distance themselves from their "apprenticeship of observation," (2) develop a personalized dance technique that could be applied to any dance form, and (3) question their roles as teachers. Though these themes clearly overlap, separate discussions demonstrate more clearly the empowerment I perceived in Glenna, Martha, and Mary and how the notion of empowerment manifested itself in their classes.

DISTANCING FROM THE APPRENTICESHIP OF OBSERVATION

One theme that arose from the cross-case study has to do with what Lortie (1975) has coined the "apprenticeship of observation." Lortie argues that time spent as a student provides prospective teachers with images of teaching that prove difficult to overcome because they tend to become so ingrained. These images support conservatism by encouraging teachers to follow a tacitly admitted way of "thinking" and "doing." Since the 1980s many authors have addressed this characteristic of conformity by dance teachers (Clarkson 1988; Gray 1990; Lord 1984). According to Myers (1989), when asked the reasons for their instructional choices, most dance teachers would answer, "the tradition, the way things are" (1). Glenna, Martha, and Mary did not follow this tendency. They did not replicate what they learned during their own training. The analysis of the data showed that for these three teachers, empowerment came partly from a greater critical awareness of their past experiences as dance students. Throughout the interviews and observational data, evidence supported that the three teachers integrated their various backgrounds to produce idiosyncratic ways of teaching. Their teaching was not a collage of dance steps or somatic exercises learned previously. They used these specific tools only when needed. Thanks to their eclectic background, their endless curiosity and desire for change, the three women challenged conformity in their teaching.

Glenna's teaching encompassed six categories of instructional tasks: locating, scanning, analyzing, hands-on, visualizing, and moving tasks (Fortin 1994). Whereas typical dance classes favor moving tasks, Glenna considered a variety of tasks to hold prime importance so that students could achieve movement efficiency through more than kinesthetic repetition. "It astounds me," she said, "how many teachers teach dance without any reference to sensory awareness. They simply teach dance from the point of view of the limb moving through space." Somatics can improve dance teaching because it places, as she said, an enormous emphasis on "attending one's sensing self by giving oneself over to a receptive mode, not only a doing, moving one." She insisted that the integration of various somatic practices was feeding her personal and professional life. Though her teaching drew from specific somatic practices, she said that she had an eclectic stance toward them:

I don't see myself ever becoming a Feldenkrais practitioner, an Alexander practitioner, an Ideokinesis practitioner. I see these body therapies as feeding who I am, what I need, and therefore what eventual work I will do as a teacher; but it is a combination of those things [somatic practices] that is integrated into what I do. Maybe one sees that as standing aloof, but I need to see myself as an individual at once being able to partake of that and then being aloof from that.

Somatics also informed Martha's teaching. Like Glenna, she presented her content through unorthodox tasks, which varied from open to closed. More precisely, four categories of tasks emerged inductively from the data: routine copy tasks, theme and variation improvisations, guided improvisations, and free improvisations (Fortin and Siedentop 1995). She explained the importance of her somatics experience to her teaching in these terms:

I made the choice to work more from concepts coming from Laban Movement Analysis and Body-Mind Centering. . . . Rather than just doing a movement that I like, I'm usually doing a movement that I feel will teach them something, a body connection, a use of dynamics and space.

The observational data indeed revealed that Martha organized the tasks around three themes derived from the conceptual frameworks of Laban Movement Analysis and Body-Mind Centering: variation of space and dynamics, developmental body part relationships, and moving from inside out. The tasks presented in Martha's class were sometimes transferred directly from her past experiences, sometimes modified, and sometimes created entirely by her. She explained that she borrowed from her past teachers, altering the material to fit the needs of her students and her own body limitations and facilities. Her background in dance, Laban Movement Analysis, and Body-Mind Centering provided Martha with a repertoire of tasks to teach. More important, her background in somatics led her to engage in a personal bodily exploration, which enabled her to relate her past experiences in a meaningful way and to keep adding some of her own. The following quote clearly reveals Martha's all-encompassing approach: "It's not a Laban, it's not a Bartenieff, it's not a Body-Mind Centering class. . . . It is a dance class. To dance is to communicate. Let's have a dance class and use all the tools that are within dance." In the publicity materials for her class she wrote this description:

[The class] is designed to experientially teach principles of anatomy, kinesiology, human development, and movement fundamentals in relation to emotional/artistic expression. The aim is to coordinate inner body focus with the outward projection needed in performance. Emphasis is on befriending unfamiliar, unknown, or taboo parts of the body and psyche, learning to include them in the creative process.

Like Glenna and Martha, Mary explained that somatics had radically changed her teaching. Talking about her teaching before using Laban Movement Analysis, she said that she was teaching the "steps" she had learned, more or less in the same way in which she had learned them:

Historically what has happened is that you learn by imitation from your teacher, and you teach what you learned, period. Teaching dance is like storytelling except we do it with our whole body. Instead of speaking the stories with our mouth and remembering them, passing them down to the families, we do this with our bodies. So we tell stories with our bodies and we do not know why it happened or where it comes from or anything. We just imitate that and take it to the next level. People blend in some of their own personal viewpoints and feelings, but it becomes still a physical interpretation, a physical mirroring of that past generation.

Laban Movement Analysis seems to have given Mary, as for Martha, a conceptual framework for making sense of her prior training. She described how her teaching is now based on concepts instead of steps:

If I was not working with Laban Movement Analysis work and exploring new ways of teaching, I wouldn't be in the dance field. If I didn't have the information that I have, sort of having a personal library of ideas and ways to work underneath the steps, I don't think I would be a performer or a teacher.

When asked directly where her knowledge for teaching comes from, her answer was clear: "Laban Movement Analysis, the combination of mentors, and just my own process of learning how to teach myself because I went back and basically taught myself how to dance."

Glenna, Martha, and Mary all spent a lot of time exploring body and movement principles in order to develop their nontraditional dance classes. Both Glenna and Martha had a dance space in their house, and they each spent hours focusing on their lived bodily experience. They continually engaged in a process of discovery to perfect their vision of what a dance technique class might be. At the same time all three teachers mentioned feeling the pressure to conform to the students' and the teaching institution's traditional expectations of a dance technique class. For example, Martha conformed to these expectations by including complex dance combinations at the end of each class. Mary also made concessions in her teaching:

> When you get a job as a teacher, you should be accommodating the students who are paying for the class, the institution you are working for as well as yourself. I'm not 100 percent fulfilled, the kids may not be 100 percent fulfilled, the administration may not be 100 percent fulfilled, but all together we come to some sort of consensus. Unless you teach on your own, and people are coming to see you specifically for your teaching technique, that's a different story.

How this sort of "institutional disempowering" may have acted as an impetus toward creating and maintaining a freelance innovative teaching practice is addressed in the last section.

WORKING TOWARD A GENERIC DANCE TECHNIQUE CLASS

Embedded in both the notion of empowerment and somatics is the development of a better understanding of one's own experience in order to recognize one's own power as a knower and a creator of the world (Ellsworth 1989). Somatics influenced Glenna, Martha, and Mary's teaching by the explicit acknowledgment of their subjective experience as a reliable source of information to be investigated systematically, then shared with others in a nondogmatic manner. This view contrasts sharply with the prevailing behavior in many technique classes, in which students are required to replicate the teacher's movements exactly. Often these movements are adopted from a specific style such as Graham, Cunningham, or Limon. Glenna, Martha, and Mary's classes differed from this image of the traditionally codified dance class in that they did not situate their classes in any particular dance style. The three women attempted to offer a generic technique class in which priority was given to sensing the body, in contrast to focusing on the aesthetic model of a specific idiom. Technique for them was not relegated to a particular style but was meant instead to enhance a wide range of skills in such a way that optimal execution of any dance style would be achieved.

Martha's desire to move away from the traditional technical class was visible in many ways. She rejected the separation of dance classes into the categories of dance technique, composition, and improvisation. For her, traditional dance technique classes are based on the mimicry of the teacher's idiosyncratic movements, which Martha saw as a barrier to the individual expression of the students. Dance, in her view, should be expressive whatever the context. In a teaching situation, even the simplest movement should convey something about the internal feelings and thoughts of the mover. The dancers' instruments, their sensitive bodies, should be developed to express and communicate their internal motivation. Martha encouraged her students to sense their bodies internally by making comments such as the following: "Do what your body needs to do," or "Take two minutes to move as you want to move. How do you feel? How do you want to feel?" To her, strict technique classes have value only in a particular context:

> If you're about to perform in somebody's repertory and you're going to really embody it, it's helpful preparation [to take strict technical dance classes] but if your goal is to discover yourself or to work on your own choreography, then for a dance training class to do that, maybe it's better if it's open-ended and less about ritualizing someone else's movement.

On that issue, Glenna believed that "repeating steps at the expense of attending to the way we might accomplish them" is not worthwhile. She explained,

> My goal is to make a technique class so I've got to put in a certain degree of repetition but repetition of a certain type that keeps the senses very lively. It may be the same movements strung together in a different way to show that there is repetition of a theme or a concept, or repetition of a sense of awareness but not of a movement necessarily.

Glenna structured her classes around six weekly themes: the pelvis, the rib cage, the abdominals, the knee and the hip joint, and the neck and the head. Each day she presented a subtheme in order for the students to learn how that aspect can support the body part of that week. For example, the week that she worked on the rib cage, a subtheme was the connection of the arms to the sternum. Glenna did not build her classes on a progression of physical skills, from the simpler to the more difficult (tendu, dégagé, battement, etc.)

because she believes in the synergistic relationship between the whole and the part. Her class emphasized key concepts of somatic education, such as inclusiveness, integration, wholeness, and connectedness. Whole-body connectedness appeared to be a central organizing principle of her teaching along with sensing kinesthetically. She believes that the body is intelligent, by which she means that the body is self-correcting if it receives new sensory information, and if the person becomes aware that options are available other than those that are habitual. While presenting different tasks, she constantly used sensory verbs and a variety of adverbs to call attention to a sensory quality and to internal movements in executing different actions: "Stay there a minute and feel where in your body the movement is traveling; what body part does not respond smoothly?" The following quote expresses her hope that the tone of her voice as well as her specific use of language might influence how students attend to their own bodies in a sensory mode:

I feel that my voice is another kinesthetic sense. My voice has to create a sensitivity that people can feel about their bodies. . . . I use my voice in a way that implies connectedness. Then they're going to understand what I'm trying to get at.

She constantly asked the students to pay attention to their inner sensations; doing so was probably as important as the specific movements they were asked to execute. Glenna felt that sensing, as an approach to teaching movement, is unfortunately impeded by the lack of social value given to sensing in general:

There is little understanding that sensing movement will in and of itself organize the movement . . . . Our culture has virtually a poverty of movement. We separate mind and body. The politics and the society is such that it does not help you. It just removes you more and more from your own sensation . . . . Of course to me, the most optimal way of learning is to have a very accurate sense of the inner body while it's moving. Visually you see the outside and visually you see the inside and the two match. Those two have to come together in such a way that you're not simply a clone of the outside person.

In a way, Mary echoed Glenna's point of view when she asked her students in class, "If you don't learn different sensations, then how can you do different people's work?" She explained in one of our interviews that she teaches students a different way of thinking about dancing than that to which they are accustomed:

I'm teaching the students to move from the inside out. Most of these students are interested in style. They are not interested in learning how to get the style. I'm sort of teaching the students what it's like to do somebody else's work from the inside out.

QUESTIONING THE TEACHER'S ROLE

By focusing on the inner lived experience of the body, Glenna, Martha, and Mary created a context in which to nurture the students' own empowerment. They encouraged the students to free themselves from the external pressure of a strict model of success proffered by the external image of the teacher. This invites a new way of looking at the teacher's role.[3] "In most dance technique classes, the teacher is the authority and the only recognized source of knowledge," argues Stinson (1994). Furthermore, Stinson adds, "The model for the traditional dance pedagogue seems to be the authoritarian father" (2). In their teaching, Glenna, Martha, and Mary encouraged their students to challenge this authoritarian view. In class Mary referred to her work as "fundamentool," rather than fundamental, explaining that:

Fundamentals gives you the tools so you can work with yourself and then can take anybody's class. In this class my interests are in three things: the relationships between your personality, your body type, and your preferences in movement. You are a person who's a dancer, not a dancer who's a person. My interest is in teaching you independence.

Mary elaborated on this idea in an interview in which she said, "Fundamentals is a way to look at movements in themselves in relationship to what the teacher is giving. It's a way to make choices not to involve the teachers and make the teachers feel as if they know everything."

Mary, Martha, and Glenna stated explicitly that the students did not have to please them by copying them but that they should discover how to express themselves and take care of their well-being by working within the limits of their own body types. They often explained that the differences in students' execution was due to their distinct body structures. All three teachers, however, noticed the students' difficulty in expressing their individuality through the movement and in acknowledging their own experience. They each talked about a certain docile attitude among dancers. "I think basically dancers are trained to respond in a particular way," said Martha, continuing, "Dance classes are really about following the hierarchy of the model of the teacher." Glenna reflects this view:

---

[3]The ways in which these three women's teaching methods had an impact on the students are beyond the scope of this research, which focuses exclusively on the teachers. An investigation of the effects of their teaching would be a promising avenue of research. The students' perspectives on these teaching methods are surely needed to build our understanding of what we should teach in a dance class and how we should teach it.

I don't know if we find this only in dance, but people are so set on doing the right thing. They like doing the exact way of doing things. I would say that above all this is the biggest frustration [for me]. To at once impart to them that they can let their own individuality come through in a movement is hard.

In one way or another, each teacher expressed the view that learning dance is a lifelong process that individuals pursue for themselves, and typically by themselves, under the guidance of or through collaboration with others who are further advanced in their own developmental process. They all expressed an awareness of being at a certain point in their own learning process and recognized their limitations. "I'm not afraid to send my students to somebody else if I feel they need something other than I'm giving them," said Mary. "I'm not afraid to say, I'm sorry, I don't know the answer to all questions. Hopefully, you will never know the answer to all questions." Talking about her strengths and weaknesses, Martha said that she sometimes deliberately displayed her technical limitations in class to convey the message that learning is a process shared by everyone. The three teachers allowed their teaching to be influenced by factors such as their own physical needs and their desire to have an enjoyable class for themselves. The first time she met her students, Glenna said to them: "I teach the class because I like this class. I need it for me."

She further explained that doing the exercises put her in touch with her own kinesthetic sensations, which helped her to provide accurate sensory descriptions of the movements and to give students feedback. Each woman allowed her sensations, emotions, and intuition to inform her teaching. When I asked Mary how she proceeded to correct the movement of her students, her answer reflected her capacity for empathy and embodiment:[4]

I observe them, and I put myself inside their skin. I devote myself completely to listening to them, and it's as if I enter inside their bodies. The two bodies become one. I put myself into their way of doing things, and I feel their internal state when they move.

It is interesting to make an analogy here with my own process of embodiment, in my role as a researcher, while conducting the individual case studies. Like the dance teachers' embodiment of the lived body of their students to better feel, understand, and act, I embodied the lived body of the

---

[4]According to Gomez (1988), embodiment "involves resonating, vibrating, echoing with whatever information we choose to focus on, either within ourselves, our breath, our ligament connections, etc., or outside ourselves through feeling empathic responses to someone else's rhythm, to the softness of a baby, etc." (41).

teachers to obtain a better understanding of them. I immersed myself completely in the reality of each of the three teachers with the attitude that we can only approximate other people's experiences and knowledge. The three studies occurred during dance festivals where I had the opportunity to be with these women from morning to night as they were engaged in various activities. We developed a sense of closeness, which became so intimate that Glenna gave me her personal diary to read in which her private and professional life were inseparable. All of them allowed me to reveal their identities, even though the initial agreement involved confidentiality and anonymity. I would say that the level of deep trust in our relationship was supported by the fact that I was about the same age as them and that I am also a dance teacher and somatic educator. I invested myself and they returned the investment. The friendship did not have personal or professional boundaries. Like Wolcott (1990), I agree that there is no compartmentalization in postpositivist research: "I personalize the world I research and intellectualize the world of my experience" (144). The close exchange I had with Glenna, Martha, and Mary remained unchanged when I returned to them later to verify the accuracy of the research, a stage postpositivist

© Joel Hauserman

researchers call *member check*.[5] In fact, there comes a point in the research when the researchers have to respect both the participants' and their own points of view, not to subjugate one to another but to try to clarify one through the other. When the points of view differ, the researchers present them for what they are: perceptions of a constructed reality with multiple facets, as varied as the individuals engaged in the action.

INFLUENCE OF SOMATICS ON DANCE PEDAGOGY

Somatics influenced Glenna, Martha, and Mary's teaching in a number of ways. The data clearly illustrates how the three teachers distanced themselves from their apprenticeship of observation, developed a personalized generic dance class, and began to question the nature of their role as a teacher. In the following discussion, I first look at these findings from a historical perspective because empowerment is a recurring theme that is played out differently in time. I then highlight aspects that somatic education and feminist pedagogy have in common. This includes, among other things, the primacy of the subjective experience as a reliable source of knowledge and the acknowledgment of a bodily level of meaning.

EMPOWERMENT IN THE DANCE COMMUNITY

Each of the three women's teaching is inspired by the work of somatic pioneers who made an impact mainly from the 1930s to the 1960s (Mangione 1993). A first generation of modern dancers attended the classes of the somatic pioneers in tandem with their dance classes. Glenna, Martha, and Mary belong to a second generation that is attempting to integrate dance and somatic practices. Their struggle to develop a new approach to teaching dance reflects a desire for change shared by many educators in the modern dance community. According to Hanstein (1990), it is indeed time to challenge the status quo of the dance tradition:

> The increasing complexity of our society requires us, and the students who will shape the future, to function in tasks that demand imaginative thinking and the ability to suggest alternatives and formulate hypotheses. Education in general, and dance education in particular, should focus on developing the ability to see the connection between actions and their consequences and between means and ends, to take cognitive risks, and to extend thinking beyond the known in order to deal effectively with what might be rather than with what is. (57)

---

[5] A discussion on the member check I undertook in the three individual case studies is presented in Fortin (1995a).

Glenna, Martha, and Mary shared the common thread of resistance to conforming to a conventional style. Ironically, the rejection of external standards for the body and a tightly codified movement aesthetic are tenets that contributed to the foundation of modern dance and still shape the development of choreography today. A similar rejection has never really found its counterpart in the realm of dance teaching. Dance teaching on the whole has remained faithful to a tradition characterized by the expert authority of the teachers over the body and movement aesthetic of the students (Gray 1990). The issue of a styleless, generic, neutral, or basic technique, however, is not new (Bird et al. 1979).

From a historical perspective, the present conception of technical dance teaching in North America originated with European ballet. The ballet masters and mistresses believed that their rigorous training technique provided a universal foundation for all theatrical dancing. This authoritative conception of dance technique was shaken by early American and German modern choreographers who developed concepts of expression closely linked to modern social issues and who eventually opened schools to teach their eponymous technique. Martha Graham, José Limon, Merce Cunningham, and Alwin Nikolais can be cited as examples. In turn the authority of these approaches were attacked by the New York-based Judson Dance Theater, whose members revolted against the academic character of modern techniques, which had become tightly codified and formalized by mid-century. The Judsonites questioned the standards of any "right" or "wrong" way of dancing or making dance. They rejected all orthodox approaches and considered all types of movements as possible material for dance. Regarding the Judsonites, Jowitt (1988) explains,

> The rejection of elitism and hierarchies and the attempted democratization of dance's processes, ingredients, and nature became the focal points—with one goal being to free the dancer from the tyranny of rules, ideals, and "technique," as it had come to be taught. (8)

The Judsonites opened the door to a dance that is still in search of proper labeling, being variously classified by critics as new, contemporary, postmodern, or experimental dance. With the exception of a few who attempted to create "new dance academies" (Davida 1996), the proponents of the new dance did not develop a codified "danse d'école" (Huxley and Burt 1987). The entire training structure is not the same as the one prevailing a few decades ago. In the past, it was typical for a choreographer to have a permanent company with an affiliated school responsible for providing the company with the next generation of dancers. Today, "new dance" choreographers work in an individualistic way, what Bentivoglio (1987) identifies as "danse d'auteur." Teachers of new dance also tend to function in an individualistic way. Their challenge is to respond to the demand of new dance choreography, which requires highly skilled dancers without any rigid stylistic imprint in their bodies. Indeed, cutting-edge international choreographers such as Larieux in France, Perreault in Canada, or Bill T. Jones in the United States are looking for dancers without the typical mannerisms acquired through long training in a single style. The current tendency of these choreographers is to show dancers performing a wide range of movements from the pedestrian and natural to the highly athletic and gymnastic. Although they require natural and athletic performers, no specific training schools teach their requirements, as did (do) schools of modern dance choreographers of earlier generations. New dance choreographers often assume both teaching and choreographic functions in an individualistic fashion.

Stinson, Blumenfield-Jones, and Van Dyke (1990) point to the nature of the ties that teachers establish with professional practice. These authors argue that within the dance community in North America choreography and performance has considerably more status than teaching. Even within the teaching profession a hierarchy is created. At the top of this hierarchy are teachers who are well-known and respected choreographers and performers. The hierarchy functions on a series of levels, access to which is not necessarily based on how effective one is as a teacher. When teaching, new dance choreographers usually direct a personalized warm-up followed by an offering of their own choreographic sequences. These choreographers/teachers, according to Davida (1996), share "an interest in innovation, body issues and new perspectives" (7). Alongside the "category" of choreographers who are teaching are renowned performers/teachers who have mastered at the highest degree the typical skills of dance idioms such as Graham, Cunningham, and Limon, and who remain faithful to these teaching traditions. Finally, it seems to me that another category is emerging. This category includes teachers, such as the women discussed in this chapter, who choose to a great extent to base their teaching in somatics. Teachers in this rapidly expanding area view technique as "the ability to use basic physical movements effectively" (Berardi 1991). Glenna, Martha, and Mary advocate working in a direction likely to answer choreographers' specific demands for highly skilled but not stylized dancers. Somatics provides these three teachers with the knowledge useful for meeting these new requirements. Their teaching, with its focus on sensory information, might well serve both tendencies of the contemporary dance scene, from the natural and pedestrian movement to the highly athletic, gymnastic movement of the new dance.

Looking historically at the development of dance teaching is enlightening. Beginning as idiosyncratic exploration, modern dance techniques became codified over time. Horton Fraleigh (1987) addresses the interesting issue of how, initially forged out of personal sensory experiences, modern dance technique became frozen throughout the generations of practitioners. Judson's avant-garde reacted, she explained, by producing "various styles difficult to combine into one, although, the style inherent in the ease and unremarkableness of sneakers comes as close (as Banes suggests in the title of her book *Terpsichore in Sneakers*)" (129). Will a teaching style based on somatics also become gradually codified, as did the practices of Graham, Cunningham, and Limon? Somatics is no longer offered merely as adjunctive training, secondary to the study of technique; more and more it is being integrated into the technique class itself. In the past, choreographers have been the main influence on the development of technique classes. Now, somatics plays a significant role in that direction. Will somatic teaching styles continue to generate new approaches and perspectives? In time, avant-garde practice often becomes part of the establishment, as was the case with so many first generation modern dance choreographers such as Martha Graham. Perception of the role of somatics may well change once the practice has become integrated on a large scale in the teaching of dance.

PERSONAL EXPERIENCE AS A SOURCE OF KNOWLEDGE

According to Sandell (1991), "feminist pedagogy attempts to foster a confirmation of self-knowledge for the knower that is not provided by teaching in the traditional academic style" (181). The assumption of a reliance on personal experience as a basis for individual and social change underlies the work of many somatic and feminist educators.[6] What constitutes a valid source of knowledge is a relevant question for dance teachers. According to Eichelberger (1989), knowledge comes from three different sources: tradition, systematic research, and personal experience. He notes that "in making decisions, or drawing conclusions, one of the weakest logical foundations for doing anything is an appeal to authority" (13). In dance, tradition has long been the main guide for educators (Clarkson 1988). That is beginning to change. In their never-ending quest for new ways of teaching, Glenna, Martha, and Mary did not reject their past experience; they did not turn away from the dance tradition. Instead they attempted to integrate into their teaching knowledge what they had gained from others with knowledge that came from personal lived experience. Belenky et al. (1986) argue that when women "move outside the given" and are able to incorporate others' viewpoints, they are in a position of strength in that they are constructing knowledge.

The various somatic approaches that the three women had studied did not simply become a new rigid frame of reference substituting for a

---

[6] For an excellent discussion about the meeting of somatic and feminist theory, read Green (1993).

dissatisfying old one. They did not rely on somatics as a "truth" guiding their teaching behavior. Rather, their somatic background encouraged them to move toward a thorough self-examination that led each woman to her own unique way of teaching modern dance. It is interesting to note that, at the time of my data collection, both Glenna and Martha were in the process of making public their own eponymous teaching programs called, "Movement Revisions" and "Body-Mind Dancing," respectively. On the one hand, working as freelance teachers gave them the freedom to develop new approaches and to affirm their differences. On the other hand, once they were hired by an institution, specifically as a result of their idiosyncratic teaching, they had to follow to a certain degree the tacit culture of this institution. These freelance teachers were in a delicate position due to their precarious status. Within the context of the institution employing them, they felt that they could not transform their teaching to the extent they would have liked.[7] That being said, they were able to progressively formulate a practice of their own design by fine-tuning specific somatic practices and acknowledging the validity of their personal experience.

Interestingly, during their journey they found that the somatic practices that had initiated their personal and professional transformation eventually became insufficient. It was in breaking with the strict adherence to specific somatic approaches that they paradoxically came closer to the meaning of somatics. Somatics is primarily about coming to know oneself; this point cannot be stressed enough. "I believe that knowing oneself is the most important thing a human being can do for himself. How can one know oneself? By learning to act not as one should, but as one does," argues Feldenkrais (1981, xi). Becoming aware of one's bodily processes as a source of knowledge is a fundamental theme of somatic educators.

A BODILY LEVEL OF MEANING

The role of the teacher, in the view of feminist and somatic educators, is to facilitate students' process of becoming an expert of their own bodies and lives by interrogating and analyzing their own experiences. Conscious awareness of what was previously unconscious is the gateway for change. Critics of current dance education practices increasingly call into question whether dance students are being helped to become dancers who can take responsibility for their own bodies (Brightman 1995; Green 1991; Shapiro 1995; Stinson 1994). In the three individual case studies, ample evidence supported this goal. Glenna continually encouraged her students to adapt

---

[7] It is probably because of my status as Associate Professor at the Université du Québec à Montréal that I have been able recently to contribute to drastic changes in the teaching structure of my institution. For more information, read Fortin (1995b).

the different dance exercises to their body types and to pace themselves according to their kinesthetic sensations. Martha invited the students to perform the movements their own way, acknowledging the emotional component of the dance experience. Mary also required the students to acknowledge their own body type and sensations. They all stressed that they did not want to impose bodily norms and that as teachers they were not all-knowing experts. Each worked at home extensively, engaging in a process of gaining knowledge about her own body and validating it through heuristic experimentation and personal study of functional anatomy. Through self-education, they were involved in a process of empowering themselves by gaining personal bodily authority. They invited their students to do the same. For feminist educators, empowerment comes with a transformation of the educational system, which is achieved by presenting the subject matter in a different way and by building a new kind of coexistence between students and teacher (Weiler 1988).

Along these lines, Johnson (1983) shows how people have been systematically alienated from their personal authority and made dependent on experts. Johnson asserts that people should trust their "gut feeling" in making important decisions and not defer to the experts, discounting the wisdom of their own senses. "The fundamental shift from alienation to authenticity," he said, "is deceptively simple: It requires diverting our awareness from the opinions of those outside us toward our own perceptions and feelings" (54).

Glenna, Martha, and Mary also believe that people know their own needs better than anybody else. In their individual practice, however, they all confronted the dance community's tendency to generate docile bodies unable to act in the world by themselves. Traditional dance classes indeed reinforce the concept of human beings as "world-receivers" instead of "world-makers." Each woman believes that awareness of bodily experience is closely tied to the development of personal authority and hence provides leverage for empowerment. They faced the implications of taking and giving personal bodily authority in technical dance classes, which are usually informed by a delineated tradition and cultured body. By different means, they tried to tie together teaching and learning dance into an unorthodox approach to fostering personal and social change. Green (1993) explains,

While much somatic theory focuses on individual experience and the primacy of the self, and works toward freeing the body through an exploration of movement possibilities and choices . . . the usefulness of somatic theory may be limited unless it is also applied beyond the self and also addresses how our bodies are inscribed by the society and culture in which we live. (317)

CONCLUSION

Several dimensions of Glenna, Martha, and Mary's teaching were influenced by their study of somatics. Their desire to break away from a conventional codified dance style was empowering in the sense that the process of becoming empowered includes the feeling people get when they move outside the realm of the habitual to develop their own vision. They shared a vision that knowledge emerges from the learner's own experiences. Their teaching was counter-hegemonic in the sense that they did not want to be confined by dance tradition. Their desire for change in the way dance technique is taught, however, was partially constrained by external pressures to conform to what is expected in a traditional technical class. Despite this pressure, each pursued with determination her vision of what dance teaching might be, and each was aware of the pioneering aspect of her contribution. Like the pioneering somatic educators who inspired them, they strove to find their own paths. Glenna shared,

> The people who really influenced me were people who followed their desire in spite of all odds. That's the model that just keeps coming back. It was the resistance of the experience, not only within themselves but culturally, that created energy to go on. And I often do feel that about myself.

None of the three women would be considered "typical" teachers teaching "typical" courses, but similar teaching approaches are likely to become more common with the passage of time. As we begin the process of integrating somatic education and feminist pedagogy into our modern dance technique classrooms, we are defining new models for dance. We are often obliged to find creative ways to work within the restrictions of our institutions if we are interested in challenging the "way things are." We have no choice. If we and our students want to be part of current choreographic practices we need to transform the content of our classes as well as our pedagogical outlooks. In a progressive art form, dance teachers and dance choreographers cannot embrace conservative ways of doing things. A new relationship between students and teachers is called for if we want to prepare dancers and choreographers for the future. Contemporary choreographers are constantly pushing the boundaries of aesthetic canons, and they are looking more and more for dancers who actively participate in the creative process. A growing number of choreographers are moving away from the authoritarian mode and acknowledging the contributions of their dancers. If dance teachers really want to engage in a contemporary art form, one that is constantly changing and growing, we must continue to question the content and the pedagogy of our teaching.

On a last note, the contribution of this cross-case study is to provide, as Shulman (1983) calls it, "images of the possible." Images of the possible are necessary in any journey toward empowerment. Glenna, Martha, and Mary's teaching approaches provide three images of the possible, specific instances in which a knowledge base composed not only of tradition, but also of knowledge gained from personal bodily experience, contributed to personal transformation and challenged the status quo of dance teaching. I hope that the insights that emerged from this cross-case study may serve to inspire the transformation of dance pedagogy and move us toward a promising new century while keeping the integrity of earlier decades.

Critical Reflections

Embedded within the tradition of dance pedagogy are the "taken for granted" (using Maxine Greene's phrase) ways of "doing things." Contrasting positivistic to postpositivistic research, we draw our attention toward "what it is that we come to know" and for what purpose. In the former, research depends on empirical evidence (those things we can see objectively), whereas in the latter research approach the focus shifts from objective knowledge to subjective knowledge. Sylvie Fortin used the latter approach to look at how a background in somatics affected the teaching of three dance educators. Postpositivist, or interpretive, research work is based on the premise that there are no right answers. Postpositivist researchers try to understand the world from the perspective of the subjects themselves, that is, how the people they study give meaning and significance to the world in which they live. To understand dance is to understand something about ourselves and our culture. This understanding, in critical and feminist pedagogies, is not simply directed toward "knowing something"; instead it is directed toward taking action through conscious choices based on sensual and experiential understandings. In the Freirian sense, it is called *praxis*, active reflection upon one's world in order to change it. As you read and reflect upon these issues try to determine the nature and relative importance of your own aims and goals.

Take a Moment to Reflect

1. What specific pedagogic or research methods do you currently use? How many of those do you follow because that is "the way things are"?

2. How would you describe the types of body exploration you have undertaken in dance? What did you learn from them (implicitly and explicitly)?

3. Does understanding the relationship of the parts of the body to the whole give us a holistic understanding of the culture in which we live? How might this happen?

4. Why might it be valuable to reflect upon your embodied experiences? (Embodied means those things, such as values, attitudes, and beliefs, that we learn through our culture and that become a part of our physical beings.)

5. Try to think of examples of what you might consider to be your own experiences of "institutional disempowerment"?

6. Why are postpositivistic, or interpretive, research methods valuable in helping us understand dance education?

Working within educational settings has entailed being faced with constant questions concerning the value of the art experience to the individual as well as the relevance of arts education to the overall school curriculum. Having "made it' into that curriculum, and being sensitive to feminist concerns for a curriculum that is more connected, arts education is now faced with the task of integrating with other arts or subject areas and working within an interdisciplinary curriculum approach. In the next chapter, Jan Bolwell looks at these issues and discusses how cultural diversity plays a role in them.

REFERENCES

Alexander, F.M. 1943. *The Use of Self*. Long Beach, CA: Centerline Press.

Bainbridge Cohen, B. 1983. *Sensing, Feeling, and Action: The Experimental Anatomy of Body-Mind Centering*. Northampton, MA: Contact Editions.

Banes, S. 1980. *Terpischore in Sneakers: Post Modern Dance*. Boston: Houghton Mifflin.

Bartenieff, I., and D. Lewis. 1980. *Body Movement: Coping with the Environment*. New York: Gordon & Breach.

Beaulieu, M., and S. Fortin. 1996. "Performance Work in the Contemporary Dance Technique Class." Unpublished manuscript. Montréal, PQ: Université du Québec.

Belenky, M., B. Clinchy, N. Goldberger, and J. Tarule. 1986. *Women's Ways of Knowing*. New York: Basic Books.

Bentivoglio, L. 1987. "Europe et États-Unis: Un Courant." In *La Danse au Défi*, M. Febvre, (ed.) Montréal: Les Éditions Parachute.

Berardi, G. 1991. *Finding Balance: Fitness and Training for a Lifetime in Dance*. Princeton, NJ: Princeton Book Company.

Bird, B., J. Jarrell, P. Mackenzie, and N. Steedman. 1979. "Some Considerations of Technique." In *Dancing and Dance Theory*, V. Preston-Dunlop, (ed.) London: Laban Center for Movement Studies.

Brightman, P. 1995. "The Dancer and Her Body." Paper presented at the Convention of the American Alliance for Health, Physical Education, Recreation and Dance, March, Portland, OR.

Clarkson, P. 1988. "Science in Dance." In *Science of Dance Training*, P. Clarkson and M. Skrinar, (ed.). Champaign, IL: Human Kinetics.

Davida, D. 1996. *Dancing the Body Eclectic: A Dance Curator Reflects on Culture and the "New Dance."* Toronto: Dance Department of York University.

Dunn, J. 1990. "Dance Science." *Journal of Physical Education, Recreation and Dance* 61 (9): 25.

Eichelberger, R.T. 1989. *Disciplined Inquiry: Understanding and Doing Social Research*. New York: Longman.

Ellsworth, E. 1989. *Why Doesn't This Feel Empowering? Working Through the Repressive Myths of Critical Pedagogy*. Harvard Educational Review 59: 297-325.

Feldenkrais, M. 1949. *Body and Mature Behavior*. New York: International Universities Press.

———. 1981. *The Elusive Obvious*. Cupertino, CA: Meta.

Fortin, S. 1990. "Mary: Pedagogical Content Knowledge of an Expert Teacher." Unpublished manuscript. Montréal, PQ: Université du Québec.

———. 1994. "When Dance Science and Somatics Enter the Dance Technique Class." *Kinesiology and Medicine for Dance* 15 (2): 88-107.

———. 1995a. "La Recherche Qualitative dans le Studio de Danse: Une Relation Dialogique de Corps à Corps." *Revue de l'Association pour la Recherche Qualitative* 12 (12): 75-87.

———. 1995b. "Towards a New Generation: Somatic Dance Education in Academia." *Impulse: The International Journal of Dance Science, Medicine and Education* 3 (4): 253-262.

Fortin, S., and D. Siedentop. 1995. "The Interplay of Knowledge and Practice in Dance Teaching: What We Can Learn from a Non-Traditional Dance Teacher." *Dance Research Journal* 27 (2): 3-15.

Gomez, N. 1988. *Movement, Body and Awareness: Exploring Somatic Processes*. (Available from Ninoska Gomez, Cabano de Puntarenas, Montezuma, Costa Rica)

Gray, J. 1990. "Dance Education in the Future: Trends and Predictions." *Journal of Physical Education, Recreation and Dance* 61 (5): 50-51.

Green, J. 1991. "A Somatic Approach to Dance." Paper presented at the Convention of the American Alliance for Health, Physical Education, Recreation and Dance, April, San Francisco.

———. 1993. "Fostering Creativity through Movement and Body Awareness Practices: A Postpositivist Investigation into the Relationship between Somatics and the Creative Process." Ph.D. dissertation, Ohio State University.

Hanna, T. 1983. "Dictionary Definition of the Word Somatics." *Somatics* 4 (2): 1.

———. 1986. "What Is Somatics?" *Somatics* 5 (4): 4-8.

Hanstein, P. 1990. "Educating for the Future: A Post-Modern Paradigm for Dance Education." *Journal of Physical Education, Recreation and Dance* 61 (5): 56-58.

Horton Fraleigh, S. 1987. *Dance and the Lived Body*. Pittsburgh: University of Pittsburgh Press.

Huxley, M., and Burt, R. 1987. "La Nouvelle Danse: Comment ne pas Jouer le Jeu de L'establishment." In *La Danse au Défi*, ed. M. Febvre. Montréal: Les Éditions Parachute.

Johnson, D. 1983. *Body*. Boston: Beacon Press.

Johnson, D.H. (ed.) 1995. *Bone, Breath and Gesture: Practices of Embodiment*. Berkeley, CA: North Atlantic Books.

Jowitt, D. 1988. *Time and the Dancing Image*. New York: Morrow.

Lord, M. 1984. "Enseigner avec Souplesse ou l'Art de s'Adapter à sa Classe." *Magazine Danse au Canada* 39: 26-27.

Lortie, D.C. 1975. *School Teacher: A Sociological Study*. Chicago: University of Chicago Press.

Mangione, M. 1993. "The Origins and Evolution of Somatics: Interviews with Five Significant Contributors to the Field." Ph.D. dissertation, Ohio State University.

Myers, M. 1980. "Body Therapies and the Modern Dancer: The New 'Science' in Dance Training." *Dance Magazine* (February): 90-92.

———. 1989. "Dance Science and Somatic Education in Dance Training." Keynote address for the Australian Association of Dance Education biennial meeting, Spring, Sydney, Australia.

Sandell, R. 1991. The Liberating Relevance of Feminist Pedagogy. *Studies in Art Education* 32 (3): 178-187.

Shapiro, S. 1995. "Toward Transformative Teachers; Critical and Feminist Perspectives in Dance Education." Paper presented at the Convention of the American Alliance for Health, Physical Education, Recreation and Dance, March, Portland, OR.

Shulman, L. 1983. "Autonomy and Obligation: The Remote Control of Teaching." In *Handbook of Teaching and Policy*, L. Shulman and G. Sykes, (ed.) New York: Longman.

Stinson, S. 1994. "A Feminist Pedagogy for Children's Dance." Paper presented at the Conference of Dance and the Child International, July, Sydney, Australia.

Stinson, S., D. Blumenfield-Jones, and J. Van Dyke. 1990. "Voices of Young Women Dance Students: An Interpretive Study of Meaning in Dance." *Dance Research Journal* 22 (2): 13-22.

Sweigard, L.E. 1974. *Human Movement Potential: Its Ideokinetic Facilitation*. New York: Dodd, Mead.

Weiler, K. 1988. *Women Teaching for Change: Gender, Class and Power*. South Hadley, MA: Bergi & Garvey.

Wilson, D.C. 1990. "The Utilization of Mind-Body Practices by Modern Dancers in Canada." PhD dissertation. York University, ON.

Wolcott, H.F. 1990. "On Seeking and Rejecting Validity in Qualitative Research." In *Qualitative Inquiry in Education*, E.W. Eisner and A. Peshkin, (ed.) New York: Teachers College Press.

TELLING STORIES

CHAPTER 4

INTO THE LIGHT: AN EXPANDING VISION OF DANCE EDUCATION

JAN BOLWELL
Wellington College of Education, Te Whānau O Ako Pai Ki Te Upoko O Te Ika, New Zealand

This chapter discusses issues in dance education in the context of international curriculum reform. The debates concerning generic arts and interdisciplinary arts education are analyzed from a dance educator's perspective. New paradigms in the education of school performing arts teachers are identified, with examples drawn from an experimental work in a New Zealand College of Education where music, dance, and drama are taught within one program. The social and cultural challenges facing dance education are addressed, using as examples the initiatives occurring among the indigenous people of Aotearoa, New Zealand, in partnership with European New Zealanders. The need for further research in dance education is discussed in the context of the teacher as researcher, reflecting on her own teaching practices. The author concludes by urging dance educators to enter into a dialogue with other educators, inside and outside the arts, to expand their vision of dance education.

These are challenging times for dance educators. The worldwide trend toward curriculum reform provides an opportunity to review our practices and philosophy and to determine the directions that dance education might take as we approach the 21st century. Thanks to advances in technology we can maintain a close and ongoing dialogue with colleagues internationally, not only in the dance field but also across the broader spectrum of arts education.

Dance will not fully serve its role within the complex social and political arena of contemporary education unless its practitioners (teachers, performers, writers, critics, and administrators) broaden their vision beyond the immediate and specific concerns of the discipline itself. As dance educators we must engage vigorously in general education debates to bring our perspectives to other forums, both inside and outside the arts. Carroll reminds us that "A rich and rewarding dialogue might be stimulated by arts educators writing for others, coauthoring articles across disciplines, and comparing conceptions and perceptions" (1993, 21). In my view such interaction needs to go beyond writing articles and extend to examining institutional structures and programs that encourage interdisciplinary debate and present challenges in a broader social and cultural framework. We would inevitably feel less isolated if we sought this collegial relationship and realized that we share common concerns with other art forms. Visiting a problem or issue in another discipline can help to illuminate the concerns in one's own, and new solutions may arise from a more lateral approach. Koroscik (1994) suggests,

> The attraction of interdisciplinary collaboration is that we can continue to pursue depth within an area of specialization, yet draw upon expertise in related disciplines when the need arises. This allows us to gain valuable input from other fields without sacrificing the depth required for innovative research in our own discipline. (2-10)

If arts educators felt less marginalized within the total education system, they might embrace more willingly the notion of partnerships across art forms and regard such interaction as a dynamic development instead of as a "watering down" or minimizing of their own discipline.

In this chapter I address dance education within the broader context of general education and arts education concerns. The topic, *interdisciplinary arts,* provides a focus for discussion on the relationship among the arts, which is currently being debated in many countries as a result of national curriculum reforms. The idea of the arts as representing a generic entity has led to some fiery and contentious arguments among arts education philosophers and practitioners. Dance educators have been largely absent from this debate, and so I raise issues here as they pertain to dance. Cultural issues are at the cutting edge of the politics of contemporary education, and dance educators have been woefully negligent, either largely ignoring this critically important area or being superficial in their approach by making a symbolic effort only. I discuss some of the cultural issues facing dance educators, particularly in the context of my own country, New Zealand. The paucity of dance education research has prevented dance educators from entering in a dialogue with professionals in other art forms, and I address the idea of empowering dance educators to become reflective practitioners and researchers of their own practice. In this way we may begin to build a body of literature that is seen as relevant and useful, which addresses the relationship between theory and practice. Of necessity, the issues discussed in this chapter are selective, but I believe that they embrace some of the most important and fundamental challenges confronting today's educators.

INTERDISCIPLINARY ARTS

Throughout the world, national curricula are being developed, a clear signal that the arts are being regarded as a collective entity. It is therefore imperative for us as dance educators to grapple with the actualities of some of these structural changes that policy makers have put before us. A starting point must be dialogue with other arts disciplines about the impact such reforms will have on the whole field of arts education and how together we might strengthen the role of the arts in the education system.

Another strategy is to work actively with arts educators from other disciplines. Interdisciplinary inquiry is often constrained, however, by the way we train teachers in colleges and universities. At Wellington College of Education, where I teach in New Zealand, we are attempting to deal with this problem both structurally and in terms of our course content. Music, dance, and drama are taught within a Department of Performing Arts Education; team teaching across disciplines is encouraged; and course planning is a highly interactive process. Issues such as setting learning outcomes and conducting assessment and moderation procedures are dealt with in a collective manner. A new advanced undergraduate course, Contemporary Issues in Performing Arts Education, allows for the exploration of specific issues as they pertain to the individual disciplines; it also provides the opportunity for performing arts staff to examine and debate matters of common interest and concern. We believe that it is important to model for our students a team teaching and interdisciplinary approach to the arts; this collaborative approach is what we expect students to follow once they are out teaching in our elementary schools.

It is important to clarify the distinction between the terms *interdisciplinary* and *integrated* arts. The latter is defined as bringing elements or parts together to create a new whole whereas the former suggests a dialogue among disciplines in which each retains its own identity and integrity. Integrated arts is now a largely discredited notion, accused of promoting directionless, nonspecific thematic work where students ended up lacking in knowledge and competency in any of the art forms. Mason suggests that although words like "integration" and "interdisciplinary" signify different perspectives, in the end the distinction is not a meaningful one because it represents a similar approach to curriculum design (1996, 263-64). We have found in the practical working situation that a definite need exists to clarify the meanings of these terms. Students need to be aware, for example, of the impact on teaching and learning when an art form is used in an instrumental way; how the particular sequencing of a problem-solving task is conducted (e.g., music stimulus → dance activity → drama activity) affects the end product. In taking a general thematic approach, many different starting points are possible, and actively experimenting with the ordering of tasks helps to illuminate both the similarities and the differences of the working processes in the performing arts.

It is significant that in recently advertised positions in New Zealand high schools and tertiary training institutions, the descriptors used are "performing arts teachers" rather than solely mentioning a specific arts discipline expertise. This trend indicates that we need to reexamine some of our long-held beliefs about the training of arts educators if we are to meet the needs of the market place.

At our college, having already set up a Department of Performing Arts Education for the training of generalist elementary teachers, we are simultaneously experimenting with an interdisciplinary model in the training of high school music, dance, and drama teachers. Within the one-year postgraduate program, all the students undertake a compulsory interdisciplinary arts course, as well as discrete modules in their respective main discipline. We are testing in a practical manner the notion that some generic basis can be established for the training of arts educators and that interdisciplinary study can enrich the teaching of performing arts to adolescent pupils. We see these students as pioneers, modeling a different way of approaching the teaching of music, dance, and drama in our schools.

NATIONAL CURRICULUM REFORMS AND DANCE EDUCATION

National curriculum reform is a trend throughout Europe, Asia, North America, and Australasia. Within this movement, the idea of arts education is a relatively new conceptual development, superseding individual curricular frameworks in specific arts disciplines.

Some writers criticize treating the various arts as a single entity (Boughton 1994; Best 1992; McFee 1994; Swanwick 1988), and others contend that curriculum reform is fundamentally about governmental social engineering and control. For example, prominent Australian arts educator Doug Boughton claims that "such imposition of common goals and assessment are applied simply as an instrument to abolish social and cultural diversity to achieve unified values through rational forms of official control" (1994, 8). This strikes me as an extreme, and unnecessarily cynical, view of curriculum reform. An optimist might counter this argument with the view that at least the arts are being considered seriously within the totality of curriculum design and implementation and that the imposition of common goals and assessment could enforce some rigor into erstwhile sloppy and ephemeral arts education practices and philosophies. Identifying individual art forms within the framework of arts education reveals considerable international variation. The Australian Curriculum Corporation arts statement (1994) lists the arts as dance, drama, media, music, and the visual arts. These arts are defined as "strands" and are commonly characterized by the following "strand organizers": creating, making, and presenting; arts criticism and aesthetics; and past and present contexts.

At the time of this writing, New Zealand's curriculum initiative in the arts is about to take place. Within the New Zealand Curriculum Framework / Te Anga Marautanga O Aotearoa, the arts are described as one of the seven essential learning areas, which also include language, math, science, social studies, health and physical education, and technology. The arts are identified as comprising dance, drama, literature, music, visual arts (including craft and design), film, video, and oratory arts (Learning Media Ministry of Education 1993). The New Zealand document embraces the literary, visual, and performing arts, and it acknowledges the cultural heritage of Aotearoa, New Zealand with the inclusion of Maori art forms. (Aotearoa, "Land of the Long White Cloud," is the Maori name for New Zealand.)

In the United States the 1994 National Assessment of Educational Progress (NAEP) Arts Education Consensus Project, an Arts Education Assessment Framework, identifies the arts as dance, music, theater, and the visual arts. Subcategories include architecture, industrial design, graphic design, and media arts. The framework identifies the processes involved as creating, performing / interpreting, and responding. In a nation that has never had a history of centralized curriculum prescription, it is interesting to note the surfacing of this unified philosophy of arts education, which has been presented in such an uncompromising manner (14).

The NAEP Framework process and National Standards have constructed a vision of arts education that integrates the aesthetic, social, cultural, and historical contexts of the arts with the knowledge and skills necessary to participate in the arts. Skills will not be considered as separable, and the achievement of students will be reported as a whole, not on separate scales of isolated knowledge or technical skills. The image of arts education portrayed by the NAEP is as close to a vision of the arts as basic, unified, and pervasive as practically possible. It remains to be seen whether the laudable vision of the NAEP policy makers of a unified approach to arts education leads to improved practice and increased opportunities for students across the whole spectrum of the arts.

In England, the National Curriculum comprises three core subjects (English, mathematics, and science) and seven foundation subjects (technology, history, geography, music, visual arts, physical education, and, from the age of eleven, a modern foreign language), which must be included in the curriculum of all students (Davies 1991). In the arts, only music and visual arts are given full status as foundational subjects and then made optional after the age of fourteen. At international conferences that I have attended, dance and drama educators have expressed dismay that these art forms have been subsumed under other subject headings.

Although some structural anachronisms are present, as demonstrated by the English National Curriculum, overall the curriculum reforms offer potentially exciting possibilities for dance to secure its place within the total school program. The field of dance also stands to benefit by strengthening its conceptual base through engaging in a dialogue with other more developed and educationally entrenched art forms such as music and the visual arts.

Now is the time for dance educators to put aside parochial concerns and turn our attention toward the more general issues affecting the development of the arts within the education system. To do this we need to inform ourselves about current issues and research being addressed by educational psychologists, philosophers, and sociologists. In other words, it is time to step into the light and actively engage in the world of contemporary education in all of its social, cultural, and political complexity.

SOCIAL AND CULTURAL CHALLENGES TO DANCE EDUCATION

It is surely a truism to state that what is valued is dependent upon its cultural context, and so it is disturbing to find so much dance education literature that situates itself outside of any social or cultural context. Freedman (1994) expounds on a number of myths associated with arts education, and it is evident that similar myths appear in the writings of dance educators. The notion that dance is a universal language is a common one, although clearly profound cultural differences are found in the attitude toward, the meaning contained within, and the application of dance across societies. This leads to complex issues for curriculum designers in dance when attempting to frame elements in abstract terms, which may be meaningless or unimportant in certain dance traditions. Freedman claims as another myth the distinction between fine art and other forms of visual culture; this myth has its parallel in dance with distinctions between dance as artistic product and dance in other manifestations. For example, McFee states that "dance used to promote cultural understanding will not typically be 'art/type' dance and/or will not be performed to a sufficiently high standard to satisfy the artistic account" (1994, 124). This statement displays a cultural myopia that is counterproductive to the development of dance and its role in education. As Freedman incisively puts it, "Contemporary visions of art and culture are too complex to be represented dichotomously" (133). Freedman further exposes the erroneous notion that all art can be understood through formalist, analytical, aesthetic models that are Western in thought and conception.

In New Zealand we are working on new curriculum developments that include the dance forms of the Maori, the indigenous people of Aotearoa, New Zealand, and those of the increasingly large community of Pacific Island peoples who are residing in this country. In partnership with Maori arts educators, Pakeha (European) educators and administrators grapple with some of these fundamental issues of developing arts curricula in a particular social and cultural context. In Polynesian cultures, for example, the arts are regarded holistically; and so the new music handbooks for schools in New Zealand include a substantial "movement" section, as it is inconceivable in most contexts for Maori and Pacific Islanders to sing without also expressing themselves bodily.

Competency in these art forms also means acquiring language skills, with the centrality of language in the dance form (through chant or song)—a direct contrast to the nonverbal traditions in Western dance. These are group rather than solo dance forms, and although much allowance is made for individual expression within the group, the concept of presentational or performance skills stems from a cultural base; for example, the leader of the troupe leads from the back, as one leads in rowing a waka (canoe), not from the front. The motivation to dance arises too from a different source, going beyond physical pleasure or creative drive into a means of identifying who one is, one's tribal base, and one's family connections. The reclamation of identity and sense of self comes through strongly in the newly developing Polynesian performing arts courses, which are springing up throughout New Zealand at the present time, providing culturally and socially alienated youth with opportunities that have substance and meaning for them.

The learning style is one in which you learn through imitation, often informally, and in a group setting. Keri Kaa, a first-language speaker of Maori and highly knowledgeable in Maori dance forms, claims she first learned to dance in her father's kumara patch. Kaa explains,

We sing and dance because we must . . . and you learn because your granny teaches you, or your grandad, and you soon learn to keep the beat when the old lady pinches your leg and says "E tu (stand), dance now." You don't get told anything; you get signaled to and you stand up and you copy what your elder's doing so that the music and dance is not seen as a separate part of your life—it's just there all the time. . . . Who taught me? Nobody taught me; I just listened and watched by being part of the scenery. There is no provision for that kind of learning anywhere. The whole thing now is that you go to classes and you parrot off. It's the new way—teach it as a skill, but then it just becomes a technical matter without the knowledge behind it.

Kaa raises pedagogical issues that we must address in dance education if we are to commit ourselves to inclusiveness and diversity in curriculum development. With reference to American dance educators, Oliver offers the following challenge:

We should revise curriculum and research to include a range of races, classes, and ages and should consider the role of gender in dance as part of any class curriculum. In addition we should make a commitment to learn and research one nonwestern dance form. (1994, 163)

© Sarah Hunter

Although Oliver's sentiments may be laudable, the dangers of tokenism and "political correctness" are palpable with statements such as these, and the retorts from conservative academics staunchly defending the Western intellectual tradition ring in one's ears. We must address the arguments of scholars, such as McFee (1994), who contends that "the educational distinctiveness of dance is related to its art status; . . . that . . . art status applies only to some dance" (55-56).

In a multicultural world do we accept this Western concept of what dance is, what art is, or do we begin to redefine these words by exploring non-Western traditions? If we could liberate ourselves from an entirely technical approach to dance and allow our work to breathe freely in the swirl of ideas and historic and social forces that exist within the "aesthetic field" of dance, then, as Abbs suggests (1994), we might just possibly broaden, enliven, and deepen the meaning and relevance of dance education.

Arts educators are developing models in other disciplines that can provide a useful leaping-off point for clarifying our own stance on such matters in dance. Pearse's (1992) structural analysis presents one example of placing the arts within a cultural context. Basing his work on the ideas set forth by the German social philosopher Jürgen Habermas, Pearse sets out a three-fold framework that is empirical, interpretive–hermeneutic, and critical–theoretic. The first component, empirical, deals with the analytical examination of technical skills, that is, the physical mastery of the elements of dance in relation to body awareness, space, shape, rhythm, dynamics, and relationships. The second component, interpretive–hermeneutic, deals with situational knowing, relating people to their own world through the creation of dances that communicate personal ideas, feelings, emotions, and attitudes. The third component of Pearse's framework is the critical–theoretic, which is about empowerment and transformation, that is, understanding dance as performer, creator, or viewer in the context of one's social, cultural, and political place in the world. Using the arts as a pathway to cultural literacy would be placed into this latter category, where learning is socially charged, leading to action. Pearse suggests that the only way through such thorny and contentious issues is to adopt what he calls a "postmodernist" stance, which is outside all three of the paradigms in his framework (251).

As we approach the 21st century, optimists envision an arts education in which local cultural practices are valued; the differences of those who have been historically marginalized by virtue of gender, race, ethnicity, or class are celebrated; and the cultural artifacts of all places and times are valid "texts" for study by art educators and students. In stark contrast, pessimists see an aimless, fragmented, relativistic arts education, cut off from standards of excellence.

Pearse summarizes the complex situation that confronts those of us working in dance in multicultural education environments. A starting point is to look at the immediate environment; question whether the program reflects the needs, interests, and background of the students; and determine whether the possibility of entering into partnerships with educators from different cultural backgrounds is a way to address issues of equity and lead toward self-education.

In New Zealand we have legal educational obligations to the *tangata whenua*, the indigenous people of the land, and the only way that we have found to meet those obligations successfully is to establish partnerships where knowledge and expertise are shared equally. This mutual exchange is often a challenging, bewildering, and painful experience; but the rewards are immense in terms of both personal and professional enrichment. As multiculturalism holds center stage as one of the key intellectual debates of contemporary education, it is imperative that dance educators grasp the issues and enter into the fray because if we do not, we will simply be further marginalized within the larger education arena.

GENERIC ARTS: A USEFUL CONCEPT FOR DANCE EDUCATION?

The framing of the arts as a generic entity is a contentious policy issue that has arisen in the development of national curriculum statements concerning the arts. The criticism of this concept has been spearheaded by David Best (1992), a British philosopher in aesthetics and aesthetic education. He claims that the idea of the arts being planned for and taught collectively because they involve the same processes is a "seductive thesis" for administrators, saving space, time, and money. To support his argument Best turns to semantics, giving the dictionary definition of "generic" as something that exhibits common structural characteristics and is distinct from other groups. In his view assertions that the arts are generic; cognate; and familial, having a "natural" affinity, have gone largely unexamined (31). Best does not deny the value of combined or integrated arts courses, but he states that the imposition of a generic theory compels people to look at arts education too narrowly. Robinson (1992) challenges Best's argument from a pragmatist's point of view. He claims (and research findings would support his claim) that schools tend to think separately about the different arts disciplines, some of which are provided for and some are not.

For dance education the idea of a generic arts program does hold some attractions, as it is a way of upgrading the status of dance in schools. For those who see the arts as already marginalized within the school program, however, generic arts structures are seen as a tool for further marginalization. At a national Teacher Education Conference held in Wellington, New Zealand, in 1994, arts educators expressed the fear that looking at the arts collectively would simply allow schools to teach students one art form only and to thereby claim that they were meeting their curriculum responsibilities toward the arts. This assumes of course that schools are free to adopt this course of action, and that may well not be the case. Abbs (1992) places himself somewhere between the polarized views of Best and Robinson and sagely takes a historical perspective on the debate. He suggests that the current attempt in arts curricula to look "holistically at the field is the slow and spasmodic evolution of this transformative idea still struggling to find its best conceptual form and practice" (267). Inevitably "old baggage" will surface during this evolutionary process. The specter of the now largely discredited integrated arts approach raises its head when generic arts curricula is mentioned, and the notion of interdisciplinary as opposed to integrated arts education has barely been mentioned, let alone thought through in a methodical fashion.

Abbs accuses Best of narrow literalism in his interpretation of generic arts, and he contends that combined or integrated arts was not the intended sense of the word. He suggests that unifying elements make it appropriate to think of the arts as a single entity (284). The arts, Abbs contends, are expressive of life, they depend on formal constructions to obtain meaning, they cannot be translated without significant loss, and they all require an aesthetic response. Apart from issues of educational validity, considerable political implications surround the idea of generic arts. In their document, "The Arts and the Year 2000" (National Arts in Australian Schools Project Department of Education 1991), Australian curriculum developers deliver a strong message about the need for a unified approach to arts education: "If the notion of dividing to conquer was the strategy employed by schools and central agencies, the results seem to have been spectacularly successful in the arts" (iii). They urge a definition of the arts with a capital "A" because without this, the arts are likely to be fragmented and marginalized in an increasingly pressured curriculum. There is a danger of the arts competing with each other for time and resources, thereby weakening the place of the arts as a domain of study within schools.

Through my work with a group of 22 New Zealand elementary school teachers who conducted surveys in their own schools about arts education provision and practices, I found that the majority of teachers had no concept of the arts as a whole and referred only to individual disciplines (i.e., music, drama, visual arts). If the "arts" as a concept are to be used by teachers in their planning and teaching, then those of us involved in teacher education in the arts must demonstrate its usefulness by such means as exploring practically new models of teaching and conducting action-based research projects in partnership with teachers.

In dance we need to think strategically about our role in generically devised curriculum frameworks, and we certainly need to attend to our political relationships with other art forms. In particular we must turn our attention toward music and the visual arts, which have traditionally held a much stronger position in the curriculum in elementary and high school education. In my experience working in a department of performing arts education, the generic model facilitates interdisciplinary dialogue and planning, and it enables us to present a holistic model to our students on teaching and learning in the performing arts. This does not, and should not, exclude students and teachers alike from engaging in the particularities of the individual arts disciplines; but within a collective entity, we can strengthen the rationale for the place of the arts in education.

THE REFLECTIVE DANCE EDUCATOR

In seeking direction on policy issues during this time of national curriculum reform and development, it is glaringly apparent that no substantial body of research on dance education has been conducted. We find no sustained investigation into the fundamental aspects of the design, planning, and teaching of dance; nor do we find much dance education research that is applied within the context of contemporary social, cultural, and political educational concerns. Swanwick's (1988) complaint that research in music education tends to be undertheorized, that it "drifts aimlessly towards the arbitrary and the irrelevant, lacking principled engagement with the liveliness of intellectual ideas" (128) can also be leveled at dance education.

Research often gets bad press among arts practitioners because it is seen as lacking relevance in their working lives. As Myers (1988) states,

> The argument that researchers should have the luxury of not being expected to translate their findings into practice simply cannot be sustained in arts education. The field is too small, the subject matter too subjective, and the needs too urgent to pretend that research can be divorced from the responsibility of program development. (21)

As dance educators we need to take the business of research into our own hands, claim our place, and make our voices heard in the world of arts curriculum innovation and development. Becoming reflective practitioners means becoming our own classroom researchers; as Schon (1983, 1990) asserts, reflection provides a pathway to self-empowerment and a means of coalescing often years of expert and wise practice into a form that can be articulated and shared with the dance education profession. Reflective teaching is a multifaceted activity categorized by Killion and Todnem (1991) as "reflection in the active teaching moment, reflection after the event, and reflection for future action" (14-16). These three modes of reflection must be expressed by dance educators, both verbally and in written form, as we deal with key issues such as teaching strategies and methodologies; the content of our program; how the program is sequenced, developed, assessed, and moderated; and the moral, ethical, cultural, and other issues that surround what and how we teach (Shulman 1987).

At my college, our newly devised postgraduate interdisciplinary program for training high school teachers in performing arts education has provided an ideal opportunity to use the reflective teaching model in assessing the strengths and weaknesses of the curriculum structure. My teaching colleague in drama education is keeping a detailed reflective journal on the daily progress of the program; this includes regular hour-long interviews with a selection of the participants as well as general class discussions. The students are also asked to keep reflective journals as part of their course requirements. They are kept well informed about this "reflection in action" project, and their views are sought as we revise and modify the program following discussions with them and among our-selves. While my colleague's project is at the micro level, with the students in the college, I am working at the macro level, investigating key policy issues that will affect the teaching of the arts in schools as the new curriculum initiative in the arts is about to be launched. It is a liberating feeling to realize that as practitioners we can follow our own research needs and those of our education community and that we can devise projects of immediate need and relevance that will lead to political change in education. Positivistic research, described by Carr and Kemmiss (1986) as research dealing with "a notion of prediction based on scientific laws established in past situations and expressed as controlled intervention, as its basis for informing future action" (70) has excluded the perceived needs of the practitioners in the field being researched. It is also a form of research that is antithetical to the personal philosophies of many arts educators who prefer to deal in the subjective world of feeling and expression rather than in the objective world of facts and proven hypotheses.

Action research is a process whereby the practitioners are themselves the key researchers, engaged in a cycle of planning, acting, observing, and reflecting on their practice. In other words, it is a means through which the focus can be placed

on the improvement of the practitioner's own understandings of their practices by involving practitioners in the systematic development of their understandings, both in the context of the practices themselves and also in the context of explicitly sharing and examining these understandings through communications between collaborating action researchers. (Carr and Kemmiss, 71)

The idea of a community of action researchers in dance education holds great appeal; such a community would provide an opportunity for national and international dialogue on issues that are pertinent to the field. The evolving conception of the arts as a whole entity will also provide opportunities for interdisciplinary research in arts education; we may at last begin to build a body of knowledge about learning and teaching in the arts that has relevance and meaning for practitioners and theoreticians alike.

In order to walk this path, dance educators will be required to make some changes in their thinking about the way in which the discipline is currently perceived. It will mean moving away from the perception of ourselves as conveyers of already set pieces of information and knowledge into the role of researchers and explorers alongside our students. Broadening the base of our work through team teaching and interdisciplinary teaching may help produce such changes. Certainly this is the obvious path if the wider social, cultural, and political issues are to be acknowledged in a dance program. Following Stenhouse's vision of curriculum "as a particular form of speci-fication about the practice of teaching and not as a package of materials or a syllabus of ground to be covered" (1975, 142) could free us from historical ideas of what should and should not be taught. Viewing curriculum as a collection of ideas that is to be tested in practice can carry us forward into new and perhaps unforeseen areas of exploration.

This journey should not be undertaken alone; it must be shared by those who value a collegial model of professional interaction, one that draws both learner and teacher into a mutual exploration. In my work with experienced elementary teachers on classroom-based research projects dealing with gender issues in dance education, it was exhilarating to witness them grappling with research data, gathering information from their children, and then problem-solving their way through to providing a better balanced dance curriculum. Teachers are empowered through these processes; they are in command of their own professional development while providing enhanced learning opportunities for the children in their classes. Bresler (1996) argues strongly for a coordinated approach where educators, re-searchers, and those devising policy and curricula come together with a common sense of purpose. Ultimately, however, the classroom teachers provide the key to successful arts education, for without their commitment, belief, and energy, no curriculum initiatives will truly succeed.

DELIVERING A DANCE CURRICULUM

Words such as creating, making, presenting, responding, performing, inter-preting, appreciating, analyzing, and so on, that appear in recent national curriculum documents indicate that some degree of international consen-sus has been reached on the design of arts curricula in Western countries. What is not dealt with so explicitly are the teaching and learning strategies that might ensure the successful transmission of such processes. This is surely the critical part of the equation, for the writing of a curriculum framework does not necessarily lead to development of improved practice in the classroom. Bresler (1994) conducted a three-year ethnographic study in three elementary schools on visual arts curricula and identified three distinct orientations in the delivery of the curricula, all of which have relevance for the teaching of dance and are worthy of analysis. One of the reasons Bresler cited for carrying out the study was a noted discrepancy "between aesthetic theories discussing goals of arts education . . . and what actually happens in art education programs" (91). The first approach noted in this study is rote orientation, which is directive, emphasizing discipline, good work habits, and a common cultural base. The second is open-ended, student centered, and based around theories of child development. Bresler explains, "The arts are seen to provide relief from social pressure and a safeguard against the routine and the uniform by promoting creativity, self discovery, self expression, and the healthy channeling of feelings" (99). The third (higher order) orientation results from the cognitive revolution carried out in the 1960s, which has led to arts education theorists (e.g., Gardner 1993; Goodman 1981; Langer 1953) characterizing art as the comprehension and manipulation of a series of different symbol systems. Bresler describes the teacher's role in this orientation as providing students with "cultural symbols and specific knowledge to facilitate students' problem solving and encourage the investment of cognitive and affective faculties in the creation of artwork which requires guidance but not prescription" (100).

It is not difficult to find parallel examples in dance education of Bresler's three approaches to delivering curriculum. A rote teaching orientation is seen in the explicit teaching of precise technical skills, which is based on a sequentially developed syllabus or program, with mastery of specific material required at each step of the way, and assessment criteria predetermined and hierarchically defined. The second teaching orientation described by Bresler, the open-ended, student-centered approach, has its parallel in dance education in the creative model. In this model what is valued is not the mastery of predetermined skills but instead the ability of the student to find his or her own movement vocabulary and to express personal ideas and feelings that exemplify the student's uniqueness and individuality. Bresler's third orientation, the use of sophisticated symbol systems and complex processes, is utilized in dance education through structured improvisations and compositional problem-solving tasks. These activities are translated by the skillful dance teacher into a learning activity that provides both "scaffolding" and a content base for the student, which can be realized in accordance with individual abilities.

Assessment in dance education also involves three distinct orientations. The first is a finite and straight-forward process of determining the level of skill acquisition. The second, open-ended, approach requires an achievement-based assessment model and the setting of criteria (often mutually agreed upon by both teacher and student) that may be multifaceted in nature, dealing with comprehension, execution, presentation, and explication. Approaching assessment with the third orientation, using complex symbol systems, raises problems for teachers in identifying what can and should be assessed. In this latter case, a mixture of self, peer, and teacher assessment might be the most appropriate model.

In my work with New Zealand elementary school teachers, I found that, not surprisingly perhaps, many resisted the whole idea of assessing children's progress. They claimed that children's art is completely individual and personal, that the arts allow children to express and share with others a part of their individual selves, and that such expression should not be compared or judged against that of anyone else. These teachers concluded that there is no fair way to gauge progress and skills attainment other than in the area of technical proficiency.

In working with beginning dance educators, I strive to put the whole business of assessment into a broader context so that it does not drive the content of the program. In the New Zealand Curriculum Framework seven essential skills are identified, which students are to develop across the whole curriculum (Learning Media Ministry of Education 1993). Four of these—physical skills, communication skills, problem-solving skills, and social and cooperative skills—are particularly relevant to dance, and using a selection of these in relation to the content of the lesson allows for a more flexible, multifaceted approach to assessment.

In Bresler's model she points out that each of the three teaching orientations fulfills very different functions and expectations. The first reinforces values of accountability, social control, and inculcation of popular cultural symbols; the second attempts to balance a highly structured and preordained curriculum by restoring creative and expressive elements that are perceived to be missing; and the third emphasizes knowledge and engagement in critical thinking (101). Bresler's orientations provide a thought-provoking model for dance educators to address, especially with regard to the manner in which we train prospective teachers of dance in our elementary and high schools. For the sake of clarity these orientations have been presented in separate categories. In reality, as Bresler herself points out, each category overlaps with the others, and it might be more useful to think of the three as a continuum of teaching orientations in the arts. Although the third orientation may appear to be the one for which to aim, based as it is on recent scholarly research in the arts and in educational psychology, we need to balance this against the current realities of school environments. The fact is that without specialist training in the arts, or extensive teacher development once in the field, it is unlikely that elementary school practitioners, and to a lesser extent high school arts practitioners, will be able to fulfill the expectations of those academics currently researching teaching and learning in the arts. The lack of arts-based theory in general education texts has been documented (Gardner 1993). Arts educators need to be proactive in challenging the content of undergraduate education courses where symbol systems that are not linguistically based (such as in dance) are virtually ignored.

CONCLUSION

We cannot expect arts educators to adopt more sophisticated and complex models of teaching if their education has been devoid of a strong knowledge base about how children learn in the arts. If the needs of arts education students are not being met in general education courses, then we must enter into a dialogue with educational psychologists and encourage a broadening of the arts curriculum. Carrol adds, "Interdisciplinary teams, teaching together, may be the strongest vehicle for reconceptualizing the paradigm that governs education" (1993, 21). The efficacy of this model was reinforced for me recently as my postgraduate performing arts students completed an intensive weeklong residency program with 12- and 13-year-old children at a local high school. Possessing a variety of skills in music, dance, and drama, the postgraduate students' ability to team teach effectively was exemplary, and their approach was greatly appreciated by the children, who remarked very favorably on the "teacher-to-teacher" interactions in their written evaluations. Collaboration among arts educators, however, does not happen automatically, nor does it happen by chance. The development of group skills, in the context of both teaching and learning, is something that is consciously learned. Participants must be given appropriate strategies that can be practiced and refined as they work toward common goals. The performing arts are a particularly powerful media for realizing such skills. Improvisational drama and dance games can focus on the building of cooperative group behavior; it is interesting to note how frequently these sorts of activities are used in business management courses where team building is deemed essential. The opportunity also exists for much incidental learning to take place as music, dance, and drama educators acquire knowledge and experience of each other's art forms through working on the same project.

Performing arts educators often complain of "burnout," as they exhaust themselves staging the school production, the music or dance concert. By reexamining the structures and curriculum models within which they work, almost certainly opportunities can be found for increased collegiality through mutual enterprises, where the burden is shared and professional development occurs in the best possible way by working alongside one another. It is commonplace in the world of professional performing arts to find composers, musicians, dramatists, actors, choreographers, dancers, and designers working collaboratively on a single project. If arts programs in education institutions wish to connect with the real working world of many artists, then a serious examination of their modus operandi is imperative. As I write this, I recall a university music educator, who, when discussing cross-disciplinary performing arts programs, looked at me in some bewilderment and said, "Yes, but how do you *do* it?"

Obviously there first has to be the desire to step outside the boundaries of one's own discipline and then the courage to experiment and possibly to fail. Learning by doing is ultimately the only way, as structures are refined and people modify and develop their teaching strategies in relation to those with whom they are working. In my view this can lead to some of the best curriculum development, for tasks that you may have taught in the isolation of the dance class, for example, now get taught in the broader context of music- and drama-related ideas. This can lead to new ways of looking at and approaching the dance material, enriching both the content and the teaching approach.

This brings me back to the starting point of this chapter, for an expanding vision of dance education entails entering into an ongoing dialogue with other general educators and arts educators. Some of the ways this might be accomplished is through joint teaching, research projects, or both; the restructuring of programs and departments to add a more "cutting edge" approach to our professional work; and enhancing the profile of the arts and of dance education by presenting papers at general education conferences. The issues confronting us are too large and complex to be dealt with in isolated subject settings. Curriculum reform is leading us toward reconceptualizing our discipline in ways that will allow for more comprehensible cross-disciplinary interactions. Now is the moment for dance professionals to take up the challenge and enter this larger world of educational policy issues.

Critical Reflections

It is hard not to smile at Jan Bolwell's reference to the music handbook now used in New Zealand when thinking of the straight backs and motionless bodies that typify many forms of European musical expression. In contrast to this formality is the inseparability of song and bodily expression in traditional non-Western cultures. Yet how quintessentially European it is that we learn to see these two things as entirely separate artistic activities. To break down the aura that separates one art form from another, and the creation, presentation, and viewing of art from life itself, it is surely necessary to ground and reconnect art to culture in all of its multiplicity of different forms. For dance to become relevant to people's lives and their educational experiences, it must not only include an appreciation of these differences, but also it should do so in a way that reveals the life experiences and historical circumstances that have helped shape and sustain people's cultures. The appreciation and apprehension of cultural differences calls for dance educators to fully seek to understand the struggle and reality of people's lives as opposed to the trivialization of having students dress up for a day and make the food of a particular culture. The process of recognizing connections and honoring differences should not be reduced to "multicultural fiestas." Building human communities is a complex process in which we teach students both about our differences as human beings and about our commonalities. The history of community in many parts of the world has, sadly, usually meant the imposition of one group's way of understanding the world on that of others. In recent times we have seen an upsurge of political and cultural expression among indigenous peoples around the world as they have come to reassert themselves after generations of "incorporation" into ruling cultures. And in the current era of multicultural education, it may be that the arts have a special role in making space for the variety of human experiences and expressions. In doing this arts educators will have to come to terms with their own implicit values as to what is considered "good" art, dance, drama, or music.

Take a Moment to Reflect

1. To what extent, within your school classroom or curriculum, are cultural differences honored?

2. How can "art" and "dance" value the multiplicity of dance forms in the world? In what ways might this redefine our concepts of what these words mean?

3. How should we prepare ourselves to work with students from cultures that are different from our own?

4. How can we reconcile our emphasis on classical forms of dance (i.e., ballet and modern dance forms) with the need to be inclusive of non-European dance forms?

5. Is it possible to teach dance as part of an integrated or interdisciplinary curriculum and retain the "pure" form?

6. How might we enter into a dialogue with other art forms for the purpose of strengthening arts education in the curriculum? What value would there be in doing so?

To apprehend and appreciate cultural differences and the possibility of the arts to give expression to all of human experience is poignantly expressed in the next chapter. Sondra Sluder shares her courageous journey of healing, addressing how dance can be empowering and create a feeling of wholeness through the mind–body connection.

REFERENCES

Abbs, P. 1992. "The Generic Community of the Arts: Its Historical Development and Educational Value." *Journal of Art & Design Education* 11 (3): 267-284.

———. 1994. *The Educational Imperative: A Defence of Socratic and Aesthetic Learning.* London: Falmer Press.

Australian Curriculum Corporation. 1994. *A Statement on the Arts for Australian Schools.* Carlton, Australia: Australian Curriculum Corporation.

Best, D. 1992. "Generic Arts: An Expedient Myth." *Journal of Art & Design Education* 1 (1): 27-44.

Boughton, D. 1994. "Confronting Curriculum Reform in Art Education: A Rocky Road to the Future." Paper presented at the Aotearoa, New Zealand Art Educators Conference, August 28–September 1, Wellington, New Zealand.

Bresler L. 1994. "Three Roles of Visual Arts Curricula." *Studies in Art Education: A Journal of Issues and Research* 35 (2): 90-104.

———. 1996. "Traditions and Change Across the Arts: Case Studies of Arts Education." *International Society for Music Education* 27: 24-35.

Carr, W., & S. Kemmiss. 1986. *Becoming Critical Education, Knowledge and Action Research.* London: Falmer Press.

Carroll, K.L. 1993. "Taking Responsibility: Higher Education's Opportunity to Affect the Future of the Arts in Schools." *Arts Education Policy Review* 95 (1): 17-22.

Davies, M.R. 1991. "The English National Curriculum: A Landmark in Educational Reform." In *Educational Leadership* 48 (5) (February): 28-29.

Dearing, R. 1993. *The National Curriculum and its Assessment.* York, UK: National Curriculum Council.

Freedman, K. 1994. "About this Issue: The Social Reconstruction of Art Education." *Studies in Art Education: A Journal of Issues and Research.* 35 (3): 131-134.

Gardner, H. 1993. "Harvard Project Zero." In *Multiple Intelligences: The Theory in Practice*, H. Gardner (ed.). New York: Basic Books.

Goodman, N. 1981. *The Languages of Art: An Approach to a Theory of Symbols.* London: Harvester.

Hargreaves, D.J. 1989. "Delta Project (Development of Teaching and Learning in the Arts)." In *Children and the Arts*, M. Keynes (ed.). Leicester, England: University of Leicester.

Kaa, K. 1993. Unpublished interview conducted by J. Whatman, 13 July.

Killion, J.P. and G.R. Todnem. 1991. "A Process for Personal Theory Building." *Educational Leadership* 48 (6) (March): 14-16.

Koroscik, J.S. 1994. "Blurring the Line between Teaching and Research: Some Future Challenges for Arts Education Policymakers." *Arts Education Policy Review* 96 (1): 2-10.

Langer, S.K. 1953. *Feeling and Form: A Theory of Art.* New York: Scribner's.

Learning Media Ministry of Education. 1993. *The New Zealand Curriculum Framework/Te Anga Marautanga o Aotearoa.* Wellington, New Zealand: Learning Media Ministry of Education.

Mason, T.C. 1996. "Integrated Curricula: Potential and Problems." *Journal of Teacher Education* 47 (4): 263-269.

McFee, G. 1994. *The Concept of Dance Education.* London: Routledge.

Myers, D.E. 1988. "Contenders or Comrades for Arts Education?" *Design for Arts in Education* 89 (January/February): 21.

National Arts in Australian Schools Project Department of Education. 1991. *The Arts and the Year 2000.* Queensland for the Curriculum Corporation, Brisbane, Australia: Department of Education.

The National Assessment of Educational Progress. 1994. *Arts Consensus Project Arts Education Assessment Framework.* Washington, D.C.: The Council of Chief State School Officers.

Oliver, W. 1994. "Are We Feminists? How Our Own Antifeminist Bias Permeates Dance Academe." *Impulse* 2: 157-164.

Pearse, H. 1992. "Beyond Paradigms: Art Education Theory and Practice in a Post-Paradigmatic World." *Studies in Art Education* 33 (4): 244-252.

Robinson, K. 1992. "The Arts as a Generic Area of the Curriculum." *Journal of Art & Design Education* 11 (1): 9-25.

Schon, D. 1983. *The Reflective Practitioner: How Professionals Think in Action*. New York: Basic Books.

———. 1990. *Educating the Reflective Practitioner*. San Francisco: Jossey-Bass.

Shulman, L. 1987. "Knowledge and Teaching Foundations of the New Reform." *Harvard Educational Review* 57 (l): 1-22.

Stenhouse, L. 1975. *An Introduction to Curriculum Research and Development*. London: Heinemann.

Swanwick, K. 1988. "The Relevance of Research: Too Little Theory." In *Research in Music Education: A Festschrift for Arnold Bentley*, A.E. Kemp (ed.). London: International Society for Music Education.

CHAPTER 5

HER STORY

SONDRA STAMEY SLUDER
Asheville, North Carolina

This chapter looks at dance as process rather than product. Sondra Sluder, through the telling of her own life story, speaks for the inclusion of art as part of the educational curriculum, not just as an extracurricular activity. Furthermore, the author sets about to challenge traditional ideas about who can dance and what is good art. Sluder addresses the power of dance as an art form that can bring wholeness through the mind–body connection, resulting in a process that is healing, educational, and empowering. This process, she argues, challenges the accepted pedagogic tradition in which knowledge is "set" upon the dancer; instead she suggests a dance pedagogy that seeks to develop self- and social understanding from the inside out. In concluding, Sluder asserts that through the healing process of seeking greater awareness, both the artist and the art are set free.

What would happen if one woman told the truth about her life?
The world would split open.

—(*Rukeyser 1973, 377*)

My grandmother, Janie Laughter, married at 22, raised 10 children, survived the Depression, buried her husband, and lived to the age of 97. College was never a choice. She worked the farm from sunup to sundown. She loved fishing and the wide world of wrestling. At 70, she worked the soil with her old wooden plow and workhorse. In the evenings she washed her clothes in an old kettle on the stove and hung them to dry by moonlight. As I lay down beside her, her stories trickled down the moonbeams . . . resting in my soul . . . where she still remains.

I spent my summers at my grandmother's farm. She was a combination of light and fire. Nothing pleased me more than hearing her laugh or tell a story. Some of my earliest memories are of her kitchen, where time seemed to hang in suspension as I stood beside her on a kitchen chair learning to make biscuits. As I would pat out the dough, Grannie would tell me stories about our family. Sometimes in the evening she would hang her laundry out on the back porch, and I would sit in the darkness and soak up her words as she spoke about events and people that hung on the branches of my family tree. I tucked these stories away until later in my life when her voice would fill my mind, calling me back to those priceless moments that I shared with one of the most important women in my life.

I did not fully realize the important part my grandmother had played in my life until I began creating the dance, "Her Story," my final year at Meredith College, a women's college in North Carolina. As I entered my final semester, I began the journey toward closure of my sojourn there. It was a time of sadness, excitement, and reflection. I needed to work through the feelings pervading my body and mind. This led me to create a dance about my journey as a nontraditional-age student; in creating this dance I realized how vital art is to me as a vehicle for uncovering what lies at the depths of my being. Through the choreographic process I can recover moments and experiences in my life that have shaped me. With my subject matter in hand, I began working on the choreography, which, much to my surprise, led me on a search for my maternal grandmother, Janie.

My search led to more questions than answers. I wondered what her dreams were as a young woman growing up in a wealthy Southern family. Her father had had enough money to send her to college. Instead, she married a man twice her age and bore him 12 children, 10 of whom survived. Perhaps her dream was to get married and raise a family. Or, in traditional Southern fashion, she may never have even considered her choices, nor even known that choices existed. The issue of women and choice confronted not only my grandmother but also my mother, myself, and my two daughters. Women, especially Southern women, are generally molded to become housewives and mothers, never considering that higher education and a career are also possibilities. After spending time with my mother gathering material for the dance, I realized that my grandmother, my mother, and myself all share a bond as women, although we represent three generations of mothers and daughters.

> *Myrtle, my mother, sold fruit in the streets with her own mother. At 11 she left home to live and work as a housekeeper for several years. She dreamed of college and of becoming a teacher. At 17 she traveled 60 miles by bus to work weekends as a waitress, returning home Sunday evenings, past midnight, to rest before returning to school the next day. After graduation, she left to pursue her dream of becoming a teacher. Yet she continued to send all of her earnings home to support her family. College was no longer a choice. Had it ever been?*

I knew very little about my mother's dreams as a young woman until I phoned her about the dance. We were not very close when I was a child or young adult because she was always working. My mother worked as a waitress all of her adult life, retiring at the age of 66. She had worked relentlessly throughout her childhood to help her family to survive, and she knew no other way to live. While she has a wonderful life full of love and friends, I cannot help but wonder how it might have been different had she lived in a society where educational opportunities are equal and ideas about women are different.

Like my mother, I, too, had dreams as a young girl. My mind was always working, questioning everything around me. I recall being 10 years old and sitting in a huge, walnut tree in my backyard wondering about what I wanted to accomplish with my life. It hit me that millions of people live and die, and nobody even remembers their names. What difference had their lives made? This question sent a tremble through my body. From that moment on I decided that I wanted my life to count for something. This urging was the beginning of a search for wholeness as a human being, as part of a community.

I had no one with whom to share these thoughts as a young child, so I kept them stored away in the pantry of my soul where they would provide me with the nourishment for my lonely childhood journey. Like my mother and her mother before her, our dreams would remain in our hearts where they would become buried with the realities of our lives.

She married a handsome, young musician . . . a victim. Beaten and threatened, she finally found the courage and left, raising four children alone.

My mother's desire to become a teacher was to be packed away with her childhood dreams; instead she accepted the role of wife and mother. As a child I was captivated by her beauty. As an adult I became aware of her independence. It took many years before I could realize the courage and strength that it took for her to leave a man she loved to save her life.

The ensuing years were hard as she worked 16-hour days to provide a home for her children. We did not share a relationship during the years of my adolescence and young adulthood because she was rarely home. There were few lovely moments between us as we were strangers to each other and to ourselves. We were a mother and daughter separated by ignorance and circumstance.

My mother and I stand together against the tide. It tries to pull us under as we struggle to stand. Holding each other, we are ready for the next wave.

When I came to Meredith, I didn't trust women. I thought, having been "properly" shaped by my culture, that women were conniving and deceitful. It was easy for me to accept this stereotypical image, as my mother was absent from my life as she was never home, and my paternal grandmother was abusive to my father, my mother, and me. The only influence and loving presence in my life was that of my brothers. It was only reasonable that I would embrace the familiar and safe, strong image of the masculine and turn away from the feminine.

All of these ideas were challenged my first semester at Meredith in a most unlikely place—a modern dance technique class. The teacher included movement exploration as part of the class. She often created combinations that left eight counts open for our own personal phrase. These phrases were always built around an issue or a movement element such as time or opening and closing.

One afternoon she asked us to bring a slip, dress, or other article of feminine clothing to the next class. The following class we put on the clothing and began to explore moving in them. In our discussion at the end of class, we talked about the images that arose during our dance. I shared my feelings toward women, which led to a discussion about why I felt this way. Others shared their personal stories as women in relationship to other women and men. By the end of the class, I realized that my feelings about women were shaped by a society that keeps women oppressed by encouraging women to compete for men—any respectable woman must marry the best man. It was interesting as well to recognize that I had been hurt by just as many men as I had been by women. Yet, because of these false stereotypes of evil, vindictive women, I had given women very little space to be anything but worthless while giving men plenty of space for human error. As we talked in the class about the struggles of women, I began to understand why my mother had left my father—why she was never home.

My mother had evolved from a victim to a survivor of abuse. By becoming a single parent, she was faced with raising her children alone without child support or the guarantee that her salary would be the same as a man's for the same work. Therefore she had to work twice as hard to provide for us. In addition, she endured all of the criticism for leaving, while my Dad became the victim even though he was the abuser. These realizations did not erase any of the pain I had endured as a small child, but they did help me to understand the challenges that my mother and other women face simply because they are women.

I have always heard that we should never judge others until we have walked around in their skin. That day in class, dressed in feminine clothing, I had the chance to do just that as I danced in their skins. As I moved through the stories of others, I began to reshape my perspectives and my judgments. Several years after this class I stood on the beach with my mother. As the waves crashed around us, we stood holding onto one another. At that moment I realized that as mother and daughter we share so many things as women. We share motherhood and sisterhood. We often stand alone. But we are stronger when we stand together.

I am a wife, mother of three, class of '95, Meredith College. I am the granddaughter of Janie, daughter of Myrtle, and I stand on the threshold of their dreams. My roots are in the Blue Ridge Mountains, where I slid down tin roofs and lost myself in the woods. I escaped into the vast playground of my imagination.

I moved through my early childhood living life to a song as I danced through trees, forests, and my imagination. I lived life completely, enjoying every playful moment. I loved school and the world it opened up to me. Despite my father's violent outbursts, my home was a beautiful place that provided me with love and security. My father's violence was just another part of that world.

My father's smile lit up my world. His songs connected my world. His pain crushed my world. As he began to die, the abandoned child inside emerged. My family went into hiding. At 15, I buried my father.

My father was a good man with a warm smile and a heart that could melt stone. He was a songbird, and he loved to dance. The two of us were very close when I was young. We would go out to the stables where we boarded our horses and spend hours brushing, shoeing, and riding. He taught me to waltz, and we would square dance regularly at the local community center. We used to dance the evenings away as he smiled down at me from his 6 foot

2 inch-tall frame. As I gazed up into his large eyes, I saw only this man who was bigger than life, this man who was my father. I was unable to see the small, abused child within him who lay hidden deep within his hazel eyes.

I met this child when I made my first dance in a composition class at Meredith. We were assigned to locate any piece of furniture and create a movement study around it. I chose my kitchen stool.

That stool is more than a piece of aluminum. Kitchen stools hold stories about women and their families. My kitchen stool holds stories about my journey as a woman. As I began to move on the stool, images filled my mind as my body moved through experiences that were stored within my body memory. Images of kitchens and family filled my mind and moved my body. The stool became the nucleus around which my life journey had developed and revolved. As I manipulated the stool it became a high chair and a walker. The images spanned a lifetime. The stool became a metaphor for my lifetime, a human lifetime, and then my father's lifetime.

During this movement process, I met the abused child who lives within me. Then I met the abused child who lived inside of my abusive father. The moment was painful, yet healing. I faced the abusive father who had haunted me throughout my life. I looked beyond my father's abuse and saw him as a human being. Healing occurred as my body released the tension and fear that it had stored for three decades. As I released the frightened child within me, I began to understand my father's release from life as he passed from the father I had known to the mentally disabled child within whose mind he remained until death rescued him from his own fears and pain.

My mother worked from 6 a.m. until past midnight to survive. PTA was not a part of her reality. At school I became a "troubled youth." No one bothered to look beyond the trouble at the pain. "I" vanished.

One night the fragile bubble of my childhood world burst, and I would face adolescence alone. I awakened one morning to find my mother gone, my father mentally disabled, and my brothers fragmented. The youthful songs, rhymes, and imaginary friends with whom I had shared my world would go to a secret place hidden away from the fear, confusion, and oppression that would quickly take their place.

It was during this time period that I became "the girl from a broken home." No one approached me from school to help me through my ordeal, even though they were quite aware of the situation. On one particular occasion I was warned by my sixth grade teacher that my father's unbalanced mother had been calling the school to report that I was leaving for school dirty and should be removed from my home and placed in an institutional home. This teacher, who had become the father figure in my life, took me into a cold hallway and informed me of the situation. He pointed out that I must be responsible to see that good hygiene was a part of my daily concerns, as well as keeping up my grades, or I was going to be removed from all that was left of my familiar world.

At the tender age of 11, I stood alone in that concrete hallway disrobing my innocent soul as I walked naked and victimized down the pathway of survival. With me would go all of the insults that would haunt me throughout my youth and still whisper into my ear today incessantly insisting that I am stupid and worthless. Nevertheless, the voices of those who taunted me, including members of my own family, grow faint as I discover that I am an individual—unlike them, and yet human—like them. I was not worthless, only powerless.

I met my best friend and married him. Together we made a family.

My husband, David, and I met when I was at the perplexing age of 20 and he was a befuddled 19. As in all relationships, our family backgrounds were also united at the altar. With us came our personal wreckage and all of the culturally defined ideas and ignorance that serve to both weaken and make us strong. Fortunately, David and I have put our energy into rummaging through the wreckage, tossing the trash, and restructuring the treasures. This process involves a cleansing of the lost self that lies broken under the rubbish and a redefining of the true self. I began my cleansing and restructuring the day I stepped into the dance studio at Meredith College to claim myself as an artist, woman, and human being.

The lack of money and interaction with adults in my family kept me from taking instructional dance classes as a child. Since dance was one art class that was not offered through the public school system, my dance studio became the fellowship hall of the Episcopal Church, the teen centers throughout the small town of Asheville, North Carolina, and the gym at the local YWCA. Every Friday and Saturday evening, the gym floor of the "Y" would support the rhythmic hoofing of countless teenagers who sought entertainment and physical art outside the studio. In that place we were all the prima donnas of dance. There were no elites—no class or caste systems. Racial and gender lines melted and created a unified pool swirling with all shades of brown, uniting us as powerful, unyielding individuals intoxicated with the rhythm of our own bodies. Little did I know then that this space would become the studio floor upon which I would leap and turn my way through a rigorous ballet class 15 years later. The very place where I kept time to Percy Sledge and James Brown would be the locus of my movement training to Bach and Stravinsky.

During those tumultuous years of teenage angst, I grew from an innocent child to a naive, reckless, young woman. Without adult shaping and direction I wandered aimlessly, looking for love in every and any direction. As my mother worked for her own sense of survival and self-worth, so I searched for mine. Feeling alienated, I lost my desire for learning and school became just one more obstacle. My eagerness to learn had been dismissed by my desperate need for love.

The teachers had no time for active love in a strict schooling environment. Finally one afternoon the Dean of Girls slammed the door shut on my education while I lay on her office couch sick with a high fever. She harshly informed me that she knew what was going on in my house including the lack of adult supervision. She placed her final blow, threatening to have me removed from "that place." Hot tears poured down my cheeks as I pulled myself up from the sickbed and stood at her office door. As I walked across the threshold, I never looked back at my injured spirit that lingered behind on the sofa. Instead, the pain that was pulling me down gradually hardened into a numbness that would sustain me throughout my struggle for survival. Several years later I joined the ranks of high school dropouts, turning to the streets for my education.

As my spirit slept through the 1960s and 1970s, my body and mind moved on through the sexual revolution and the women's movement. Having an unhealthy view of the human body and an enormous ignorance of sex, I found myself drowning in a sea of confusion. I was trapped between the innocent, helpless image of the Southern woman that had been carefully instilled in me since birth and the resourceful, sexual, female image that I was encountering in the world around me. Without wise mothers to guide me down this spiritual pathway of sexuality and female identity I went blindly forward, and in my search for love I was often painfully hurt. One day a soft, playful creature danced into my life. His sensitivity and respect, coupled with his warm face and heart, slowed my tumbling world and together we embarked on a new journey.

My marriage to David brought with it considerable stability and order. As wife and mother, I found purpose in creating a home and shaping our children into loving, responsible individuals. David and I worked diligently to develop their independence. In addition, we fought to keep our marital relationship alive so that when the children left home, our relationship would still breathe. It was during this time of stable instability that I decided to dance again.

I was a young mother when I entered the technical world of dance. I cherished every moment of class, so thrilled at the opportunity to dance that I gave no thought to the external development of my technique. I worked hard and advanced quickly. It was an exciting time. Not only was I shaping a family, but I also was being shaped.

As the body moved, so stirred the spirit. I found myself needing more, but I could not define what "more" I wanted. One thing was for certain, I wanted my dancing to move beyond ballet barres. I felt a strong desire to leave and venture out into the larger world of technical training. I was convinced that the "more" was a physical place. I did not know then that it was a spiritual place for which I was looking.

The yellow pages led me to a studio that was for the "serious student of dance." I enrolled and found myself in the old gym and entrance hall of the old "Y." I felt at home.

Within three weeks, I noticed a man was standing at the door of my class. At the end of class, he came over and invited me to join his company as an apprentice. For the first time in my life, I was more than a pretty girl with long legs or a wife and mother. I was a dancer. My time with the company was to be cut short, however, by the calling of another voice.

The year I danced with the Asheville Civic Ballet was also the year that I began to seek reentry into the institutional church. I was fulfilling my need to dance, but I still felt an emptiness in my life. This emptiness was the voice that kept calling me, propelling me forward on a journey that would change my life in unimaginable ways.

I was raised in the Bible Belt of the South, so I felt right at home in the Right Wing Fundamentalist Church. It seemed only right that I would give up dancing when David and I felt a "call" to ministry. This call was very intense for both David and me, yet I was quickly reminded by my elders that the call to serve God was David's, not mine. My call was to serve . . . David. In true Southern fashion, I submitted, giving up dance and everything else outside of church and family to do what was "right by God." David did the same.

I have been told that God gives us the desires of our heart and that we all have special gifts with which to serve God's community. It was this knowledge that eventually caused me to question the institutional church, the institutional God, and my decision to give up dance—the thing my heart desires.

Then Sue entered my life—educator, prophet—bringing a fresh set of colors.

Dr. Sue Fitzgerald was one of the many miracles that touched our lives while David was studying for the ministry at Mars Hill. As David's professor Sue set about to meet the needs of the whole person—David, not just her student. This relationship between Sue and David led Sue to me, as she discovered from David that I was once a dancer.

Sue began to reach out to me by sending books home with David that dealt with dance and spirituality. One particular book she sent dealt with dance as worship. While the book nudged my dancing soul, it was Sue's belief in me that began to arouse my slumbering spirit. While I had never trusted women, Sue, with her gentle, nurturing spirit, aroused my curiosity. It wasn't long before I accepted Sue's invitation to attend her class along with David. She began to tenderly stroke the young woman that lay dormant beneath the oppression of society and the church. She became my friend and mentor. I did not recognize at the time what Sue already saw. She could see the gifts that I possess that offer hope and healing to others as well as completeness to myself. My limited vision caused me to see ministry as becoming a pastor or shelter worker. I had no creative method for seeing beyond the usual models of pastors, missionaries, and "preacher's wives." Sue saw more. She saw a minister whose gifts were those of a dancer.

Supported by Sue and my husband, I got my GED and enrolled at Meredith College.

David and I moved our family across North Carolina so that David could attend seminary after finishing up at Mars Hill. During this time my youngest child entered school, letting go of my hand and never realizing how much I needed her to hold onto me. While I mourned her passing into her rightful independence, I was forced to face my own lack of independence and my soul yearned for a life of its own. This was when Sue called and suggested I get my General Education Diploma.

The idea of seeking anything outside my home was frightening to me, as I had contained my life within the walls of my home and family. I also believed that I had very little value as anything other than a wife and mother. Sue's call was timely, as I was struggling with this need to create my own life apart from my family. So I gathered up my courage, swallowed my pride, and went to the local high school to begin the process of acquiring my GED. I passed the test, received my diploma with my family by my side, hung my diploma on the wall, and went on about my midlife crisis.

Earning my GED had given me a new confidence, which resulted in my taking a dance class at a local studio. I was six years older and out of shape, as well as intimidated by all of the young, firm ballet bodies around me; yet just taking class was rekindling the desire to dance that had been smoldering within me. Once again the phone rang. It was Sue.

This time Sue suggested I consider going to college. I immediately dismissed this idea, as I knew I was not "smart enough" to attend college. Then Sue got my attention when she mentioned that Meredith College has a dance program. From that moment on my memory of the progression of events that landed me in an orientation class in continuing education at Meredith College is like a dream. I will never forget the moment I first stepped foot in the old dance studio at Meredith. It was like stepping through the looking glass. To my delight, life was wonderfully different on the other side.

They unlocked the door to my spirit. Sherry set me free.

I was soon to learn that a vast difference exists between schooling and education. Schooling lacks creativity, whereas education is creativity. School teaches about freedom in a setting where students passively collect information and theories. Education sets the student free as it engages the teacher and the student in a collaborative process. Entering college I was attending school; I left with an education.

In the beginning, I celebrated, struggled, and cried through my technique classes at Meredith. The multitude of voices in my head kept reminding me of my inabilities. The culturally defined dance image loomed before me pointing out that I was no longer strong enough, young enough, or slim enough to be a dancer. It was hard to tune out this voice when I was surrounded by beautiful, young women who, although they sometimes lacked confidence, still had each other. I felt like an intruder who had invaded their space as a nontraditional-age student, even though my younger friends welcomed me. This feeling would weaken through the years, but it would not go away completely.

In the classroom I faced the monster of a grading system that set about to determine the value of a human being based on her academic performance. The measuring stick for intelligence in most learning institutions is based on memorization skills and one person's opinion of what is important knowledge and what is not. I spent five years watching the "grade monster" devour women, draining them of their energy and self-worth. I fought hard for my own sense of worth, reminding myself daily that a grade was not the determination of my value as a human being. My victories were only won when I got so involved in learning that I forgot about grades.

Meredith is a liberal arts college, and so I received a well-rounded education. I loved soaking up knowledge that informed me and broadened my world view. I welcomed the diversity of ideas and perspectives. As a religion major I was able to better understand history. As a dance major I was able to connect and relate my academic courses to my daily life. Through art I learned to take what is often a narrowly viewed black and white world and see its colors. My general education and religion classes in turn broadened my intelligence and world view. My dance classes breathed life into both, creating a colorful wisdom that allowed for flexibility and possibility.

My creativity and confidence began to blossom through improvisation and composition classes. Up to this point, dance had been about the physicality of the movement, not the spirituality that lay beneath the movement. In addition to these wonderful developments, all of my other general education classes were coming together in dance. On a trip to the North Carolina Museum of Art with an improvisation class, I saw the "big picture" as a culmination of my exposure to literature, Western civilization, and sociology. I began to see the paintings and sculptures as more than just pretty pictures or unusual pieces. I began to see them through educated, creative eyes as stories and images of people and their lives. I felt deeply connected to my world and to myself. Something was occurring inside of me that I could not see. I was beginning to think for myself. My true self was emerging.

I have always been strongly opinionated and passionate. The problem was that my opinions were often formed out of ignorance. My opinions were changing, however, as I processed new ideas and information. I was soon to discover that a vast difference exists as well between memorizing information and thinking deeply about information. I also realized that we often follow rules within our society without ever questioning the rules or who spoke them into being. With all of these realizations rooting their way into my consciousness, I became acutely aware that education is not something that someone or something gives to you. On the contrary, education is something you must take for yourself.

It was during this time of recovering my consciousness that I began to understand that dance was more than simply movement; it is a means of speaking one's voice as well. I began to recover my personal voice through improvisation and composition. These classes unlocked the door to my spirit as the teacher, Annie, led me through a wonderland of movement possibilities. Annie introduced me to Laban Movement Analysis, a movement theory developed by Rudolph von Laban, where I gained a new insight into the body and its movement as I explored the various elements of movement identified by Laban: time, weight, space, and flow. I became more conscious of how I moved as well as how others moved.

Through these explorations I discovered my personal kinesthetic world. I recognized how my body was bound, and I released it through free flow. I experienced time as I found stillness and rested in it. Through weight exploration, I found a new strength that is bringing balance to my light, timid way of being.

Annie's improvisation classes were both a playground and a hospital. The studio would be transformed into an operating room as I was sometimes "cut open" while exploring movement that took me through feelings and images related to painful life experiences. As I moved through the images, I physically worked them out and healing occurred. Healing occurred through playing as well. Improvisation became an endless playground as I played with new perspectives, becoming objects and other characters, experiencing their world views. I discovered creative problem solving by finding various ways of moving from one point to another. I learned about leading and following as I experienced both roles. The list of experiences is endless as I continue to improvise as I move through my life. As I respond to the world around me, I am conscious of my responses and how I can shape them to shape myself and the world around me. Annie awakened in me the spirit of my own creativity.

These varied experiences, like my technical training years before, were being stirred by my desire to act on them. I loved moving and experiencing. I yearned to share my awakened spirit with others, like myself, who need to dance in order to live. I wanted to help others increase their range of movement, develop and broaden their kinesthetic language, and discover the richness of abilities that lay unrecognized by a world that sees more disabilities than possibilities. I wanted to show others such as the elderly, the blind, and people with mental disabilities that they too have an artistic voice. I wanted them to see and feel the world through new creative eyes and bodies that look and move beyond what is to see what can be.

© David Kohl

Around this time, Liz Lerman came to Meredith to do a residency with her company, the Dance Exchange. As a choreographer, dancer, and teacher, she introduced me to a method of bringing dance to various populations of people through "movement games" that develop the spiritual, artistic dancer within. This approach does not exclude dance technique, but it adjusts the teaching method to fit the physical capabilities of the students.

As a storyteller, I am most affected by dance that is about something rather than just a study of pure movement. Liz Lerman's approach to choreography utilizes descriptive movement of the details that exist within a story. This approach gave me a strong and vast choreographic language. Liz Lerman's choreographic process compliments my love of dances that tell a story and builds on the creative foundation that Annie Elliott and Dr. Sherry Shapiro have imparted to me through improvisation, composition, and creative movement.

Liz Lerman challenges the traditional images of dancers through the members of her company, which is made up of people of all ages who possess a range of movement abilities. Liz brings validity to individual movement, with a philosophy that everyone can be a dancer. I was exposed to her company at a critical time in my dance education. I drank in her wisdom and boldness, allowing my thirst to be the foundation of an artistic view that is supple and elastic. Liz's residency at Meredith would set me on a new course that would be shaped and stretched by Dr. Shapiro who, like Liz, sees possibilities and abilities instead of limitations and disabilities.

Annie Elliott opened the door to my spirit. Other teachers and professors had shaped me. But Dr. Sherry Shapiro set me free through an educational process that seeks to develop the whole person. Sherry's teaching approach recognizes the unity of the mind and body. She does not set out to shape just the mind but recognizes that the mind is one part of a human being whose spiritual makeup includes feelings and emotions as well. Sherry does not see her students as a collection of clients and grades. They are human beings, mothers, fathers, daughters, and sons. She recognizes their humanity and their uniqueness, and she celebrates their diversity, recognizing within it strength and richness.

Sherry wants the students who pass through her life to be more than a regurgitation of her thoughts and ideas. She hungers for the students to think for themselves, to become empowered individuals who act as responsible citizens within a world community. She encourages them to develop a wisdom that bridges education with real life, making the "knowing" applicable. Sherry validates each person's wisdom, challenging students to think and act. This continues in the studio, where she encourages the dancers to move from the inside out, celebrating process rather than product.

One of the most freeing and profoundly affecting experiences I have had as a dancer occurred during my participation in a dance piece that Sherry choreographed entitled "Eating," a piece that deals with the issues surrounding women and eating. I was the oldest dancer in a group of five, being about 20 years older than the others. Sherry supplied us with many articles and movies that dealt with the facts and true life experiences of women and their relationship to food. Before we read anything, however, we began by discussing our own personal relationships to food.

Through this process of discussion, sharing, and emptying ourselves of our personal frustrations and pains, we put together a dance that speaks volumes. As women and dancers we struggle with image, starving ourselves in an attempt to become that thin-figured woman who smiles at us from the television and movie screen.

Once again, age is not a part of this issue. As women we are oppressed at any age because of a society that is more product oriented. Our society continues to hold American women hostage with its focus on the product rather than the process of wisdom and the beauty of a person's life. As a result, we are all oppressed—men, women, young, and old; we are our own oppressors, mindlessly sustaining the oppression by searching for ourselves outside ourselves. We look for ourselves in our external possessions or in some narrow definition of intelligence and validity. As artists we are oppressed by a narrow definition of what is good art, putting more emphasis on the product than the process. This narrow definition of art has stolen our artistic power, a power only accepted when it is used by those who meet the qualifications of the product-oriented artist. In creating "Eating," we moved beyond this ideology into one where pure art erupts as we submerged ourselves in the process of physical and spiritual creation.

As we created movements that came out of our life experiences and emotions, we brought the issue of women and our relationship to food to life. As we struggled, laughed, and cried through the process, we gained strength and community. We were not aware of the profound product that we were creating. When the process is real and honest, the product will not only be good art, but it will also be art that is valid, exceptional, and skilled. This process allows dancers to perform with honest emotion and energy, to perform from the inside out, as opposed to the outside in.

On a hot, sunny afternoon in Washington, D.C., at the Latin American Youth Center (LAYC), I sat watching the three, dark, beautiful creatures weave and step magic with every ounce of their spirit. I began to ask myself what my role was as a dance teacher. I had entered their lives, their space, with an agenda full of good intentions, wanting to "bring" art to them so that they might gain power in their lives by becoming creative, productive people. I had come to bring them a voice. Instead they were bringing art, they were bringing a voice, to me. It was their art and their voice. As I sat watching their dance, I realized that I was only providing the crayons and the paper; they were creating the picture.

I had arrived in Washington that summer by way of a Summer Study Scholarship I had been awarded by the Meredith Dance Department. Liz Lerman's residency had spawned an interest in the Dance Department to offer a class in community outreach, and I had spent my last three years at Meredith focusing on an outreach effort involved with bringing dance out into the community to populations of people who generally are not targeted for dance because of age, disabilities, or economics.

The community outreach class proved to be a valuable teaching experience. We met once a week in a retirement setting where we worked with the elderly. The experiences were satisfying in their richness of reciprocity between the class members and the leaders who included Annie, the teacher of the outreach class, myself, and another student. Through the movement exercises and games we played, the class members came alive as they were exposed to a variety of new experiences in dance. Through the process of exploring movement shapes, stories, and combinations, these elderly individuals were acting as choreographers, creating their own dances and defying the stereotypical definitions of who is a dancer and artist. As witness to their experiences, I was being fed as observer, artist, choreographer, and teacher. This reciprocal relationship was humbling and satisfying. My philosophy on teaching was beginning to change and develop on a subconscious level through this class experience. It would begin to take a conscious and verbal form when I embarked on the journey to Washington in the summer of 1994.

I also arrived in D.C. that summer on the heels of a summer course in Dance Appreciation. I entered the Dance Appreciation class never realizing the part this class would play in my search for a personal dance philosophy. I knew what I wanted to do as a dance teacher in the community; I wanted to bring art to the people. I had no clue, however, that my approach as a teacher was about to be challenged in a profound way.

The Dance Appreciation class exposed me to a world of new questions as I watched a broad range of films from documentaries on young people dancing on street corners to technically trained dance companies. I watched movies that dealt with issues surrounding the morality of dance to issues within the professional dance world relating to definitions of who can dance and what is good art. I read articles addressing the historical era in the evolution of dance and various dance disciplines. After the films and readings, we wrote in our journals and discussed the ideas, answers, and questions that were evolving due to our exposure. More questions than answers were emerging in my search.

As I sat watching the film "Ballroom Dancing," where a young man was being excommunicated from his dance family simply because he was stepping outside the boundaries of what had been determined as the only appropriate steps, I could not help but compare this to the modern dance pioneers who, like the young dancer in the film, challenged tradition. Yet although modern dance is rooted in a language of self-expression and personal freedom, I wondered if in some ways modern dance has become as confining as ballet in its definitions of dancers, technique, and choreography. This question would take more reflection than I was ready to give as I prepared for my study with Liz Lerman and the Dance Exchange. I decided to put it on the back burner of my mind to simmer until a later date, while I packed and planned for my journey.

I arrived at National Airport an eager and frightened woman. I was eager to begin my studies with Liz and the company; but, as a woman who had never ventured too far from home, much less completely alone and leaving behind her husband and children, I was terrified. Weeks before, however, I had determined not to let fear control me. I had waited all of my life for the moment when I would fly on my own, and it was going to take more than my fear of being an inexperienced traveler to keep me from boarding that plane. As I fearfully, yet determinedly, boarded the plane, I did not notice the spirits of my mother, my grandmother, and other women who had shaped my life who were there beside me. I was not truly alone.

So there I sat, witnessing the beautiful choreography of the neighborhood youth in the old sanctuary of a church that served as a youth center in the heart of Washington, D.C. I sat in the midst of history where decisions are made that can either build or destroy a nation of people. I sat in the place that determines whether this country is indeed a land of equal opportunity, or merely a land of opportunity.

The questions that had lain dormant since the Dance Appreciation class were now surfacing in the LAYC. As teacher, was I helping these teens to discover their artistic voice by defining for them what that voice would sound like? Certainly as a teacher my purpose is to lead students in stretching their boundaries. But am I stretching their boundaries or limiting their boundaries if I do not first investigate what their boundaries are? I must have a class plan, but should that plan be one that allows a sharing of power among students and teacher? As I gave the students directions, they followed along, albeit reluctantly. I saw that I was not bringing them a means of expressing their own artistic voice; I was bringing them my voice. I was discovering that I cannot narrowly define art with my own personal language. If I attempt to do that, then I am no longer bringing art to others. Instead, I am bringing them dogma, and I am stifling their creativity.

My experience with these teenage dancers caused me to reflect on my own dancing experiences. I was denied dance as a youth because it was not a part of the educational system. That has not changed very much over the years. Art is still extracurricular, tagged on as an elective, mainly in the form of music and visual art. Children's minds are the focus of education, producing disconnected children and adults as the body and spirit are left undeveloped. The result is a society of people who are fed information in a vacuum where it is sucked into a dust bag of uselessness; instead children should be learning to think creatively about knowledge in a collaborative environment. When children are taught creatively, their own creative powers are developed, producing a society of connected people with the power to create a life for themselves.

Education is still about creating factory workers. It is still concerned with product as opposed to process. Of course, there are exceptions to this rule, just as there are teachers who strive to change the current educational system. These teachers, however, are at the mercy of the State whose politicians are the products of the system. These politicians do not see the need for creativity as their creativity has never been developed. And so the cycle continues.

Another result of dance being excluded from public education is that art remains accessible only to the middle- to upper-class elite; unless, of course, parents of lower-class children make sacrifices so that their children can develop artistically. This situation leaves little hope for the lower class to escape poverty, since it is denied access to achieve its creative potential. This loss of power is not exclusive to the lower class—the art world itself strips most of us of power through its oppression of the arts.

As I move within the dance world, I am confronted with these same issues. Dance classes are often taught by teachers who are abusive to dancers (see the next chapter). They destroy the dancer's spirit to develop the physical technique, either due to ignorance borne out of their own training experiences or to stroke their own egos. One of my most disappointing experiences has been attending dance festivals to see the work of major dance artists whose work I have either studied or admired over the years. Through my college experience, I have been given various opportunities to meet people close to these dance masters as my friends have taken classes with them or through my personal dance experiences with these artists. These same artists create an abusive classroom and choreographic environment; in many ways, some of these dance artists are no more than rock stars of the dance world. These choreographers make dances about oppression when they are the oppressors destroying the spirit of dancers, making their art nothing more than a sterile, physical product.

After this period of reflection, I returned to the youth center the next day with a new approach. I asked the teens to show me how they like to move. With brilliant beauty and energy the young women began to move with a rhythm and emotion that went far beyond anything they had done the previous day. When they finished, I proceeded to stretch their boundaries with an agenda that now incorporated their movement choices with my preconceived movement elements—the result of this process was art.

This struggle of teacher as student is tied up in the same struggle I have in ministering to those in need and being ministered to by those in need. If I am to be a true minister, I must be open to letting those whom I lead to lead me as well. In doing so I am forced to acknowledge that I, too, am needy. Only under these circumstances will a reciprocal experience occur that brings true help while maintaining dignity and creating an atmosphere of shared power. We must search for the answers together. Likewise, in order to be a competent educator, I must not lead students blindly and powerlessly along. Instead, I must lead them, too, to think, search, and move powerfully. As educator, I must share the power. Teaching is like looking into a mirror; at times one is never quite sure which side of the mirror one is on.

> I stood on the island of Meredith College on a cloudy day reaching for my Bachelor of Arts degree. It was as if I was moving through a dream in slow motion. But as I felt the smooth, leather folder that contained the piece of paper that held my name, I knew it wasn't a dream. I had come to Meredith a young girl in a woman's body who was existing in an illusionary world of fear and oppression. I was leaving a woman who had been set free in a real world that was unpredictable, sometimes unsafe, yet fully alive.

As I moved slowly in the line of women who restlessly waited for their names to be called, I reflected on how I had come to this point in my life. How had I, a frightened, powerless woman, made it into an institution such as Meredith, let alone standing now as a graduate with other women? No sooner had I asked the question, than I answered it. I had gotten to this point by my determination to live fully; through the encouragement of others who also were determined to live fully; and by hearing, dreaming, holding on, taking, and giving. I had gotten to this point by my need to dance.

I came to Meredith a frightened, fragmented woman. I loved my role as wife and mother, and I still do. This is a part of the beauty and honor of being a woman. Yet, these roles are extensions of other people. I had no strong center as an individual, as a woman. I had become unsure of myself, and I would panic when I was out with other people. To say I had low self-esteem would be an understatement. I was desperate and lost, imprisoned by the voices of my past. I believed that I was not as smart as others and that what I thought was of very little value. It was the small child within me that wanted so desperately to make a difference that gave me the strength and courage to take that first step to register for classes. It was that small child who wanted to live fully that would move me forward on the one hand and hold me back on the other.

The inner child that played in the woods at Grannie's, rode horses across the mountaintops, and danced through the trees, moves me deliberately through life. This artist child hungers to live like an eagle hungers to fly. This child is afraid of nothing because she is more afraid of dying than she is of living. However, she is part of a dichotomy; she is also the inner child of abuse, rejection, and abandonment. Her fears are borne out of the pain of others who stepped on her while fleeing from their own pain. She is injured and afraid of further injury. She fears she will disappear in the darkness and be exposed in the light.

I carried this inner dualism with me as I entered college, it was with me when I graduated, and it goes with me now. Yet, through the process of dance education, the fearful child is slowly healing. In the halls and studios of Meredith, the darkness within me was illuminated. Each time I entered the darkness, feeling my way through, I gained strength for my journey into the light. With each courageous step, the dancing, artistic child emerges and the fearful child is healed. Through my education at Meredith I gained knowledge; wisdom; creativity; and, finally, power.

Through knowledge I develop my mind and my world perspective. Knowing replaces ignorance, requiring me to be more responsible as a human being and citizen. Knowing coupled with life experience manifests itself as wisdom. Wisdom is the meeting of my body, mind, and spirit. I am a "created" and "creative" creature. I draw my life from creation, and I give life back by creating. My spirit is the substance of my being, the breath of my mind and body. My body is the storehouse of my experiences, thoughts, and emotions. I shudder physically at certain thoughts, my neck stiffens and my muscles tense when I am under emotional stress. I weep when I am feeling sad. I want to run or hit something when I feel mad. My body is the storehouse of my mind and the pipeline of my spirit.

Dance is the power that propels me through life. Through art I find my power. I can know and feel many things intellectually, but it is through my artistic voice that I can articulate these things. My power lies in my ability to process, create, and produce.

Entering college was the bravest thing I have ever done. There were days throughout the five years I was there that I did not think I would make it, as I was often tired from working part-time and taking care of a family in addition to being a full-time student. Sometimes school was a challenge as I came up against people who were hard and degrading. When I was in these situations, I would remind myself that I had allowed other people to rob me of the first half of my life, and I refused to give up the rest of it. Although many people reached out and helped me, I learned that there are times when no one can help you but yourself—you must take control and make it happen.

As I encountered situations much like the ones in my past, I began to recognize that I was not responsible for many things in my past as I was not responsible for many things now. I set about to deal with the ghosts that haunted me, and I was able at last to move ahead. And while we cannot ignore the past, neither can we let it continue to drain us of our energy. We must learn to name our past mistakes and forgive ourselves for making them. I have to accept that I make mistakes just like everyone else and that I have to work to change what I need to change, disregarding other people's wrongful criticism, often borne out of their own lack of power and self-esteem. I began to no longer see myself as a bad person but as a normal human being. I learned at last to love myself.

I struggled to refocus my energy at school. My determination to survive, my love of life and people, and my sense of justice kicked in, and nothing could stop me from getting the education that would supply me with the tools to help myself and others. Meredith led me to the gateway of freedom by providing me with a well-rounded education that developed my intellect and my creative spirit. Now Meredith and I stand together, struggling to pass on into freedom.

We are both seeking true freedom, me as a woman, Meredith as an institution for women. We both struggle with masculine language that keeps women from moving ahead. As educator and educational institution we struggle with a linear educational methodology whose primary concern is developing the rational, thinking mind in a competitive environment where intelligence is defined by test scores. As woman and school for women we struggle against the maintenance of female images that keep women oppressed. We strive to be educators of the whole person, intellectually and emotionally, in an atmosphere where intelligence has no boundaries. We are the messengers, the mothers, the followers, and the leaders.

I don't want to be a man; I just want to be a woman. That is a strong statement, because the feminist movement often, in its striving for freedom and equality, unknowingly abandons the feminine. I am, finally, *proud* to be a woman.

Dear Grannie . . . thank you for your stories, and for teaching me to hear.

My grandmother had something that no institution can give to you. She had wisdom that comes from listening to life. She taught me to listen to the wind if I wanted to know when a storm is coming. She taught me to respect the wisdom of the soil if I wanted to eat. She taught me the value of stories as she connected me with my heritage, weaving a tapestry of family lineage with design and richness. Now, through the wisdom of an elder, I am weaving my own story into the tapestry of my family.

During the dark period of my life I had stopped listening. I had locked myself away in a safe place deep in the recesses of my mind and soul. Dance unlocked those recesses as I learned again to pay attention to the details, to see and hear the movement and the stories behind the movement. Through dance, my story emerged and I found my true self. Now I want to pass this on, to help others to find themselves through their stories and movements.

I want my story to be for others a story of healing and hope. In return I want to hear all of the stories that lie beneath the words and the movements. I want to hear the stories of the elderly, the wisdom and the poetry of a life long lived. I want to hear the wisdom of children as they experience life with a freshness each new day.

I am always teaching myself to hear others. When I am with other human beings, they are not just a face or a client. They are people with joys and struggles. They are people who need love and power in their lives. Through my work in dance as a choreographer, I am witness to people's stories. I am witness to the recovery of their personal voice. Through art I have seen people recover their own creativity as artists, realizing that art is not just the province of a special few. Through art individuals are freed as they discover their worth as people with creative and valid thoughts and ideas. Through dance everyone can satisfy a primal need to move in celebration of their physical and spiritual beings. Through dance they are given life.

Dear Mother. . . thank you for showing me to hold onto my dreams for dear life.

My mother may not have lived her dream to become a certified teacher, but she has lived her dream to become a teacher of life. She has taught me, and she continues to teach me, the joy and fulfillment of compassion and passion. Through her acts of compassion she has taught me that it is in giving that we receive. Through her passion, she has taught me to never give up on my needs and desires, nor the needs and desires of my family. Dancing is a need and a desire of my heart. Dancing, for me, is breathing. It sustains me and gives me life. I inhale air and energy; I exhale art. When I am dancing, I am wholly and fully experiencing my true self. Dancing is my dream and my life. I am holding onto my dream for dear life.

Dear Sue . . . thanks for the new box of crayons.

Sue gave me new crayons to color new possibilities. She did not tell me how to draw the picture. She just provided the wisdom and guidance that I needed to define what that picture is for me. As educator artist, Sue taught me to see each opportunity with fresh eyes, using the gifts that I possess to create and shape my life in a way that honors these gifts.

I was sharing my desire to lead others to recover their artistic voice with a spiritual artist and leader, when the minister of the progressive Jubilee! Community Church in Asheville said to me, "Do you know that you are a missionary?" I was taken aback with this thought. I had struggled for so long to make sense of how this strong desire to dance fits with my faith and my need to work with people. I could not see how dance and religion fit together.

Yet as I moved beyond technique to dance as authentic movement, I found the spirituality of the dance. My friend, my minister as prophet, had spoken truth to me. His words pierced my heart where the voice of God, the Goddess, the Mystery, the Wind, truly speaks. At that moment, I could see the journey in all of its twists and turns. The day that I answered the "calling," it wasn't the calling of the church. It was the inner voice inside me of God, the Creator, calling me to fulfill my creation as an artist, as a dancer.

I no longer look for myself outside of myself. For it is inside the breath of every human being that the mystery, the wind of God exists. It is the spirit of the creator that breathes through me, bringing light and color to me as an artist. If I want to be with God I need only dance or take the hand of a fellow human being.

> *To my daughters, as you journey through life, look where you are going so that you do not step on anyone else along the way. And remember . . . education is power, faith is in the living, and wisdom is in the questions. As human beings, live responsibly. As women, live deliberately.*

In the spirit of the women who have gone before me, those who go beside me, and those who will follow me, I wish for all daughters the peace that comes from dancing with the pain and dancing with the joy. I have found that true peace comes from living responsibly, courageously, and fully.

May my daughters live responsibly. May they, as women, live deliberately. May they rise to the challenge of living up to their artistic potential, and dance all the way to the top. May they make a difference in the world, seeing color and embracing it. May they in their ability to set others free, be freed themselves.

> *To my husband and my son, thank you for your strong, soft, nurturing, male dance.*

The men in my life bring a strength and tenderness that completes me as a woman. They achieve this by making room for, and developing, the feminine within their masculinity. They are the linear thinkers who bring order and rationalism into the chaotic and irrational parts of my life. They are not the opposite, antithetical part of me. On the contrary, they are the part that complements all that I am as woman, joining the circle of my spirit that is connected and moving as I grow and spin in my dance to, and through, life.

Dear Sherry, thank you for the wings.

I was recently asked to do two things. The first was to list three things that others have done for me, and three things I have done for others. I chose to list love, hope, and power. These three things have led me to the moment when I was ready for the most important gift of all—wings. Many people breathed life into me at Meredith and throughout my life, but one woman, provided me with the gift of flight.

Three years ago I would have listed my work with people who were in crisis as the most important thing I have done for others. That has changed. Without hesitation I wrote, I have helped people find freedom and power through dance. I have spent much of my adult life in trying to help others feed and clothe themselves and their families through my work with the church and as a private citizen. These homeless people taught me about grace and beauty through their humble existence. As I worked with them I wanted to give them something more lasting than just a bag of food or clothing.

Through dance I help people to heal their emotional wounds with a healing, creative, and lasting power. I help them to find that they can have a choice through a restoration of power that rests in creative thinking, problem solving, and a sense of self-worth. Through working as part of a group, creating dances from the stories of those with whom they dance, people who have been isolated in their need are finding a new way of seeing. Through creative movement, they discover their own movement preferences and ways of being. Through this process people also unmask spiritual pain that has been stored away in their body memory as they release through movement images.

I lead them to recover their power by helping them to recover the artist that lives within. I teach them that who they are is valid. As they act as choreographers, creating movement, they become confident that how they choose to move and be is worthwhile and important. The artist surfaces and they become powerful, productive people. I help them by leading them to restore their power and dignity. Then they can move beyond dance to create their lives as parents, laborers, students, human beings. In return, they help me by allowing me to witness the beauty and depth of their individuality as creators and human beings, touching and teaching me.

Through dance, stories are being told. As dancers share their movement stories, those who witness their stories are gaining new insights into the realities that other people live. This approach can help to bridge communities, destroy ignorance, and eliminate prejudice.

Dance, as all art, is about life. When we dance we share our lives and our stories. By dancing we can hear the voice that touches and speaks to us in that deep place where words can neither explain nor reach. Through dance, I express who I am, learning from the past, living in the present, shaping my future.

Through dance I recovered my story. It is the story of women. It is the story of a woman. It is the story of family, children, loss, and gain. It is the story of lost innocence, harsh realities, and shattered dreams. It is also the story of growing up, dreaming dreams, taking chances, and re-creating life. This is my story.

It all began on the back porch of a house nestled in the Blue Ridge Mountains. An artist lived there. Her name was Janie. She was the mother of a daughter named Myrtle. Janie was a storyteller. You could find her most evenings out on the backporch with the moonlight shining on her silver hair. If I listened closely, I could hear her stories trickling down the moonbeams . . . resting in my soul . . . where she still remains.

I am the granddaughter of Janie. I am the daughter of Myrtle. I am a dancer . . . .

I am Sondra. I am. I.

Critical Reflections

For many of us, the concept of human freedom seems so abstract, something that we read about or hear in songs and see in movies. Words of liberation can also ring of war and bloodshed. To bring these words into the everyday, or life world, enables us to begin to understand just how they shape the experiences of our lives. Freedom and oppression are inextricably related like two sides of the same coin. Every situation, like Janus's face, provides us with possibilities for both freedom and continued domination. Marxist and feminist theories have helped us to think about freedom in terms of our everyday social and material worlds. Feminist theory in particular has alerted us to the everyday world of women, in which we are constantly confronted with obstacles and limitations on our capacity to live rich and full human lives. Feminism has shown us how women's lives are disfigured by sexual objectification, economic exploitation, lowered expectations, and stigmatization of what it means to be a woman. We have come to see how everywhere, from the bedroom to the workplace, women must constantly struggle to assert their own needs and humanity. Freedom in this context means to continually struggle to go beyond the limits and obstacles that contain our lives. These limits are not merely externally imposed; we impose them on ourselves as part of our own understandings and self-perceptions. Women learn to devalue their own knowledge and wisdom and to discount their voices. In a world where women continue to have little power they obsess about the appearance of their bodies as perhaps this is the only place where they feel able to exert control over their own lives. For many of us dance can be a place of liberation, a lifesaving vehicle in which we as women have felt the sublimity of transgressing the boundaries of the body, sexuality, and creativity. Dance can also be a place of transformation where we become empowered, moving beyond the distorted cultural images of perfection to those of real women, beyond silence to speaking the stories of our lives, and beyond self-doubt to respecting ourselves and courageously addressing our most deeply felt convictions.

Take a Moment to Reflect

Write descriptively and freely about your own history as a woman in dance. After writing without censoring, reflect upon experiences in which you felt oppressed or liberated and what structured those experiences.

In the following chapter Clyde Smith draws on his own experiences in dance as a dancer, observer, and researcher, interviewing a professional dancer to analyze relationships found within the dance classroom. This is an example of interpretive research wherein the author situates him- or herself in the conversation, situates the subjective responses of the participants within the cultural context, and draws upon his or her understandings of the research to assist in "making meaning" of those experiences.

REFERENCES

Rukeyser, M. 1973. "Kathie Kollwitz". In *By a Woman Writ*, J. Goulianos (ed.): 373-378. New York: Bobbs-Merrill.

CHAPTER 6

ON AUTHORITARIANISM IN THE DANCE CLASSROOM

CLYDE SMITH
Ohio State University

This chapter considers professional dance training with implications for dance pedagogy at all levels. The author draws on personal experience and interviews with a professional dancer. Citing the work of Michel Foucault, the author discusses the body in terms of social coercion and surveillance and how these are directed in and through the body/subject. The dance classroom is analyzed in relationship to these issues, and the relationship between dance teachers and dance students is questioned. The author also draws parallels between characteristics of cults, citing here the work of Arthur Deikman, and elite dance conservatories. The author concludes by recognizing that, although authoritarian behavior appears to be imposed upon the students, often the students themselves expect and accept such treatment.

The photographs included with this chapter are illustrative only, and are not intended to imply that any of the persons or places depicted are directly or indirectly involved in any of the behavior described or criticized in the text.

This study is an initial consideration of the operation of authoritarianism in the dance classroom, centering on how authority is imposed by teachers and how students participate in their own oppression. However, I only consider the issue of why people behave a certain way in passing because this is a much larger issue than this study can encompass. Although I focus on specific instances in professional dance training, this chapter illuminates issues that are more generally relevant to dance education and to education as a whole.

My methodology involves a qualitative search for meaning rather than the testing of a simple hypothesis. I chose this approach because the issue of authoritarianism is complex, even when limited to a setting seemingly as straightforward as a dance classroom. A quantitative approach would not provide the kind of understanding that could begin to account for human involvement in oppressive situations; such an approach does not allow for a full consideration of the complex interrelationship of individual and environment that influences human behavior. Although this study cannot fully account for said involvement, I do establish a solid base for further study.

My exploration is divided into three sections. I begin with a consideration of my own formation as an anti-authoritarian, in part to visibly situate myself in my own research. I draw on my journal and personal essays to clarify how my theoretical perspective developed in relation to my everyday life. In considering my past I also explain how I came to this project and what my questions were in the context of my own experiences. This section is followed by a discussion of the literature I found most useful in clarifying my opinions and in moving from personal reflection to a more analytical state. Here I draw upon Michel Foucault's *Discipline and Punish* (1979) and *Power/ Knowledge* (1980) as well as Arthur Deikman's *The Wrong Way Home* (1990).

I then turn to my dialogues with a dancer who studied for two years in a conservatory setting with teachers who had a deserved reputation for authoritarian behavior. I chose her, in part, because she is a person whom I know to be honest and thoughtful and with whom I could engage in active conversation rather than simple questioning. This dancer is a very successful performer who critiques her past training quite clearly, yet she does not have a fixed analysis of her experiences. This set of circumstances allowed us to enter readily into a rich dialogue.

This project does not end with a simple finding but with a more complex conclusion. I hope to provide a clearer understanding of authoritarianism in practice, which reveals not only that extreme situations are at hand but also that these situations exist on a continuum of authoritarianism that pervades the dance world. Furthermore, the underlying principles of such extreme situations are evident in much typical dance teaching. In a very real sense, we are all implicated in authoritarian practices whether we ignore or replicate such practices.

A NOTE TO THE READER

The reader should understand that this ungainly hybrid of personal experience, theory, and dialogue is not a traditionally objective consideration of data. Although I question the validity of the concept of objectivity, that questioning is too large a topic for this study. Nonetheless, it is important to recognize that I approach this project with a clear agenda of attacking classroom authoritarianism. I fully embrace Michel Foucault's suggestion that books such as his might be regarded as "toolboxes" with which "to short circuit or disqualify systems of power" (Eribon 1991, 237). My purpose in writing this chapter is to short-circuit what I consider to be authoritarian behavior; the reader should bear this in mind.

HOW I BECAME AN ANTI-AUTHORITARIAN

My arrival at this project followed a long, circuitous route that, in many ways, unites my artistic and political activities. I became a dancer in the late 1970s and an anarchist in the late 1980s. But before any of this I became an anti-authoritarian. The word *authority* usually refers to one who is an expert or one who is in a position of power. When I use the term *authority*, I am referring to one who is an expert. When I use the phrase *authority figure*, I am referring to a person in a position of power who may or may not be an actual expert. The term *authoritarian*, according to *Webster's New Encyclopedic Dictionary* (1993), means "relating to or demanding total submission to authority especially as concentrated in a powerful leader."

For me, authoritarianism and authoritarian behavior entail enforced submission to an authority figure, often accompanied by abusive behavior. Abusive behavior consists of verbal or physical acts that express disrespect or contempt and cause injury or damage. I think of authoritarian behavior as existing on a continuum, with one end being the absence of enforced submission and abusive behavior and the other end being the equivalent of a kidnap and torture scenario. I believe most human behavior involving power relations exists somewhere between these two poles. Whether someone is or is not an authoritarian is not what I am considering. Instead I am looking at authoritarian behavior and relationships as they are manifested in daily practice.

As an anti-authoritarian I am against the total submission imposed by authority figures. I believe in individual autonomy, or the power to make one's own choices in any situation. This power to choose can and often does include the choice to participate in work directed by another, for example, to dance in a piece choreographed by someone other than oneself. Choosing to follow another's lead can also be a way of learning, as in a dance classroom. The issue of consent is important here. I do not necessarily believe that an authoritarian situation is produced when we freely agree to do what someone else is telling us to do. The issue of the authority figure recognizing the ultimate autonomy of the individual in a situation is also important. We may agree to let someone else direct a situation and find that the person is not respecting our boundaries. If an individual cannot set boundaries in such a situation because she or he is not allowed or is emotionally unable to do so, then an authoritarian situation may occur. Unfortunately such distinctions are not clear cut. More issues are at stake and more levels of meaning to be explored as is demonstrated in my personal story.

AUTHORITY FIGURES

In looking at my various writings, I see many authority figures emerge, including God, bosses, and teachers. My parents, however, are noticeably absent from this list, although they are obviously authority figures, because they rarely exhibited authoritarian behavior. They did set boundaries, with which I sometimes disagreed, but my parents ultimately recognized and supported my autonomy. They let me make many decisions as a child and listened to what I had to say. As I became an adolescent and relations inevitably became stormier, they clearly showed that they cared about me no matter what I believed.

My parents' behavior helped me to understand that authority figures do not have to be authoritarian. Their support of my differing views also informed me that I do not always have to agree with authority figures to be a good person. This description does sound rather rosy, but although there were some hard moments, overall my parents exhibited much less authoritarian behavior than the majority of authority figures whom I encountered outside my home.

EARLY DISILLUSIONMENT

I think junior high school was the turning point for me. As an adolescent in a violent setting, I found that being "good" and following the lead of authority figures did not protect me from those petty authoritarians we call bullies. This recollection is my first memory of a series of realizations that stretched from seventh grade to my first years out of college. During this time I discovered that following the rules did not guarantee reward. I found that I did not believe in a hovering male god. I found that the United States government was not always right and that the prominence of America was built on foundations of blood. Perhaps my first encounter with authoritarianism was at birth when the doctor, my first authority figure, immediately hit me as I emerged from my mother's womb.

For me to reject the implicit validity of the authority figure and clarify when I was being subjected to authoritarian behavior, I had to experience over and over again the betrayal of my autonomy by authority figures. This betrayal happened many times in my dance experience. I can easily remember instances when, to be part of a program, I had to study with teachers with whom I would not have studied unless so required. After many years of periodic bouts with abusive teachers, I clearly saw that dance is no haven from an authoritarian world. In fact, it is often a focus for the worst forms of authoritarianism.

Let me clarify again that I do not consider the situation of a teacher directing students to be an authoritarian situation in every case. I have learned much about myself and about dance by following the authoritative lead of a master teacher. I have only been able to give myself fully to those experiences when abusive behavior did not occur. For me, one abusive moment can transform a classroom into an authoritarian setting. Certainly what is acceptable and unacceptable varies for each individual, and I am in no way attempting to set absolute guidelines for or proscriptions of behavior. Again, I am only trying to illuminate an area of consideration that has by no means been fully addressed in the field of dance.

DANCING WITH AUTHORITY

One center for authoritarian training in dance that I attended briefly was what I will term in this study the "Conservatory." This institution is the same one that the interviewee I call "Catherine" (not her real name) and I discuss in the third section of this paper. References to the Conservatory teachers are combined in a composite figure I call the "Teacher." The Teacher was legendary in the unrecorded oral archives of Conservatory history. Over the years I met many people who studied with the Teacher on an ongoing basis and told horrific stories of classroom abuse. I only had one class with the Teacher during my years of training. At one point during that class he came up to me when my arms were in second position, put one hand on my chest and one on my back to encourage me to widen in my upper torso, and then whispered that he could crush me "in an instant" before stalking off. Perhaps now somewhat amusing, this incident was a minor one in the legends of the Teacher.

Certainly by the time I finished my undergraduate dance training, which included attendance at two universities as well as many workshops and summer programs, I had many anecdotes to share about the behavior of my teachers, though none quite as peculiar as the Teacher story. I understood the dance classroom to be an ideal climate for authoritarian behavior. The student has already consented to being in a situation in which he or she is usually attempting to replicate as perfectly as possible the example and the demands of the teacher. Because most choreography involves a process in which dancers become the material for the choreographer's work, this form of training is often appropriate. With a caring teacher who respects the physical and emotional limits of the students, the dance class experience can be a powerful and positive one, as I have often found. The dance class situation offers so much power to the teacher, however, that this power is readily abused, as I myself later discovered when teaching a large group of nondancers (see "Enacting Authoritarianism").

Because dancers are generally scantily clad, evenly distributed in space, and eager to please, they are easily observed and controlled. A dancer who will not or cannot participate at the general group level is easily picked out. In addition, because dancers are typically dependent on the teacher's feedback, any comments or lack of comments take on exaggerated import. I remember when being told I was doing something wrong was a sign that I was worthy of attention. Unfortunately the line between what we as dancers term a correction and what others might call an insult can be quite thin.

Though I was quite good at replicating what I was to do with teachers I believed in, I eventually rebelled at teachers who exhibited authoritarian behavior. In my first few years as a dancer, however, I was often drawn to authoritarian teachers and the absolute power they wielded. As I look back, I see that in a consistently authoritarian setting like that at the Conservatory, abusive behavior can continue for years, remarked upon by those who study at such institutions and yet rarely questioned except in personal conversation. So, as much as I have developed a critique of authoritarian behavior, I also wonder at how dancers, including myself, often participate in and even believe in the authoritarian approach. This participation in authoritarianism means that we cannot simply blame the teacher but must look at what everyone involved brings to the situation.

ANARCHISM

In the mid to late 1980s, I discovered anarchism. I was involved in grassroots political work in North Carolina and experienced a fair amount of authoritarian behavior on the part of leadership figures in local organizations.

During a brief period in Seattle, I found a publication called "Direct Action," which discussed anarchist activity in the San Francisco Bay Area. "Direct Action" often contained critiques of leftist politics from an anti-authoritarian position that articulated much of what I was thinking. "Direct Action" also introduced me to a milieu in which an attempt was made to allow for multiple viewpoints without forging a false unity. A concern for individual autonomy coexisted with a belief in collective responsibility. In many ways, I felt that these were my people. As I learned more about anarchists, I found that some did refer to themselves as anti-authoritarians. I also gained insight from a variety of viewpoints concerning what defines anarchism, almost as many viewpoints as there were anarchists.

An important aspect of the forms of anarchism to which I was drawn was an articulation of what I had only known of as feminism or woman-centered politics. Though feminism was an important part of my political orientation, the binary gender focus often left me in the camp of the enemy. In anarchism I found a similar focus on anti-hierarchical organization and consensus decision making without the restrictive essentialist stances of many branches of feminism. I eventually found that some anarchists also exhibit authoritarian behavior; however, anarchism was clearly a philosophy that included my brand of anti-authoritarianism in its eclectic patchwork of humankind.

As a political person of anarchist persuasion, I critique whatever setting in which I find myself. I often notice on the job, at school, in arts settings, or in social scenes that people are in some ways complicit with the various forms of authoritarianism they encounter. It is true that, at times, trying to affect our circumstances might cause us to go to jail or lose our jobs over issues that may not be worth the cost. It is mere prudence to recognize these situations for what they are, duck one's head, and prepare for future struggles instead. But I also see a reluctance among my peers and others around me, wherever I find myself, to change what can be changed; instead, people tend to complain outside the setting and yet return again to a barely tolerable situation. This pattern takes many forms and seems to be the normal state of being in this culture at this time.

Beyond these mundane situations, we all know of more extreme examples of people who are heavily abused and do not resist, even if we only hear of them by word of mouth or in the media. In the case of students of the Teacher, this abuse was both mental and physical and usually, but not always, focused in the classroom. I wonder why so many students simply accepted such behavior without speaking out.

In the remainder of the chapter I focus on authoritarianism in the dance classroom and how we as dancers participate in our own oppression. In the following section, I examine the work of Michel Foucault and Arthur Deikman and explore how their theories relate to the dance classroom. Later, I present one dancer's experience of the regime of the Teacher at the

Conservatory as a practical example. And I wonder how our collusion with petty tyranny makes such extreme cases possible and what we can do to change this state of affairs.

USEFUL THEORY

Upon beginning this project, I thought of the situation of authoritarianism in the dance classroom as one in which teachers hold absolute power over students and through abusive means disempower students, breaking them down and then building them back up in the teacher's own image. Because of this viewpoint, I chose to look for theorists whose work dealt with prisons, the military, educational discipline, cult formation, and brainwashing. A wide range of literature can be found across disciplines that is relevant to my concerns, and a few of these are included in the reference list for readers who wish to pursue this subject further. Rather than attempting a literature review, for the purpose of this study I am taking useful theory and using it to illuminate the situation at hand. I found the work of Michel Foucault and Arthur Deikman to be particularly enlightening in studying authoritarianism. I begin with Michel Foucault.

DISCIPLINE AND PUNISH

References to Michel Foucault's *Discipline and Punish* (1979) appear repeatedly in much contemporary work that considers discipline of the body. This book, subtitled *The Birth of the Prison*, also considers armies, hospitals, and schools. The body under discipline is one of the key themes of this work; and so both it and a book of related interviews with Foucault called *Power/Knowledge* (1980), became important resources for me in understanding the functioning of disciplinary power in the dance classroom.

Discipline and Punish is a dense text that is in part a historical study. Foucault focuses on the changes in the French system of punishment from the early 17th century to the late 18th century. He identifies this period as one in which the modern prison system was created as part of changes in human activities, which also produced modern forms of the army, the hospital, and the school. His argument is complex and includes the concept of the subject, or self, as something that is created rather than existing a priori. Social constructionists have made much use of this material, whereas critics have attacked these same ideas and raised questions concerning the historical accuracy of Foucault's work.

Foucault's concepts of power, discipline, surveillance, and the docile body are useful for this discussion, whatever the faults of Foucault's larger work. Furthermore, although I intend to be clear regarding Foucault's use of terminology as opposed to my own application, I am emboldened by Foucault's statement in an interview entitled "Prison Talk":

For myself, I prefer to utilize the writers I like. The only valid tribute to thought such as Nietzsche's is precisely to use it, to deform it, to make it groan and protest. And if commentators then say that I am being faithful or unfaithful to Nietzsche, that is of absolutely no interest.(1980, 53-54)

Power Produces Docile Bodies Under Surveillance

Foucault views power as a force that produces. Power only exists when being put to use, unlike electricity, which is a force that can be stored for use at a later date. One does not hold power; instead one exercises power. In addition to Foucault's use of the term power, I use the phrase "power over" to apply to situations in which a person or institution controls an individual or group with all the negative implications of authoritarianism. Foucault discusses how the military man's body became something that was created through discipline (1979, 135). He later specifies that "discipline 'makes' individuals; it is the specific technique of a power that regards individuals both as objects and as instruments of its exercise" (170). Through the exercise of disciplinary power (or power over), the "docile" body is produced. As Foucault states, "A body is docile that may be subjected, used, transformed and improved" (136). Docile bodies are also the goal of much dance training as dancers become the material for the teacher's or choreographer's vision.

Foucault reveals that surveillance is a key disciplinary tactic in forming and controlling the docile body. According to Foucault, surveillance is a form of observation that is most effective when it is applied to the self. In other words, an atmosphere of constant surveillance must be created by the observer, so that the observed always feels watched. This feeling in turn creates a situation in which the observed ultimately maintains a state of self-surveillance whether or not the surveilling power is actually present. The dance classroom, with its mirrors, watchful teachers, and self-critical students, is a key site for both the external and internal surveillance of dancing bodies, as evidenced by the following discussion of my experience of my own authoritarian tendencies in teaching dance.

Enacting Authoritarianism

Shortly after I began grappling with these ideas, I taught two short movement classes to groups composed primarily of nondancers. There were around 40 students in each class, some of whom considered this experience only a slight remove from playtime while I considered it a serious exploration of movement. At a certain point in one class I realized how vulnerable these people were. In the regular classroom, although I was in charge, the students were sitting behind desks clustered together around the edge of the room. They were in a familiar environment wearing everyday clothes that concealed their bodies. In the dance studio, however, they were in an alien setting, wearing more revealing clothing, separated from each other, and easily observed.

Although I was teaching from a somatic perspective, I used traditional techniques of demonstrating and then observing. When I saw students talking to each other or not fully participating, I got their attention in order to let them know I was always watching. I felt these tactics were necessary to be able to lead such a large, disparate group through a focused experience. In short, I was disciplining docile bodies under surveillance, commanding and observing them in order to improve them. I was acutely aware of the potential for abuse in this situation. Though I tried to speak in a caring manner, by the second class this manner was breaking down. The second class was rowdier and less focused. I was wearing out and on at least two occasions verbally snapped at students. Though I apologized, it was obvious to me that I was sliding along the continuum from caring, supportive behavior toward authoritarianism and power over.

What should now be obvious is that the generally given conditions of dance teaching readily allow for authoritarian behavior. In a situation with perceived discipline problems or simply a teacher in a nasty mood, these conditions facilitate authoritarianism. The question of why I or anyone would choose authoritarian behavior is a question for further study. Following Foucault's lead, I am "not [asking] why certain people want to dominate," I am researching "at the level of those continuous and uninterrupted processes which subject our bodies, govern our gestures, dictate our behaviors" (1980, 97).

Foucault and Agency

Michel Foucault's conception of power disciplining the body is extremely useful in looking at dance settings. Critics of Foucault, however, are often concerned that his work presents a model of power acting on bodies without agency, without the ability to act for themselves. Does power or power over actually create human self-awareness from a blank slate or do humans participate actively in this process? Foucault, in *Power/Knowledge*, shows that he is conscious of human agency in the form of resistance to as well as complicity with disciplinary power (1980, 162-64). In *Discipline and Punish*, he focuses on issues other than human agency, but he makes it clear that power does not merely repress in a negative way but is a positive force in that it is productive (1979, 194).

Foucault is looking at how the application of disciplinary power creates the self-awareness and even the physical being of the subjected; he is not focusing on how power over can restrict individuals. This argument addresses, in part, my awareness as a dance teacher that my use of power in the classroom produces dancers, for better or for worse. Because Foucault does not address agency more fully, we turn to Arthur Deikman's study of cult behavior to begin to understand the dancing being's involvement in this process.

THE WRONG WAY HOME

My interest in considering cults to understand how dancers participate in their own oppression grew, in part, from a comment made by a Conservatory student. He described the Teacher's teaching process as one in which the dancer's ego is broken down and then built back up in his (the Teacher's) image. In the 1980s, as I studied various social and political organizations, I came across accounts of numerous cultlike groups that were based on psychotherapy or drama therapy. Participants who left told accounts of ego breakdown and reconstruction that resonated with the Conservatory student's comments. So, in considering the use of power in the Conservatory, I decided to also consider the literature focused on cults and brainwashing and discovered many connections between dance training and cult-like behavior.

In the area of cult formation, I found Arthur Deikman's *The Wrong Way Home: Uncovering the Patterns of Cult Behavior in American Society* (1990) to be most relevant. Here Deikman focuses on a psychotherapy cult composed of well-educated people like himself. He shows how even the elite elements of contemporary American society can enter into cult settings and accept extreme authoritarian behavior as the norm. He goes further and points to the prevalence of cult-like behavior throughout American society. This work became a key resource for me in understanding how dancers participate in their own oppression and how this participation is not aberrant behavior but instead is part of a larger norm.

Deikman explains the willingness of people to follow authoritarian leaders as indicative of a "longing for parents" that

> persists into adulthood and results in cult behavior that pervades normal society . . . a yearning for parents in the most general sense. This longing results in fantasies of wise powerful guardians . . . [which] may be superimposed on people who occupy real positions of authority, success, and power. (2)

This explanation is compelling and is based, in part, on Robert Jay Lifton's classic study of totalitarianism and brainwashing in China, *Thought Reform and the Psychology of Totalism* (1961). However, Deikman takes Lifton's theories further by applying them to a less totalistic system, in this case the United States. My focus here, however, is on the *how* of cult behavior, not the *why*, although the difference between the two is often unclear.

Cult Behavior

Deikman identifies "four basic behaviors found in extreme form in cults: compliance with the group, dependence on a leader, devaluing the outsider, and avoiding dissent" (48). He also points to recurring early experiences of people who join cults, which are "interpreted as validating the claim that the leader and group [are] special" (4). These experiences of "transcendence" or the like cause individuals to accept limits imposed by the leader to become members of the group. The leader is identified as someone who can provide the experience necessary for the individual to achieve particular goals such as "enlightenment," which the initial experience with the cult has shown to be possible. Within the group, members view themselves as an elite and devalue the beliefs of those not in the cult.

Dissent is avoided and suppressed forcefully whenever it arises. Individuals "surrender" to the leader because "obedience is the prime virtue in all authoritarian systems" (85). Because "the leader is accepted as having special powers and/or semidivine status," his or her actions are "outside the behavior norms of the ordinary person.... similar exemptions from the rules and the accompanying claim to infallibility enables many a leader to perform unethical acts that would otherwise not be countenanced" (79). Clearly the participation of cult members is necessary for authoritarian behavior to occur on an ongoing basis. Does this participation create authoritarianism or is such participation merely a necessary component that in and of itself does not signify an authoritarian setting? This question is an important one to keep in mind as we apply Deikman's ideas to dance training.

Cults in the Dance Classroom

Just as Deikman points to similar patterns in less extreme situations, so too can we find parallel observations in the dance classroom, particularly in a setting like the Conservatory. In such a setting, the group consists of the students with the teacher as leader. One is there because one believes that this teacher can provide the experiences necessary to become a good dancer. Surrendering to the directions of the teacher is a standard mode of behavior. Those not in the elite—not members of the class—are considered lesser beings and looked down upon. Although dissent may occur outside the classroom, in the classroom no dissent is tolerated. Students idolize such teachers and hence extreme behavior by the Teacher is considered acceptable, particularly if the teacher is viewed as having special insights.

I experienced all these elements to some degree throughout my dance career. Certainly as a dancer I felt special, not least because nondancers or outsiders viewed me as special. When in technique class or in rehearsal, I was obedient and thought of myself as the artist's material. My fellow dancers and I were cooperative and complied with our teachers' demands even when we were critiquing those same teachers outside of class. Individuals who did not follow suit were ostracized to varying degrees. Authoritarian or not, the typical setting of most classes I took involved these cult-like behaviors. Fairly recently I danced with an individual who was periodically unstable and whose sometimes unacceptable behavior I tolerated because I considered him an important artist. Certainly my acceptance of such a situation could be said to fit aspects of Deikman's analysis.

Disturbing as these thoughts are, they fall into place quite readily. The dance classroom is a setting in which obedient students present themselves for improvement. The teacher has absolute power, and surveillance is a key tool for administering that power. While cult-like behavior is found in negative settings, it also occurs with much-loved teachers who rule the class benevolently. Usually these situations are not absolutely good or bad as we see when we turn to specific examples. The work of Foucault and Deikman is the basis for the interviews I conducted with "Catherine" regarding her experiences at the Conservatory.

CATHERINE'S STORY

After a period of reflection on my past and a study of related literature, I interviewed a woman I call "Catherine." Catherine is a former Conservatory student who went on to further training and then a professional career. She is an ideal source for me because she is a successful graduate of the Conservatory who nonetheless is highly critical of her training there. Much of what I consider to be abusive behavior in Conservatory training, including harsh, demeaning language, is justified by some faculty and students as necessary for success in the competitive world of professional dance. I wanted to speak with someone who is extremely successful in Conservatory terms and yet views her Conservatory training as problematic, at the very least. In addition, Catherine's later study of somatic practices, particularly Alexander Technique, afford her a broader vocabulary for discussing the long-term effects of her original training than the Conservatory trained dancer without such a background.

Of course, Catherine's interpretations of her experiences are not shared by every student who studied dance at the Conservatory. Some students consider intense assaults on the trainee's psyche to be necessary for them to advance to higher levels of practice. I recall one rationale for such an approach, put forth by more than one Conservatory student, was that if they survived the Conservatory they could then survive anywhere. So behavior that Catherine and I might consider abusive and therefore worthy of condemnation might be considered an opportunity to test one's courage by another. In addition, Catherine's own account makes a straightforward attack on the Teacher's behavior problematic.

TEENAGER IN TRAINING

Catherine came to the Conservatory to escape her home situation, which she describes simply as "abnormal." In her two years at the Conservatory, the first in the ballet department and the following in modern, she describes herself as "young and vulnerable and very depressed." In fact, she feels that many of the other young students with her were also depressed. After a year in ballet, she remembers, her "sense of identity was crushed." She recalls that she felt as if she was a "non-human being" because she could not live up to her teacher's physical expectations. Transferring to the modern department was better for her because it was somewhat less painful; because she was not a favorite, she was not targeted for "really psychotic games." She ultimately described the difference between departments as one in which "the ballet thing was sick but the modern thing was twisted."

Catherine left the Conservatory because she was not invited to continue as a college student. She went to another training center largely because the Teacher suggested she go there. He called a teacher at this other school and helped her in that transition. She remembers wanting to stay at the Conservatory, not because she liked it there, but because she "would rather stay there than go home." She recalls that she was sent away, however, because she was perceived as being unhappy. In many ways she is now grateful to the Teacher for sending her on because at the time she was largely unaware of other possibilities for training. She describes herself then as not being mature enough "to know the difference between what [was] bad for me and what [was] good for me." She returned to the Teacher's act of sending her on at various points in our discussion, often at moments when her account was most critical of his behavior. Her feeling that he did something "good" for her and that she "didn't really fit into the groove" (i.e., that she not he was the problem) is the clearest example of how Catherine's own interpretation is not a clear-cut condemnation of the Teacher's authoritarian approach.

During our discussions I maintained a mode in which any such discordant information was merely grist for my interpretive mill. Catherine concurred when I suggested that because other people could cope with the situation it does not necessarily follow that the situation was good for them. I also put forth the possibility that sending her away was a form of damage control in that the Teacher saw that Catherine could not thrive on his abusive behavior, which would make her a potential liability. In any case, her choice to be, in her words, "tortured" because she "didn't want to go home," and then being shuttled between institutions hardly sounds like an example of free will or consensual behavior. Yet I imagine that it is as close as many young people get to freely choosing their options. The issue of consensual behavior is complex in any case, so I will leave that for now and turn to the classroom environment and the production of docile bodies.

CONSTRUCTING DOCILE BODIES

In speaking with Catherine, I was alert to traces in her account of Foucault's docile body under surveillance. In particular, how was the docile body produced in her time at the Conservatory? The basic conditions of the classroom, as I discussed earlier, were evident in her classes at the Conservatory. These conditions involved the tradition of a roomful of young people in revealing clothing obediently following the direction of a knowledgeable teacher who, at least in the immediate setting, was the final and total authority. Students were quiet, responsive, and evenly arranged throughout the space. Presumably all were there of their own free will with the shared goal of becoming professional dancers. Most of these details were barely touched upon in our discussions; such conditions are unremarkable and the norm. It is taken for granted that the individuals present are docile bodies following orders with the goal of strengthening skills and technique. In fact, to become even more docile is to become a better dancer in most teacher's eyes. The teacher observes and the students behave as if always under observation.

Each day in the modern dance department began with a standardized warm-up at 7:30 a.m. under fluorescent lighting, which Catherine believes "should be taken out of the whole institutional system" for health reasons. Technique class with the Teacher then began at 8 a.m. Catherine describes how the Teacher always began the class in the same way, directing students to take a deep breath and "get everything collected." He then would make a sarcastic comment about their inability to rise to his standards. She further describes this opening as a prelude, the purpose of which was to establish that, as students, they were "devalued" and they were expected to prove themselves worthy of value in the class in some form. She states that the Teacher "never started a process from a place that there are seven or eight human beings in the room trying or they wouldn't be there."

Referring to how the Teacher began class, Catherine points out that "once you come in and present yourself in that way, it's established." She speculates that this behavior was intended "to bring about a strong intense focus" and "present some kind of challenge." This beginning set the tone for the rest of the class. Catherine estimates that over half of the feedback from the Teacher involved some form of derogatory treatment. Although the verbal abuse was not always directed at the same person, someone was always being derided, and that abuse could turn on anyone in the class at any moment.

TALES OF ABUSE

One obstacle in clarifying Catherine's memories is her lack of specific details. She maintains that she blocked a lot of it out of her mind because "it's the kind of thing where you just want to forget." But more than once she returned to an instance where the Teacher told one girl she looked like a beanbag. This student immediately burst into tears. Although this example is certainly the mildest I associate with the Teacher, it resonates surprisingly deep. As Catherine points out, for a young teenage girl, it can take weeks to get over such a comparison. In fact, many students might continue to carry such a self-image with them in their daily lives, thus creating a form of continuous internalized or self-surveillance.

Catherine believes that the abuse was more intense in more advanced classes, abuse she heard about rather than witnessed. One vivid memory she retained was of a good friend who was her same age but in an advanced class. Catherine remembers this friend, who felt she had established a good relationship with the Teacher and was progressing well, "crying hysterically" because she claimed that he had punched her in the stomach during a contraction. Though Catherine did not witness this incident, she found it to be quite believable in that it fit the general atmosphere established by the Teacher. Whatever the accuracy of specific details within the wealth of oral history, a consistent picture of the Teacher's regime is one of ongoing verbal abuse and, at the very least, the imagined threat of physical abuse.

As I mentioned earlier, such behavior is rationalized as somehow ultimately strengthening the dancer. Furthermore, dancers want feedback, even negative feedback, as it means one is worthy of consideration. In an environment in which much feedback comes in abusive forms, being ignored may at times feel worse than receiving abuse. Catherine recalls that

© Linda Vartoogian

dancers often felt ignored and wanted attention; the feeling among students was that "if you didn't get attention that day or that week then there was something wrong with you." Catherine concurs that dancers often view negative attention as being better than no attention at all. But more important, she agrees that it was a "standard thing" for students to feel that their teachers saw everything, and if a student was ignored she or he was likely to feel that nothing the student had done in class had been worthy of notice.

Although such feelings are primarily psychological effects of abuse, there were physical effects as well, to which I now turn.

PHYSICAL IMPRINTS

The Teacher taught Graham technique, one of the more traditional modern dance techniques with its emphasis on attaining specific bodily positions and learning standardized movement sequences. Catherine characterizes the Teacher as lacking a clear understanding of how bodies function: "Instead of looking at really how to be connected to the floor anatomically, he just let you sit there and grab on for dear life and struggle with it physically." She draws an analogy of the daily experience of class as being like a nonswimmer struggling in the water: "If you can't swim that well [and yet] you're not going to die . . . think about how you [would] struggle in the water." Catherine considers this struggle an inevitable result of forcing bodies into forms that they are not yet capable of achieving. In fact, she says, the experience was "like I had all this movement in my body and I squeezed all my movement to fit my body into a technique." Furthermore, she relates that she "developed terrible muscular habits from that in one year."

The physical experience of her teenage years at the Conservatory is still with Catherine in her early thirties. Catherine shared, "I think I'll spend the rest of my life trying to let go of this physical imprint." She further describes herself as feeling "physically scarred" and "totally maimed." The lasting effects of her experiences can be attributed to their deeply somatic nature. She believes that the combination of poor training and the "intense and . . . frightening" classroom "setup" left an imprint on her nervous system as well as her muscles.

The difficulty of leaving such an experience behind is startling when one recognizes that Catherine began her study of Alexander Technique shortly after leaving the Conservatory. As a dancer who has a highly sophisticated background in improving her body-mind functioning and releasing the effects of dysfunctional experiences, one might expect that she would find herself leaving those experiences behind with some ease. On the contrary, Catherine says that "training at that school affected me emotionally and physically in ways that I wish that I could let go of." One only wonders at the effects, both conscious and unconscious, on those students who did not go on to discover healthier possibilities for the study of movement.

A LITTLE PRISON

But what of the larger environment of the Conservatory? Catherine states that it was "like being in a little prison, that school." She describes the Conservatory as a "whole system" in which "you are regulated." She points out that "you have room checks, you have hall checks. You have the cafeteria that you ate at three times a day, the class, the schedule." Beyond the physical environment, she feels that the Conservatory is "a kind of emotional prison." And this larger prison surrounded "that little room that I took class in every day," which she described in confining and even suffocating imagery as being like "an incubator, or a greenhouse, or a prison" of its own.

Catherine remembers that most students perceived life outside of class "as a party." She recalls, "It was like one big party away from home, especially . . . for a high school student." She herself "did so many drugs" while at the Conservatory that she "stayed . . . far away from drugs and alcohol for…years after that." Certainly what I have always heard, beyond the Teacher stories, are the stories of wild behavior by many of the students. Perhaps this image of bacchanal does not fit one's image of imprisonment. However, it is likely that this behavior is, in part, a form of recuperation that allows one to release stress and tension. The carnival-like nature of such behavior forms an inversion of the social order. In such an inversion, students have riotous control over their own lives. As critics of this sort of analysis put forth, this release via carnival maintains the dominant social order rather than fundamentally subverting that order.

PRECARIOUS ELITE

Such experiences of release and abandon did not necessarily relieve distress at the Conservatory. So how did students maintain their equilibrium in such a destabilizing environment? One possibility is by producing a sense of elite status. Catherine points out that it is somewhat natural to perceive of oneself as a member of an elite group when one has passed through such a program. Certainly the Conservatory's status as a major center for dance training would support such a viewpoint. In addition, many students considered the Teacher to be "like god." An attitude prevailed that "god is my teacher." Catherine feels that the Teacher encouraged this attitude through his "overconfidence" and his assumption that what he had to offer was "the best." She typifies this attitude as "not, I'm doing the best I can. I am the best. So lick my feet and learn." Certainly the students of such a godlike teacher must themselves feel close to the gods.

Ultimately, however, this elite self-image is somewhat precarious. As Catherine notes, in such a situation, "you're totally replaceable." Because one is in a minority of dancers accepted to the school, then one is considered privileged instead of deserving. In fact, Catherine points out that this situation creates an "abusive setup" or "syndrome" that stays with the dancer as she moves into her professional life. As a company member, one faces a director who can say, "You're lucky to have the job because I could give it to anyone else." Catherine further believes that this situation lends itself to complaining about problems that are never addressed. Instead, "you take it in" and vent those feelings outside the particular setting. Catherine feels this dynamic causes dancers to be "a complaining lot of people." Perhaps such a dynamic also leads dancers to consider extreme levels of abuse as acceptable, or even typical, aspects of a dance setting.

Thus far I have presented a rather harrowing account of the educational environment at one center for dance training. Although this is only one person's description, it resonates with most of what I hear from both proponents and opponents of the situation at the Conservatory. But beyond what this account reveals about one particular school are the insights these revelations bring to what many people consider the norms of dance training. The situation at the Conservatory is interpreted in many ways; certainly less obvious authoritarian settings are likewise subject to diverse interpretations. My own understanding is problematized by this interpretive diversity as well as by recognizing that I am by no means objective. I find that I now have more questions than answers, and so I conclude with a consideration of where I find myself in this attempt to make meaning out of the complexities revealed by this study.

CLOSING CONSIDERATIONS

I began this study with a desire to expose what I considered to be the authoritarian regime of the Teacher at the Conservatory. I quickly realized that my desire was more appropriate for an investigative journalism project, and I settled into a wider ranging exploration of authoritarianism in the dance classroom. This reorientation focused my attention on the larger phenomenon of authoritarianism, with one person's account of life at the Conservatory being only one important aspect of this study. This choice allowed me to conduct a qualitative study to illuminate typical dance practices, rather than limiting myself to exposing a particular situation.

In recounting my own formation as an anti-authoritarian, I began to clarify the focus of my search. My conception of authoritarianism focuses on a behavioral continuum that involves greater or lesser degrees of enforced submission to an authority figure, often accompanied by abusive behavior. Because I do not consider the authority figure as inherently authoritarian, this shift from labeling individuals as authoritarian to considering how authoritarian behavior functions allowed me to consider the full ramifications of my exploration. This perspective enabled me to implicate my own behavior, which became an important aspect of my understanding. In the course of examining my own experiences, I recognized that the power structure and typical environment of the dance classroom readily lend themselves to authoritarian behavior.

I still had an agenda that included revealing authoritarian behavior as a negative aspect of dance training, and so I assembled an appropriate toolkit of concepts. From Michel Foucault's *Discipline and Punish*, I took the image of the docile body under surveillance. This image was drawn from Foucault's analysis of prisons, the military, hospitals, and schools. He claims that aspects of institutional life that we often consider as humane developments in Western history, for example, the shift from torture to incarceration of prisoners, actually represent a deepening and extension of disciplinary powers. His model of a body that is disciplined in order to be improved readily fits the daily realities of dance training in the West.

The institutional setting of an arts conservatory also relates to the environments Foucault considered. In addition, his dismissal of progress allows one more freedom to consider the possibility that contemporary developments in dance may not be improvements after all. The familiar image of an ancient ballet teacher disciplining students with a little stick is replaced by more subtle approaches to control that rely, in part, on the dancer's role in self-discipline. Jock Abra claims in *The Dancer as Masochist* (1987) that the psychological dimensions of dancing in a ballet corps "has but tenuous applicability to expressive dancers such as . . . Martha Graham" (33). This claim is shown to be false, however, once one has experienced the authoritarian possibilities of the Graham technique.

Foucault's model of disciplinary power relies on the involvement of those disciplined rather than simple power over. The implication for this study is that authoritarian behavior may involve submission that is enforced with the dancer's knowing participation. Though I was not attempting to explain why dancers readily involve themselves in authoritarian settings, and even welcome authoritarian behavior, I did want to understand more about how they accept such behavior. Because my own stance focused on the idea that a process akin to brainwashing was occurring, I turned to the work of researchers who study contemporary involvement in cults.

Arthur Deikman's *The Wrong Way Home* offered a convincing model of how cults operate. Deikman identifies four basic cult behaviors: "compliance with the group, dependence on a leader, devaluing the outsider, and avoiding dissent" (7). I perceived this model's relevance to the typical dance classroom, as a dancer must follow group behavior that is dependent on the overt or covert directions of the teacher. In the classroom the dancer is part of an elite, and although he or she may express dissent outside, when in class, little or no dissent is possible.

I found Deikman's model even more applicable to the setting of the Conservatory. My own brief experience of the Conservatory, my casual conversations with other students, and my talks with Catherine made it clear that the Conservatory produces an elite. Such an elite considers non-members to be outsiders and so less special. The function of the teacher is elevated to godlike status, which, as my dialogue with Catherine reveals, was how many students at the Conservatory perceived the Teacher. Total obedience was required and so no dissent was possible. In applying Deikman's model to the Conservatory, one finds that authoritarian power functions readily when cult-like behavior is present.

My dialogue with Catherine illuminated much about the situation at the Conservatory. Catherine, a student at the Conservatory who has now danced for many years with an important dance company, readily critiqued her experiences with the Teacher. Her account illustrated that in an authoritarian educational setting a docile body is indeed produced by the flow of disciplinary power. She revealed how dancers desire observation and so they participate in their own surveillance. She also clarified the somatic effect of this disciplining of the body-mind. In her case, these negative effects stayed with her even after many years of work with such disciplines as Alexander Technique.

Talking with Catherine also revealed the mixed feelings even an outspoken critic of authoritarian dance training might have. She perceived the Teacher's decision not to allow her to continue at the Conservatory as a supportive move. Because he helped her go on to study elsewhere, she sometimes felt that perhaps he did have her best interests at heart. Certainly other students interpreted the intense behavior of the Teacher as being for their own good. Such rationalizations of what I consider to be abusive behavior are another indication of how dancers participate in their own oppression. This perspective fits Deikman's model of cult thinking, which posits the leader as the "strong, wise, protective parent." Deikman continues with the observation that in extreme instances this "fantasy" leads to "exploitation," while in everyday settings it "impairs" the ability to think "realistically" (1990, 7).

This impairment of realistic, everyday thinking brings us again to the implications of this study for dance settings, which are not as dramatic as the situation at the Conservatory. Yet, here too, we find an emphasis on obedience to the leader with little or no dissent. Even in settings that are not abusive, submission is a typical student behavior. The docile body is revered as a sign that one is a good student. Whether or not a teacher demands obedience, the student who wishes a professional career or simply a good grade recognizes that obedience is assumed. This dynamic creates an atmosphere that is fertile ground for the abuse of such power. The occasional sharp comment or disdainful look by an otherwise caring teacher reminds the student of the implicit power relationship that requires students to submit to disciplinary power.

I am now struggling with questions regarding the nature of the traditional dance setting. Have we encouraged authoritarian behavior in our pedagogical models? Is a setting inherently authoritarian, even if no visible force is present but obedience is still prized? Does student idolization of exceptional teachers create authoritarian situations? I do not know the answers to these and many similar questions. I do believe that we, as students and teachers, are continually recreating a dynamic that allows for the ready emergence of authoritarian behavior. I also believe that until we analyze our mundane assumptions about what it means to study dance, we will continue to produce dancers and dance teachers who assume that abusive behavior is also a mundane component of dance training. Ultimately, we must find new ways of being in the classroom. We must recognize the ultimate autonomy of each participant as well as the relative wisdom of teacher and student. Perhaps extreme situations like that at the Conservatory are not aberrations but are instead indicators of the worn out and destructive paradigms in which we all participate.

Critical Reflections

The deeper you go into understanding the life of one human being the more you understand the world. By accepting this premise, you can begin to understand the importance of research that does not simply observe but inquires into both the surface and the multiple layers of things. Art/dance has often been the place in society where human imagination and creativity have been nurtured. It has served as the "repository of possibility" of these human characteristics. Nonetheless (or perhaps because of this), arts education is constantly threatened with reduced funding and support. In our efforts to promote arts education we are often reluctant to publicize its sometimes harmful consequences. Yet, we do need to consider not simply *how* dance is done or *who* has done it, but what are its purpose and effects. What justifications can we make for participation in oppressive forms of pedagogy whether by teachers or by students? "Questions of meaning and justification," Peter McLaren states, "ultimately are not isolated from questions about power relationships" (1989, 256). Thus art must be problematized and brought into a critical discourse that considers how hegemonic practices that maintain authoritarian or hierarchical social relations become a part of its curriculum. In such a discourse hidden assumptions and interests can be better understood so as to inform our choices and actions. This process can break down the barriers, or aura, that surround art and that inhibit us from truly questioning its purpose or value whether on the stage or in the studio.

Take a Moment to Reflect

Consider the following statements. Decide whether you agree or disagree and explain why. Note your reactions.

1. Drawing on personal knowledge and subjective experience invalidates research.

2. Social relationships always imply the presence of power.

3. The monitoring of the body in dance is much like the monitoring in schools, prisons, and military institutions; such surveillance is used to create docile and disciplined individuals.

4. In many dance experiences one can identify the four basic behaviors found in cults: compliance with the group, dependence on a leader, devaluing an outsider, and avoiding dissent.

5. Anyone who wants to become a professional dancer may do so if she tries hard enough.

6. The tougher the training the better the dancer.

These questions may seem quite simple, yet when fully explored they can help us to understand much of the accepted traditions in dance that are oppressive and sometimes destructive. How we give value and respect to particular dance experiences and dismiss others relates to our chosen aesthetic code. In the following chapter Christine Lomas examines the deeply felt and fervently defended traditional aesthetic codes and how they shape our attitudes and actions concerning community dance.

REFERENCES

Abra, J. 1987. The Dancer as Masochist. *Dance Research Journal* 19 (2): 33-39.

Ball, S.J. 1990. *Foucault and Education: Disciplines and Knowledge.* New York: Routledge.

Benjamin, J. 1988. *The Bonds of Love: Psychoanalysis, Feminism, and the Problem of Domination.* New York: Pantheon.

Coser, L. 1974. *Greedy Institutions: Patterns of Undivided Commitment.* New York: Free Press.

Deikman, A. 1990. *The Wrong Way Home: Uncovering the Patterns of Cult Behavior in American Society.* Boston: Beacon Press.

Eribon, D. 1991. *Michel Foucault.* Translated by C. Wing. Cambridge, MA: Harvard University Press.

Foucault, M. 1979. *Discipline and Punish: The Birth of the Prison.* Translated by A. Sheridan. New York: Vintage Books.

———. 1980. *Power/Knowledge: Selected Interviews & Other Writings 1972-1977*, C. Gordon (ed.). New York: Pantheon.

Goffman, E. 1961. *Asylums: Essays on the Social Situation of Mental Patients and Other Inmates.* New York: Anchor.

Lifton, R.K. 1961. *Thought Reform and the Psychology of Totalism: A Study of "Brainwashing" in China.* New York: Norton.

McLaren, P. 1989. *Life in Schools*. New York: Longman.

Miller, A. 1990. *For Your Own Good: Hidden Cruelty in Child-Rearing and the Roots of Violence*. 3d ed. New York: The Noonday Press.

Ross, J., and A.M. Watkinson, (eds.). 1997. *Systemic Violence in Education: Promise Broken*. Albany, NY: State University of New York Press.

Ryan, J. 1995. *Little Girls in Pretty Boxes: The Making and Breaking of Elite Gymnasts and Figure Skaters*. New York: Doubleday.

Webster's New Encyclopedic Dictionary. 1993. New York: Black Dog & Leventhal.

WRITING NEW STORIES

CHAPTER 7

ART AND THE COMMUNITY: BREAKING THE AESTHETIC OF DISEMPOWERMENT

CHRISTINE M. LOMAS
Faculty of Arts, University College Bretton Hall,
University of Leeds

Lomas offers a vision of dance as a mediator of culture in our rapidly changing contemporary society. The devaluation of the natural world, others, and community is connected to a sense of loss of individual significance. Drawing upon her work with a community-based dance company, she discusses how individual significance is dependent on the ability to give meaning to ourselves within a cultural context. Further, she suggests, dance offers a way of "making sense" of ourselves through that context. Lomas argues that in valuing context and intent over form and content, dance has the potential to enrich, inform, and evolve both in performance and nonperformance contexts. She concludes with a discussion of how improvisation can be used to create an inclusive dance aesthetic through the community context.

This essay has been adapted in part from a paper and separate presentation included in the Proceedings of the Dance and the Child International Conference held in 1994 in Sydney, Australia.

Since 1984 I have been involved with the work of Jabadao, a community dance resource company based in West Yorkshire, England. Jabadao's work prioritizes groups that have for many years carried the label of the disenfranchised, for example, the elderly, people with mental and physical disabilities, people who are isolated whether in their own homes or in residential care, and others devalued by our society. The prioritization of these groups draws specifically upon the Company's philosophy, which aims to redress society's devaluation of individuals and groups. The Company is committed to providing dance opportunities and experience for everyone. Participation in Jabadao's work and two decades of work with undergraduates in Dance have led to seek to understand why, on the one hand, the Company is admired and supported for its work, and, on the other, its work is not considered to have any relationship to Dance Art. In effect the work is devalued in the same way that the people with whom Jabadao works are devalued.

Our culture's existing theatrical aesthetic emphasizes form and content as the key to unlocking meaning; what it ignores is the social context from which form and content derive their meaning. I wish to propose a more appropriate aesthetic, one that emphasizes context and intent rather than form and content; this is the way a dance company such as Jabadao works. If one acknowledges that all cultural behavior is adaptive, then the aesthetic that places emphasis on the dancers' authenticity and intentions and stresses collective resonance challenges our ways of viewing dance. Jabadao's work acknowledges the distinction between nature and culture and recognizes and celebrates the vitality and importance of dance in all experience.

The following table is a heuristic model of the ways in which an individual interacts with dance making and dance viewing in the non-theatrical performance context, Community Dance. Celebratory activity draws predominantly upon authentic responses celebrating self and community. It stresses individual significance within collective resonances. Ceremonial and Ritual activities occur as a result of our behavior being shaped, adapted. Adaptivity informs our responses whether to the State (Ceremonial) or the codified religious, belief systems (Ritual). Both the Ceremonial and the Ritual indicate prescribed behavior and limited change.

A Heuristic Model to Illustrate Non-Theatrical Performance Contexts

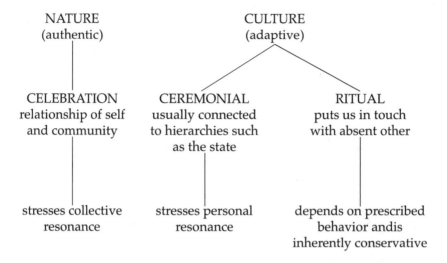

NATURE
(authentic)

CULTURE
(adaptive)

CELEBRATION
relationship of self
and community

CEREMONIAL
usually connected
to hierarchies such
as the state

RITUAL
puts us in touch
with absent other

stresses collective
resonance

stresses personal
resonance

depends on prescribed
behavior andis
inherently conservative

In different ways, celebration, ceremonial, and ritual reconcile the past, present, and future. They occur in the present, have a sense of history, and prescribe continuity. The degree of apparent rapidity of cultural change is a direct consequence of technological development and the growth of first-world monetarist materialism. The change of culture, the consequent effect on community, and concomitant disenfranchisement of the individual has occurred in both first- and third-world societies. The opportunity to reflect on cultural change is a luxury afforded by economic and political life. The model presented in this chapter offers a framework for understanding how the individual responds to culturally learnt ideologies and for redressing the impact of the first world's political–economic emphasis on the disenfranchisement of the individual.

The role of community dance in fueling a fire of opposition requires an understanding of the relationship between the authentic and the adaptive and the acknowledgment that celebration, ceremonial, and ritual all contribute to the reconciliation of past, present, and future. In emphasizing the importance of celebration we emphasize the relationship of self and community We are all bearers of our community experience as individual participants in collective resonance. We have to address for ourselves that which has shaped us, in particular in terms of our value systems. Values are inherited and constantly reshaped by individuals attached to a particular culture In acknowledging this we see that the preeminence of the ceremonial and ritual, which are dependent on prescribed behavior and inherently conservative, can be aligned to the first-world predominant monetarist perspective that has distracted us from our natural need to grapple with and express our hopes and fears. Because of this distraction we have become disenabled in the midst of peripheral successes.

The political–economic emphasis on power through possession, aggression, and dominance, which is associated with the promotion of the individual—it was ever thus—has resulted in a disenfranchisement of individuals. We have suffered the loss of our own community, our sense of the integration of self. We have become entrenched in terms of "them" and "us," and we have suffered a loss of hope for self and for society. As individuals we have become impotent, less proactive; and, to support our inherently pessimistic and conservative position, we label others negatively. As members of the first world we have to address the disempowering effect on our own experiences of a world that devalues those who are defined as not having achieved, aspired to, or are not capable of appropriate cultural behaviors.

Facilitation of community interaction is not something we should do for others; it is something we ought to recognize as a need in ourselves. The validation of ourselves in our actions and interactions is dependent on an understanding of how we define "we," which is demonstrated by my self, my family, my community, and my state.

Consider how first-world attitudes, actions, and reactions towards the third world disenfranchise self and community. The very use of the expression, "third world," devalues and dismisses the nature and culture of those who are its members. Add to this the preferred label several countries use to refer to the third world, the label "underdeveloped countries," and the devaluation is made even clearer. As with a great many linear forms of expression, the label serves to support the labelers' power and superior value and to control the position and actions of the labeled. The labels "third world" and "underdeveloped countries" serve as an indication of first-world monetarist power; at the same time they enforce the belief that the destruction of third-world nature and culture is appropriate and acceptable in their adoption of and adaptation to first-world ideologies. Having identified the huge resources, the natural riches, for example, gold and chemical deposits, we identify these as "world" resources. We destroy rain forests, gain access to these riches, and support our rape of nature and the concomitant destruction by the employment of local labor; guaranteed income; and the imposition of first-world style community activity (e.g., self-help projects, the building of schools and homes, animal husbandry, farming). We destroy cultures and seek legitimization of this act through our own value system, which is monetarist materialism. Monetarist materialism, confident in the rightness of its dogma, seeks to control and shape culture and cultural processes, denying our human capacity to interact with the natural world, to grapple with our hopes and fears, and to express and share our hopes and fears with others.

Culture and cultural processes are not fixed; they are modified by individual significance. The destruction of culture and therefore cultural processes creates anomie for the individual and for community resonance and has a cyclical effect. Without individual significance, culture is experienced as empty and cultural experiences become generalized. Culture is the attempt by human beings to reconcile the authentic, that is, nature, with life experience; as such, culture carries with it the meanings that correspond to individual significance.

I believe it is possible to redress the negative experiences for the individual in a rapidly changing world and to respond proactively to disempowerment and disenfranchisement by using dance as a mediator in relation to nature and culture. Dance, like all art activities, offers the individual the opportunity to organize experience, make sense of self, problem-solve, and represent self-expression in metaphor. It can afford self-directed and increasingly self-mastering experiences. In dance one is in the world of the nonlinear, the felt rather than the thought experience, the soul and spirit; individuals in this world are informed by their authentic self instead of their wholly adapted self.

The tools for the dance activity reside in the natural world. Natural body movement interacts with the environment and with the forces of gravity. The immediacy of the natural physical self as part of the natural world and homo sapiens' capacity for expression is basic to symbolic formation. The tools for dance expression—energy, time, space, and flow—found in or as nature, allow us through dance activity a means by which we are able to reveal our authentic selves to ourselves and others. This revelation occurs through an encoding wherein the body does the knowing, creates, communicates, and learns through dance. A process of reclamation can occur where our adaptive self, which we build in order to be acceptable to our perceived world, is challenged and reshaped; and understandings occur that are more acceptable to our inner, deeply intuitive self. Seen in this way, dance can be said to be therapeutic. I propose here that all dance has the potential to be a combination of artistic activity and therapeutic activity, to offer individuals the opportunity to self-discover and to share with others.

I am using this notion of self-discovery and sharing with others in a very particular sense. For example, while working with a Jabadao dance company of adults with learning difficulties called "Being Ourselves," I danced with them and became involved in an intimate knowing of the individuals in the company: There was knowing of them in relation to me, and me in relation to myself. On some occasions I found myself unable to continue dancing. I was unwilling and at times unable to receive them, their authenticity, or to share myself in my authenticity. Nevertheless, this process was a celebration of being ourselves, and it is undeniable that celebration with dance as mediator reconciles the natural and the cultural.

CULTURAL CONSTRUCTS, COMMUNITY, AND CELEBRATION

To many people art and therapy are mutually exclusive categories, but surely this is a distinction without a natural difference, just as the work/leisure distinction is a cultural construct. This is a matter of emphasis. The "Being Ourselves" company was involved with the creation of dance; the therapeutic experience was a by-product. What predominated in our work was celebration. The core was authenticity. Surely art, by virtue of attempting to reconcile nature (birth and death) and culture (life), is inherently therapeutic. The function of art within the traditional aesthetic is to reconcile nature and culture; because it emphasizes content and form, it fails to embrace the authentic behavior of celebration. The vast majority of our potentially celebratory experiences have become ceremonial for the individual and the community, adapted rather than authentic experience, an embracing of that which is imposed and accepted unthinkingly. The ceremonial is experienced as artifice, requiring obligatory interaction by the individual; however, obligation rarely makes available or strengthens a sense of ownership or belonging. This disempowerment of the individual, a loss of self-intimacy, of significance, clearly negatively affects community experience and interaction.

MacIver, in his major work on community written almost 70 years ago, offers sentiment as a starting point for the reinstatement of the concept of community (1924, 209). By "sentiment" he means an understanding and a recognition by others of the significance of the individual, which, in turn, affords a sense of community solidarity. Although significance may be wide-ranging and disparate in relation to others, the acknowledgment and embracing of individuality support a community of solidarity and facilitate identification of sentiment. We are born into a community and are intimately dependent on community for life. In 1934, a decade after MacIver, Simpson writes,

> Community is no circumscribed sphere of social life, but rather the very life-blood of social life. Community is not simply economic, nor simply political, nor simply territorial, nor simply visceral. Nor is it all these special elements added together. Ultimately, it is a complex of conditioned emotions which the individual feels towards the surrounding world and his fellows. (quoted in Clarke 1973, 34)

As Simpson implies, communities do not empower communities; individuals empower communities. Community dance does not empower communities; individual empowerment, self-intimacy, interaction with one's authentic self, a sense of fulfillment, a feeling of achievement all contribute to the larger whole, the community of solidarity, the "we" and the "ours"; this affords a sense of security to individuals and communities of individuals.

For the individual human being, although drawing upon the limited category distinctions shared by all animals (e.g., recognition of our own species, recognition of what is edible), individual survival within the human environment is not sufficient. In our capacity to create and communicate metaphor we can see a shift from animality to humanity, which is a combination of our determination to reconcile nature and culture. If art is viewed as mediator in relation to nature and culture, then we may also view it as mediator of the authentic (nature) and the adaptive (culture) behaviors. In this sense, it becomes clear that viewing art from the traditional aesthetic is a consequence of adaptive rather than authentic behavior. Proposing an emphasis on celebration—behavior that is least inherently conservative and certainly least dependent upon prescribed behavior—implies a possible aesthetic that is inclusive rather than exclusive, optimistic rather than pessimistic. In such an aesthetic meaning results from intent and context rather than from form and content alone.

My involvement in Jabadao's work with people with special needs led to my search for understanding how these people are able, via dance, to share themselves, to interact in deeply moving and energizing ways, to perform in the traditional aesthetic and at the same time bring to the performance an empowering experience for themselves and for the audience. Jabadao works with groups of people who do not belong to the community as defined by locality, economics, institution, and geography. Instead, Jabadao works with "threshold people" (Turner, 1969), "liminal" people, on the margins; those who elude, I would suggest in some cases by necessity, the generally imposed classifications of kinship, economy, and so forth. Via dance, Jabadao involves these people in social bonding over and above any that occurs as a result of regulated social relations and organized social groups This social bonding is a condition referred to by Turner (1969) as *communitas*: bonding people over and above socially imposed units or formal ties.

On this basis, the work of the animateur movement (whose predominant concern is community dance; see the next section) can be identified as largely responding to regulated, organized social groups and being required by funding bodies to work with dance in an "appropriate" way. These funding bodies support the teaching of dance via technique, emphasizing content and form and supporting adaptive behavior, rather than exploring the potential of dance to capitalize on the authentic experience via celebration and concomitant communitas that community dance should offer. I am not advocating for the dismissal of form and content per se as aesthetic criteria, but I do wish to see the inclusion of intent and context as meaningful criteria. Likewise, I do not advocate the dismissal of organized social structures, but the recognition that being on the margins of society may be a condition experienced by us all and that the positive elements of communitas can inform our culture and cultural change. All of us, by virtue of our age and experience, know what it means to be on or at the margins. The people with whom Jabadao is concerned are in perpetual liminality; therefore, we must seize the by-product of liminality, communitas, and exploit it.

The recent experience of a final year undergraduate at University College Bretton Hall serves to amplify the nature and response of individuals to the physical and social engineering of communitas in relation to the elderly. The building of residential homes is society's recognition of and response to the "preliminal" in the aging process and offers a constructed communitas— the home for the elderly. During her first visit to such a "home" the student discovered that its members did not know each other's names, did not know who was living in the room next to them, that they were isolated from one another. Some individuals chose not to speak at all; others spoke only of their sadness at being taken away from their own homes and being put in a "home." The student introduced dance to the elderly residents and used it as a mediator with an emphasis on the individual, and the experience of communitas for these isolated elderly people began to emerge as they started to bond with one another.

SHAKING OFF THE SHACKLES OF TRADITIONAL AESTHETICS

Further issues that I believe are crucial to the arguments in this chapter are raised by the animateur movement in Britain. (The Arts Council of Great Britain defined "animateur" in its national report in 1986, as a professional community dance and mime activist working in a community context whose post was funded either wholly or in part by public arts subsidy.) The animateur is essentially someone concerned with increasing awareness of and participation in dance in a variety of contexts. Thomson proposes a general definition of the community dance movement in the U.K. as, "offering dance to everyone in a given community, on the premise that dance is the birthright and the potential of all human beings, and that this fundamentally human activity is in our rational and logocentric culture undervalued and marginalized (Thomson 1989). Working with people with special needs has come about as a result of some community dance practitioners responding to the notion of dance being "the birthright and potential of all human beings." Clearly, the funding by local education authorities, the Calouste Gulbenkian Foundation, the Arts Council of Great Britain, and Regional Arts Associations in supporting this movement has positively affected the dance experience of many people in the community.

Consideration of the nature of these experiences clusters around two key approaches: the didactic approach and the facilitator approach (Thomson 1989). Predominantly the first group of animateurs came from the dance education (schools) route, confirming the philosophy of dance as creative instead of emphasizing craft and theatrical platforms. Where funding allowed, technique classes were led by invited company dancers / choreographers as part of the animateurs' response to the brief to encourage people in the community to dance. The topic of creative dance in the community had to be circuitously approached in an attempt to minimize the so-called "threat" to interested but uncertain individuals and groups who responded to the class offerings by saying, "I can't dance," "I can't be creative," or "I'm being asked to be a dancer."

These early pioneers were working at a time when people were culturally uninformed in terms of dance. Isolated dance workers, with the broadest of briefs, were struggling to equate public and private subsidy definitions of Art with their work, often having been appointed to localities of which they had little or no knowledge. Simultaneously the education sector was seeking to establish dance as an arts subject (creating, performing, appreciating) in the schools. Established dance companies were defining for themselves an education role, touring the regions, teaching technique classes, creating choreography and inviting groups to watch, in effect, adopting a didactic model. Whether being taught in the schools or introduced by a touring company, both approaches emphasized the didactic model, an instructional approach, concerned with the craft of dancing rather than imaginative, expression-based work.

For some the safe forms, techniques in the broadest sense, are an end in themselves, whether the activities are based on aerobics, fitness, physical / social therapy, or person-centered dance techniques. Technique itself is adaptive, and it has been adapted by the animateur, requiring adaptive behaviors from participants. The dance worker is more "at risk" in emphasizing the authentic: How will people respond? What do I do? How do I handle it? Teaching technique is safe. Although teaching technique offers a challenge, is it truly a dance challenge? With dance that emphasizes adaptive rather than authentic behavior, a paradox is implied in the role of the dance animateur because an adaptive form is being used in an attempt to encourage natural behavior. Why do animateurs focus on adaptive forms of art when the capacity exists to celebrate authenticity? We must shake off the shackles of conventional aesthetics with its focus on technique that consigns the "unskilled" dancer to being a nondancer and subliminally emphasizes the second-rate in terms of those involved in community dance. If they, the "unskilled," do dance, they are dismissed, not even to be considered; they are dismissed like those of the third world, except for those transitory periods where anthropologists or reporters choose to spotlight them.

Confusion about the precise meaning and function of the animateur has led to a variety of job titles: animateur, community dance worker, dance artist in the community. That we cannot find a commonly understood job title and description indicates confusion and the outcome that community dance means all, yet on even superficial inquiry, it means nothing. From its conception to the present day, the community dance movement is essentially flawed from three perspectives. First, the emphasis is on identifying communities as geographic localities with boundaries that can be defined and community that represents a social structure with regulated social groups. Second, it fails to acknowledge who shapes our taste in terms of Dance Art. Third, community work sounds good, and so it has been hijacked as a way of gaining income by professional dance artists, encouraged and in some cases obliged by their funders to work in the "community." Learning how to do this work has come about by having to do it and by writing it into funding applications, without conceptual understanding of community or understanding of the role of the facilitator. That the community dance movement has achieved so much is largely as the result of some young, highly motivated individual dance workers who subscribe to the community dance ideology, to communitas, which is a radical position standing in opposition to a political–economic climate that emphasizes individual competitiveness.

In practice, the vast majority of the animateur work falls short of its ideological aim. Many of those appointed were, and to some extent still are, largely from the backgrounds of training in the adaptive, subscribing to the traditional aesthetic emphasizing content and form. Their roles as defined by appointing bodies are ill-defined. The employers who are at one and the same time the funders, shape and require particular outcomes, yet are vague and imprecise in their understanding of the concept of community. The "Republic" (McFee 1992), whose members include the theorists, the critics, regional and central funders, academics, and so on, determine for us what is good Dance Art, who the true artists are, and who should be supported and given exposure. Those who celebrate and experience the authentic through art are victimized by High Art/Low Art distinctions.

Community dance is devalued because the established traditions; the established theories of art; and the control of our taste, our aesthetic, and our range of interpretive skills are the province of the High Art Republic. The production of any art is the result of the endeavors of human beings and is essentially concerned with the urge to express and create, to make sense of, to bring into being that which comments upon our interaction with ourselves and our experience. Existing concepts of High Art have to be challenged because they are a vehicle for the devaluation of the individual. In aspiring to permanence, regular funding, respectability in the arts environment, many community dance workers forego choice and freedom. They relinquish the space in which to realize and release the authentic with its emphasis on celebration, the relationship of self and community, and collective experience.

Limited resources, the political nature of the animateur's funding (e.g., Regional Arts Associations and local authorities with their concern for their own priorities), conspire to define the animateurs' response. A great deal of animateurs' work has traditionally been with those communities that may be described as ready-made, more often than not with people who may be identified as being conventionally marginal as defined by institutions. Unfortunately, because of the combination of funders'/employers' requirements, the formal lack of definition of the role, the animateurs' own subject-centric training backgrounds, and the definition of community as locality the animateurs' task is difficult.

INCLUSION VERSUS EXCLUSION

To empower implies a challenge to prevailing systems, with emphasis on the authentic, on nontraditional aesthetics, and on a way of working predominantly concerned with facilitation. Although groups may be identified largely via institutional definitions, the focus is on recognizing the liminal experiences of the individual and group and on seizing the by-product of communitas. In turn, our perceptions of the traditional dance aesthetic are challenged; we may relate the experience of the dance to a wider social context and address the tyrannies of disablement and disenfranchisement. It is not surprising that a great deal of project work and on-going initiatives are with those who are readily identifiable as already motivated and interested in dance and who are likely to share only their dance interest, for example, schools, colleges, and youth dance groups. I am not suggesting that work with such groups is inappropriate, but that, again, it is a question of emphasis. The opportunity must be taken for working with communities where dance may truly be a means by which individual creativity and expression occur, where celebration occurs, and where the sharing of individuals instead of material wealth occurs.

Earlier I asserted that the community dance movement is essentially flawed. Nevertheless, the Arts Council of Great Britain's most recent progress report, entitled "Community Dance" (Peppiatt and Venner 1993), details some excellent progress and development in the animateur/community dance movement:

Within less than two decades community dance and mime have exerted a special influence in the arts. They have also begun to make significant links between amateur, private, commercial and professional sectors, opening the way for a greater unity and advocacy, and amplifying the national and international roles of dance and mime. (8)

The Arts Council report also suggests, however, that community dance should articulate its own new aesthetic, which appears to underline the second-class nature of that which has achieved so much. Sue Hoyle, as the Dance Director of the Arts Council of Great Britain, states that "community dance" is no longer a useful term; in making such a statement she contributes significantly to the emphasis debate. She continues,

> to improve the conditions in which dance is created and performed, our priorities must be to ensure that dancers are properly paid and supported to create, rehearse and perform, and to promote their work professionally so that audiences will have access to it. (1994, 3)

In identifying this as her priority, she clearly resides in the theatrical context, with the emphasis on the values of content and form, on the adaptive. The call for a new aesthetic and for the abandonment of the term "community dance" may readily be articulated when viewed from the perspective of the traditional aesthetic. However, placing the emphasis on authenticity, nature, where the activity and way of working supports and reveals intent and context changes our perspective. Dance can now be viewed with an acknowledgment of its emphasis on process, responding to the relationship of self and community and stressing collective resonance. A narrowed theatrical aesthetic limits our capacity to view the dance. When the product—adaptive responses—is the major emphasis, "community dance" as a term becomes irrelevant.

To call for the abandonment of the label "community dance" is worrying indeed, for I suggest it is to abandon more than just the label. It is to abandon the concept and ensuing activity. This is process-based work not confined to one form or style. It offers enriching experience and encourages people to find their own dance forms and express their own needs. To abandon the concept would be to abandon a way of working that challenges the marginalizing effect in both the theatrical and nontheatrical contexts.

It would be more appropriate to call for an articulation and better understanding of the following: (a) the way in which the most recent community dance developments have linked community practice with professional practice, (b) how the nontheatrical performance context offers a way forward to liberated and liberating dance making in both theatrical and nontheatrical performance contexts, and (c) an aesthetic that informs our creation, performance, and appreciation of dance without the divisive constraints of adaptive worthiness. This aesthetic is one in which notions of access, empowerment, and enablement are not the sole province of the nontheatrical, establishing an inclusive rather than an exclusive aesthetic.

Thus far I have presented a broad-based perspective on nontheatrical contexts and discussed the devaluation and disempowerment experienced as a consequence of the apparent rapidity of cultural change and the consequent isolation of the individual. The process and purpose of dance improvisation in creating an inclusive aesthetic are investigated next.

DANCE IMPROVISATION: PROCESS AND PURPOSE

Dance improvisation is critically important to both a theatrical and nontheatrical context, as it is employed by practitioners in both arenas. Improvisation offers a method with which to readdress marginalization in our exclusive aesthetic inheritance by facilitating individual proactive responses to disempowerment. Dance improvisation is a way of working, a process described by the following definitions:

"to do or create something without preparation, practice" *(Heinemann English Dictionary* 1979, 320)

"Dance improvisation fuses creation with execution" (Blom and Chaplin 1989, 6)

"a way of tapping the stream of the subconscious without intellectual censorship, allowing spontaneous and simultaneous exploring, creating and performing" (Blom and Chaplin 1989, 6)

"the spontaneous fusion of the mind and movement" (Blom and Chaplin 1988, 15)

The definitions suggest the idea of improvisation as a method for exploring and discovering movement by dispensing with a predetermined structure and simply moving, that is, "the spontaneous fusion of the mind and movement." Looking at these definitions, the common denominators appear to be spontaneity, creativity, and a lack of design and polish, concerns that may seem distanced from dance as a selective, structured, and practiced filtration of movement ideas. A participant in dance improvisation is drawing on a basic framework of experience in order to interact with self, others, or both. This personal framework involves beliefs, experiences, emotions, and knowledge, which are drawn upon in a spontaneous process. This process is in contrast to an emphasis on shaping the dance product, a process of planned intention that involves forethought and a greater interest in design and polishing.

A key concern of this chapter is natural, authentic behavior. If we accept that a great deal of what we do, what exists, is shaped by a fundamental source/property common to us all, nature, then art that is authentic, that utilizes suggestions from nature, offers us a link with dance improvisation. Dance improvisation works by drawing from the learning resources of nature: one's own experience and understanding at that particular time and in that particular situation. In highlighting the spontaneity of the process, dance becomes accessible because product is not the main concern. More people may participate because less emphasis is placed on technical competency, promoting the idea that everyone can dance, everyone has resource, everyone has facility.

Surely though, some form of codification does occur. If we can define the workings of improvisation, then certainly we are codifying it in a similar way to other forms of dance and therefore undermining the basic principles not to contain or restrict. Blom and Chaplin (1988) refer to improvisation as "to dance with the option, but without the pressure, to take on, to imitate, the style, impulses or ideas of someone else." An example of a dance performed by John and Janet, two members of "Being Ourselves," the Jabedeo performing company, may help further the debate of the process and purpose of improvisation. John and Janet have both been influenced by their visits to ballet performances. In the dance, John opens the "pas-de-deux," encourages and invites Janet to join him, and they dance together. Some of the movement vocabulary, particularly John's rotating hands and arm gestures, we see occurring and reoccurring. Their contact, balances, and presentation are reminiscent of ballet. The impulse for the pas-de-deux is love, their love for each other. They selected their own music for this dance, and the movement vocabulary seen in this dance is present in a variety of dancing sessions. Their signature is clear. However, no dance is ever polished to a finalized product form; each has some new material. The process is always paramount, often fresh and innovative. It is possible, however, to say that this is how John and Janet improvise, to recognize, therefore to codify, their content and form. Within spontaneity movement is filtrated. John and Janet have a particular style of moving; they have selected not only music accompaniment but also movement content, which responds to and interprets the music, and the subject matter of their dance, their love for each other. In this is practiced filtration. Improvisation then could be seen as a form of technical study as it has a particular style and structure.

The structure depends on a variety of influences, including the leader's (or leaders') facilitation skills and the music, if used. The style is subject to change depending on the individuals involved. At the end of an improvisation session with "Being Ourselves" and Bretton undergraduate students, John and Janet continued to improvise together. During the session, John had danced with Sandra, a Bretton student, for quite a long period of time. It became clear, toward the end, that Janet was becoming distressed by this. She was jealous and she began to cry. As we were beginning to say goodbye, John invited and then led Janet into a space and they danced together. He held her hand, and he encouraged her to follow him. Eventually they opened away from each other and closed in toward each other; this opening and closing went on for some time. Janet's tears dried; the dynamic changed from tentative, gentle, and sustained and became more powerful, more certain, and more assured; and they finished together in a tight embrace, smiling. What began as a reaffirmation of his love for her moved through into a celebration of each other and of their love. Movements do not speak louder than words; they simply say things differently. Both Janet and John can, and do, communicate through the spoken word. In this instance, however, movement was their preferred means of communication. What we were witnesses to was authentic, natural, and celebratory, two people tuned into a dance of the moment, a creative consciousness. We could discern the content and form, that they owned the dance, that here was—simultaneously—process and product. The meaning of the dance was dependent on our ability to recognize, via an emphasis on intent and context, this dance of love. Here was virtual reality, understood by us because of our own experience: feelings of love.

VIRTUAL OR REAL: TAKING RISKS WITH THE AESTHETIC

In the same way that community dance has been "encouraged" to respond to traditional aesthetics by concentrating on adaptive forms, then inevitably what we call dance improvisation has also become subject to content, form, and performing outcomes. In recent research-based teaching, second-year undergraduates and members of an Adult Training Centre for adults with learning difficulties worked together over a period of five weeks, for one day a week. The key concern of this community project was an investigation of improvisation as a way of working in dance. I have observed and participated in many improvisation workshops and often been left pondering whether these have been improvisations or some other kind of creative process. Any element external to the activity introduces developing devices. We should be aware of their impact on the honesty called for as the essence of improvisation, as this is impeded. In the case of the leader who is outside the activity providing verbal input, the didactic questioning, the intent, is no longer intrinsically part of the moment of movement; a structure is being imposed. The process then begins to be more aligned with shaping a product, creative devising instead of intrinsic improvisation. The potential development of the initial material is the creative process, and the aesthetic and cultural form that emerges is the performance.

The emphasis in the research-based community project, creative process via improvisation, was concerned with the dance experience as intrinsic to the creation, drawing upon the authentic, the natural, and the intuitive. In improvisation, the known is explored and reformed as an expression of the individual; through this activity "the experiential body of knowledge" (Blom and Chaplin 1988, 16), that is, other experiences, sensations, and memories, is developed. So intuitive responses are used to create, and as we take part in or observe, we see the formulation of the creation. We see virtual reality, not real feelings.

As mentioned earlier, the project between the Bretton students and the adults from the Adult Training Centre lasted for a period of five weeks. We worked as a whole group for five Tuesdays, for two sessions each Tuesday. Bretton students shared in leading the session, and we all participated and danced, with the freedom to move in and out when we chose. It is important here to emphasize that the Bretton students were involved in the project not only as the facilitators of the improvisational event, but also it was my intention that they were wholly involved with the improvisational challenge, with the associated development of their own movement range. Without exception all students struggled with freeing themselves from preconceptions, the tried and tested; each student was engaged in her or his own struggle for spontaneity. Initially they all carried into the sessions a notion of what it is to "dance well," and this, at least at first, informed their responses. The emphasis was on facilitation from without and within the group. The main external structuring device was music. A range of music was taken into the sessions, and the whole group listened and was invited to select which pieces they wanted to work with in each session.

In the project we were particularly interested in the movement range of the participants; we recognized as the project progressed that learning to function creatively in movement results from greater involvement, experience, and responsiveness. The opening session's major movement idea was exploration of shape. The response was positive in the initial session to coming together as a group. The groups ranged in size from groups of three to activity involving all participants. This group work became the pivotal dance idea, that is, movement, shape, and size; group shape and size; traveling; arriving; dissolving; and traveling on. Physical contact ranged from small, limited contact to larger contact and evolved into weight taking and giving. Movement range increased and responses became more free, more explorative, and more experimental.

Alma Hawkins (1982) describes two different types of expression: naive, simple, responsive movements and mature, organized, reflective movements. In improvisation these two types of expression do not occur in a logical sequence from the naive to the mature; although we can, I think, assume that the more experienced dance improviser will have mature, organized, reflective movements more often and over a longer duration. An example of the naive and simple, drawn from the Adult Training Centre and Bretton project was the response of a diffident man named Nestor. He had, in the first and second workshop, predominantly kept himself separated from partner work, small-group, and whole-group dance activity, placing himself on the edge of the space where he mostly stayed close to the wall or at the edges of the room. In week three he began to pay more attention and tentatively became involved in building small- and whole-group shapes, making physical contacts, touching other group members, and allowing them to touch and make contact with him. Also in this week, he contributed to the discussion around the music selection. In weeks four and five we could see his individual response to music rhythms; his greater and increasing involvement in the "wall" shape; and, in a quartet, development in his interaction with others.

Nestor's progress over the five weeks was in increased physical activity, dancing with others, and remaining inside the improvisation for longer periods of time. His movement range developed as well. The Bretton students' ongoing observation and analysis of Nestor's response showed that he was, throughout the five weeks, involved either as an observer or a participant. His breakthrough in week three could be linked to his involvement in choosing music; however, the experiences of week one and week two facilitated his growth and more recognizable involvement from week three onward. Nestor's process indicated a range of response from naive and simple to reflective and organized.

To support and further the development of movement range in relation to sculptural, shape work and the arrival, contact, and dissolve, the students leading the final workshop decided that traveling activities would be challenged. Members of the group had developed skills in their partner contact work, and the aim was to support and challenge this further. For example, at the first workshop, Richard performed his dance for the group, a robotic-type dance styled after Michael Jackson, with isolated hands and lower arms, angular gestures, and spatially symmetric moves limited to the front of his upper body. He also did some limited stepping, foot and ankle articulation, on and around the spot, all with emphasis on arrival. He performed his dance fully costumed in black shoes and trousers, white shirt, black hat, and dark glasses. By the fifth session, Richard had come far from this first dance, as shown in an improvised duet with Wendy, a Bretton student, in which a different movement range and spatial and rhythmic dynamic was observed.

After a tentative beginning, Wendy and Richard opened up to more experimentation and exploration. Richard became less concerned with holding and positioning, and he began to move more freely, spontaneously. He began to move with his whole body, along with more lower body, feet, and leg involvement. What also began to emerge was his capacity for making sense in the moment, shaping a duet, sharing fully in the interaction. In the fifth and for us the final session, we could see both process and product in improvisational terms in Richard and Wendy's partnership. What we could also see was the beginnings of a duet that had the potential to become subjected to content and form selection and structuring devices, taking the improvisation into the realm of the traditional aesthetic.

As the project progressed, I made the decision that because of our emphasis on process, our work would not culminate in a performance as understood in the traditional sense of a project's outcome. In deciding against performance I wondered if I was denying a finale, a sense of completion, of arrival. For example, in what we observed in Richard and Wendy's dance, could we decide that the performance element embraced by the intent and context is enough? I think not. Nor though, is the alternative wholly satisfactory. I feared that had the decision been made to work *toward* performance, the riches afforded by the process, the experimentation, the new-knowing would have been halted; Richard would have returned to his representation of Michael Jackson, denying a wealth of movement range, dynamics, interaction, and growth.

My own understanding of value, my own critical judgment of dance, has as its starting point the traditional aesthetic; herein abides my nemesis. What needs to be constantly tried and tested and reflected upon, is the outcome, the performance. The one arrived at for this particular project was an open workshop format at which some performance outcomes were revealed. Dance Art does not exist without performance, and so an audience was invited to our final afternoon. They were invited to participate in the opening of the workshop, and the music selected became paramount in informing the progression of the dance activities. Very little outside leading occurred, except for the music selection in the first 15 or 20 minutes; the project group took the movement initiative. The audience was then invited to watch the group perform the "wall" improvisation, some small-group sculptural shaping, departure, arrivals, and contact duets. These were not rehearsed in the traditional sense, although they were rehearsed in terms of the material being explored, experimented with, organized, and refined throughout the duration of the improvisational workshops. The performance climax began with the duos collecting the audience and encouraging them into participation; the dance, whole-group traveling in circles and lines and forming group shapes. The piece finished with all participants in physical contact in a large-group shape.

The final workshop then was the final experience of all that had gone before in the five-week duration of the project. The workshop involved risk, uncertainty, trying, and testing, as well as "intended performance" with the constituent elements revealed in content and form. Victor Turner describes experience as "living through" and "thinking back"; perhaps more relevant to the participants, performers, and spectators involved in the project is Turner's description of experience as also "willing or wishing forward," that is, "establishing goals and models for future experience in which, hopefully, the errors and perils of past experience will be avoided or eliminated" (Turner 1982, 18). As art, dance has aesthetic significance; that is, it has meaning of an aesthetic kind, one acquired by virtue of its symbolic content. The meanings are to be found in both content and form—the traditional approach—and, I suggest, in intent and context as revealed by content and form. An inclusive aesthetic for dance activities is found in the community context.

Are we prepared to continue to allow dance to be affected by a status quo imposed by notions of appropriate, adaptive behaviors? Some years ago I had the good fortune to be invited to watch the Kirov Ballet performing outdoors at the Wolf Trap in Virginia. The environment was magnificent— a warm evening, a delicious meal, the skills of the dancers excellent. Altogether the performance was a very enjoyable experience, but it was not, for me, a dance experience.

Critical Reflections

Questions raised in this chapter do no less than challenge the way we think about, explore, create, experience, and give value to dance. Of particular importance here is the issue of meaning, that is, how we make sense of the dance experience and what we choose to focus on, whether as critic, observer, creator, dancer, or educator. This question of meaning touches the core of all that we have explored in the preceding chapters. There is a poignance to the dominant European model for "Dance Art," with its predilection for individualism, abstraction, and separation that are so characteristic of North American and Western European cultures. These traits are embodied in ways that are contrary to lives of compassion and community. I am reminded of the story told by Clarissa Estes in *Women Who Run with the Wolves* (1992) of "La Mariposa, Butterfly Woman." In this story, many people come to see the dance of the "Butterfly Woman." They wait with anticipation for hours; some (not those who are a part of the native culture of the Butterfly Woman) wait with visions of a woman with ethereal litheness, of purity emanating from her limbs that barely touch the earth. Yet, astonishingly, she appears with an abundance of weight that seems to shake the earth, waking it to her presence. She moves in her own time, taking up an unusually large amount of space, with a robust sense of self, connection, and spirit. The dance of the Butterfly Woman, like the dance of community dance, is of another aesthetic. This aesthetic is a "fire of opposition" to the traditional image of dance. We are compelled to question whether we see community dance as an example of an aesthetic experience that is "other" or "lesser than," something that doesn't measure up to our standards, dance that is lacking in skills and training. Clearly different cultures (whether within our own "territories" or beyond) have different aesthetic codes. Whether we affirm or dismiss these ultimately defines what kind of ethical community we are.

Take a Moment to Reflect

1. What criteria are used to allocate funding for dance in the community?

2. Should we teach dance as a therapeutic activity?

3. What changes might occur if the aesthetic code valued improvisation as much as a planned, intentional product?

4. What role should the teacher have in community dance?

5. Should we value professional dance over and above the kind of community dance engaged in by Jabadao?

This chapter challenged the aesthetics of traditional dance. In the concluding chapter, Isabel Marques deconstructs the work of Rudolph Laban and Paulo Freire, and she examines how these dance theorists influenced her own thinking and work as a dance educator. This deconstruction helped her to understand how their theories contributed to as well as hindered her pedagogy for her Brazilian students.

REFERENCES

Blom, L.A., and L.T. Chaplin. 1988. *The Moment of Movement*. London: Dance Books Ltd.

———. 1989. *The Intimate Act of Choreography*. London: Dance Books Ltd.

Clarke, D.B. 1973. "The Concept of Community: A Re-Examination." *Sociological Review* 21 (3): 32-33.

Estes, C. 1992. "La Mariposa, Butterfly Woman." In *Women Who Run With the Wolves*. New York: Ballantine Books.

Glick, R. 1986. "Dance and Mime Amateurs: A National Evaluation." London: Arts Council of Great Britain.

Hawkins, A. 1982. "Modern Dance in Higher Education." *CORD Proceedings*: 63.

Heinemenn English Dictionary. 1979. London: Heinemenn.

Hoyle, S. 1994. "No Time to Dance: Interview with Sue Hoyle." Interview conducted by Richard Ings. *Animated—The National Community Dance Magazine* (Winter 1994).

Lomas, C. 1994. "Kindle the Fire" In *The 7th International Dance and the Child Conference Proceedings*. Sydney, Australia, July 12-20.

MacIver, R.M. 1924. *Community*. London: Macmillan.

McFee, G. 1992. *Understanding Dance*. London: Routledge.

Peppiatt, A., and K. Venner. 1993. *Community Dance—A Progress Report*: 8. London: Arts Council of Great Britain.

Thomson, C. 1989. "Community Dance: What Community . . . What Dance? Dance: A Cultural Phenomenon and Community Dance." *Proceedings of the Dance and the Child International Conference*, London, England. Paper presented at 4th International daCi Conference, "Young People Dancing," July 19-28. London, UK: daCi.

Turner, V. 1969. *The Ritual Process*. London: Routledge.

———. 1982. *From Ritual to Theatre*. New York: PAV Publications.

CHAPTER 8

DANCE EDUCATION IN/AND THE POSTMODERN

ISABEL A. MARQUES
University of Campinas

Reflecting on the separations of dancer and dance educator, dancing and teaching dance, the author deconstructs her own history in becoming a dance educator. Marques challenges these separations and assumptions as she traces the influences of her own "masters" in dance. She finds that those teachers who most influenced her found their grounding in the modernist tradition, which sought universal positions and concrete answers. Marques discusses how modernism leads to the devaluation of ethnic and cultural backgrounds and limits one's power of imagination. Situating herself in postmodern theory, the author suggests that reality can be spatially divided into three distinct spheres: the living, the perceived, and the imagined. The intersection of these spheres allows for a context-based dance education as opposed to one that is discipline based. Context-based education, Marques concludes, connects the dance body of knowledge with contemporary society.

In 1990, I started teaching dance education as a visiting teacher at the University of Campinas (UNICAMP), Brazil. I had just come back from a long stay abroad, where I had completed my MA in Dance. Upon returning I began to ask myself and my students questions about the value and meaning of dance education in a country such as Brazil. Brazil is supposedly a "dancing country," a geographical space and culture in which dance is very much a part of our everyday lives. With that in mind, I soon understood I had to go further and deeper into my questioning and thinking about the teaching of dance in Brazil. Why didn't dance education students dedicate their time to the subject of education as much as they engaged themselves in their dancing projects?[1] By the end of that year this question was partially answered: My students wanted to . . . dance! They were much more eager to learn and practice the art in which they had chosen to become professionals, that is, to choreograph, train their bodies, and express themselves through dance, than they were to discuss "the processes of children's learning," "the aims of dance education," "the role of a dance teacher," "the ways to plan a lesson," and so forth. I realized that I was expecting future artists not to focus on *their* art.

I began experimenting the next year with a new group of students. I was searching for ways to understand education through dancing—through the creative process in the classroom (see Marques 1994). This was a very rewarding experience. I began to see that not only were my students coming to classes more often but also that they were excited about becoming dance teachers. The dances we created to discuss and to understand the educational process made me start thinking critically[2] about my own role as a dance education teacher at a public university in Brazil and the role of dance teachers in society.

---

[1] At UNICAMP, dance education is a complementary option to the BA in Dance. Dance students who also wish to become teachers take six extra education subjects while earning their BA degrees. The dance curriculum therefore is the same for all students.

[2] I use here Terezinha Rios's (1995) definition and explanation of critical thought/philosophy as the attempt to see clearly (with rigor), deeply (radically), and broadly (with perspective, within a context) the issues and relationships among human beings and their social, cultural, and political reality.

My doctoral research developed from further questioning of these issues: Do we really have to choose between becoming a teacher or a dancer? Can't we teach and yet be active in the dance world? These questions arose when I realized that students who considered themselves "weaker dancers" were the ones who chose to take the dance education course. They were also the most frustrated ones; and frustrated people, in my opinion, could never be good teachers. Years later I asked myself why couldn't we be dancers and, while actually dancing, teach our students all they needed to know, to understand, and to deconstruct about dance and the world?[3]

I needed to consider other issues to understand and to deconstruct my own theoretical assumptions and practices as a dance education teacher, which arose while I was taking classes for my doctoral work at the University of São Paulo, Brazil. While there I studied the new conceptual framework for art in society (see, e.g., Benjamin 1985; Favaretto 1985, 1991; Huyssen 1990; Lebrun 1983) and the artistic/aesthetic transformations that had taken place in dance since the 1960s (e.g., Banes 1987, 1993a, 1993b, 1994; Copeland 1983; Kaye 1994; Ramsay 1991; VanDyke 1992). As I furthered my research, I started to think about the relationship between dance and dance education in Western postmodern[4] society.

I found that art had changed over the last few decades. In fact, the very concept of art had changed. After Duchamp and his *ready mades*, Warhol and his Campbell's soup cans, Cage and his 4'33", Paxton and his *Walking Pieces*, among so many others, we can no longer say that the Work of Art (the Art of Dance) exists, ready to be contemplated and admired from a distance by a selected audience. The work of art has lost its "aura"; it is no longer unique and eternal (Benjamin 1985). Since the experiences of the Judson Dance Theater, dance has also lost its aura, inaugurating a new period in which not only did dance reject modern dance styles, but they also questioned the assumptions which animated the whole idea of the modernist project (Kaye 1994).

It was intriguing to me to attempt to explain why this radical conceptual transformation in the dance world did not affect the concepts of dance education in the same way. I even started to question the term *dance education*: Is it a different kind of dance? Why is there "dance" on one end of the spectrum and "dance education," "creative dance," and "educational dance" on the other? Why do educators tend to separate and isolate themselves from the dance produced in society? Why do we keep alleging that the dance we teach at schools has nothing, or little, to do with educating future artists? These questions led me to understand one more reason why

---

[3] See Marques (1996) for further discussion on this topic.

[4] For a thorough consideration of the term *postmodern*, which has had multiple readings and interpretations in the educational literature, see Giroux (1996), Lyotard (1989), and Yeatman (1994).

my university students were not so interested in dance education: Dance education is typically isolated from our society and from art being made in the so-called "postmodern world."

DANCE MASTER-NARRATIVES

"There is no reason, only reasons."
—(Lyotard, as cited in Yeatman 1994, 106)

The distance between the concrete world of dance and the school classroom relates closely to what Jean-François Lyotard (1989, 1990, 1993) calls the "restoration process": Instead of rereading and rewriting modernity, there is now a movement toward restoring its principles of universality, progressive and linear development, transcendent reason, consensus, essentialism, foundationalism, and evolution. Lyotard explains that postmodernity is understood by some as a period of "come back," "flash back," or "feed back" (1993).

During my doctoral work I discussed Lyotard's theories to dance education. I discovered that many university-level dance courses and dance academies are returning to modern principles, premises, and philosophy. I consider "modern" to mean the philosophy and theory of knowledge conceived during the Enlightenment period of the 18th century and continuing today, which defend the supremacy of universal Reason and Truth (see also Habermas 1983; Harvey 1992; Huyssen 1990).

As an example, I cite the fact that many teachers and choreographers are again considering ballet to be the basis for dance training. Valuing ideal bodies, performance, virtuosity, technique, and spectacle has again become essential in the process of the dancer's education (Van-Dyke 1992). Likewise, creative dance is being taught and thought of as the basis for children's educational process (Marques 1996). Although considerably different in their forms, aesthetics, educational aims, and methodologies, I considered the possibility of both dance modalities being master-narratives, that is universal truths, about dance and education, as they encompass claims for universal, collective subjects. In ballet we learn about what it is to be a woman in this world in a "perfect" white, skinny, flexible, light body (Brady 1982; Gordon 1983; Vincent 1989; and others). Many dancers in companies and schools still pursue the quest for an ideal body in terms of shape, color, physical abilities, size, and weight. Like the notion of the universally "perfect" woman's body promoted in ballet, creative dance promotes the universal myth of the innocent, creative, natural, and spontaneous child (Marques 1996; Stinson 1993; Taylor [Shapiro] 1991).

I found out in this investigation that in different and yet similar ways both dance modalities embed modern concepts of time, space, and education. Time in contemporary society has come to mean the perpetuation of the present, simultaneity, and the predominance of speed and quickness (Calvino 1990; Jameson 1991; Marcondes Filho 1994). In many dance classrooms, however, time is often perceived and experienced as an endless linear progress of past, present, and future, determined by sequential and serial body training. Contemporary society exists in the domain of technology and virtual reality, where spatial barriers and limits are effaced. We live today a nomadic sedentarism in which spaces and places blend and tend to disappear (Marcondes Filho 1994; Trivinho 1995). In spite of this phenomenon, dance lessons often deal only in fixed boundaries, concrete places, and nonmultiple rooms and stages that constitute the eternal "sacred" dance space.

At last, working with dance educators, I saw that many envisioned establishing national standards for dance activities based on universal aims, curriculum, and evaluation. I understood that they were in fact seeking universally "good" contents for the "Menkind" in the dance educational process. In order to propose a different approach to dance education that would not formulate its own master-narratives, I had to understand and question critically the theories of Rudolf Laban and Paulo Freire, whom I have for so long considered to be my own "master" teachers.

REVISITING RUDOLF LABAN

"We are always reading our bodies according to various interpretative schemes."

—(Bordo 1993, 289)

Laban's theory taught me an approach to dance and dance education that enabled a more objective, clear, accurate, and attentive look at dance and students' movements. It brought me body references that enhanced and opened possibilities to create and teach dances as I had never experienced before. After almost 10 years working with Laban's theories and practices I realized I should reconsider some underlying assumptions present in his work, not to abandon and exclude his vast work from my classrooms but rather not to be naive[5] about what I was teaching and how I was dancing.

Laban's educational discourse is rooted in both modern dance and John Dewey's ideas on education (Hodgson and Preston-Dunlop 1990), which claim that every child has the right to express his or her inner human emotions through a process of self-autonomy, experience, imagination, and individuality. Laban supports the idea that any human being can move,

---

[5] I adopt Freire's (1982a) concepts of a naive consciousness in which one's conclusions are hasty, superficial, and fast; the past is often considered better than the present; the humble man or woman is underestimated; magical explanations are accepted; investigations are not thorough or deep; the individual believes that he or she knows everything and imposes his or her opinions; and reality is not considered to be mutable.

therefore dance, and explore his or her human "spontaneous and inborn" abilities. During his lifetime Laban tried to formulate a central theory that could encompass this universality of movement forms in order to master the contemporary aspects of dance and human experience (Hodgson and Preston-Dunlop 1990; Laban 1975, 1985).

I had some difficulties in applying Laban's theories to my work with young Brazilian dancers. I recalled that Laban, a white European man born at the end of the 19th century, imprinted into his movement analysis his own views of the body, movement, and dance that were inseparable from his personal, cultural, historical, and social condition. Understanding his work as a claim for universal movement, as Laban himself pledged at that time, meant to me resisting and opposing in many ways diversity, multiplicity, and a polyphonic educational process in which I believed. Above all, I concluded that Laban's belief for universal movement patterns did not meet or complete the needs of the multicultural Brazilian contemporary society.

In my doctoral work I came across contemporary discussions of the body that compelled me to look closer at Laban's educational proposals. Social scientists in the 1960s and 1970s challenged the notion of the body being only a biological entity and therefore "natural." To them the body was seen, perceived, and studied as a phenomenon socially and culturally constructed, interpreted, and idealized. In Shilling's words, "if we recognize that the body is unfinished at birth, all bodies are socially constructed to some degree" (Shilling 1993, 198).[6] Likewise, the mass media and communication nets are now in charge of inculcating and prescribing bodily ideals and images about race, gender, class, and culture that normalize and homogenize our bodies (Bordo 1993).

Another difficulty that I could not ignore was the presence of the new technologies in society that have also altered our own body perceptions, including the notion of a harmonic and integrated body so often present in Laban's work. Body surgery, lifts, liposuction, transplants, artificial limbs, and so on, "exacerbate [the] uncertainty about the body by threatening to collapse the boundaries which have traditionally existed between bodies, and between technology and the body" (Shilling 1993, 4). We no longer know and control our bodies, in as much as we are no longer certain about what is "natural" about the body. In fact, if financially supported, I can be "any" body I wish. Therefore, our creative potential in dance can never be totally "free, natural, and spontaneous" as Laban argues; it is always shaped by our experiences, relationships, education, and so on, as we go through our lives (Marques 1996).

It has become difficult for me to work with Laban's principles while also explicitly thinking about and working in my classrooms with the meanings

---

[6] I will not in this work argue in favor of any of these theories. See Shilling (1993) for a more complete account on this subject.

conveyed by movements and dances in Brazilian society, a country known to embrace multiple cultures, bodies, and dance heritages. I have realized that working with Laban's movement analysis for its own sake could be as fruitless as a dead tree. Therefore, I see Laban's work today not as the foundation for dance education but as a starting point for open-ended possibilities to explore and create dances in different contexts.

I have in my agenda numerous questions to discuss through the use of dance and intellectual exercises that examine gender, class, racial, and ethnic diversity. I encourage my students to observe and ask questions that relate to their own understanding of themselves and their bodily experiences in society. I ask them: "What do you want to convey in your dance by using these movements?" "Does it mean the same to everyone?" "How did you come to these movements?" "What do they mean to you?" "Where have you learned them?"

I often ask myself and my older students what it means to be and move strong, direct, and sudden in this world. What kind of attitude (verbal and bodily) does our society value the most? Why? Do you want to change it? Or also, what does it mean to use different body levels, spatial relationships, eye focus in different cultures? Brazilians usually occupy the high level and the wheel plane to demonstrate friendship when greeting, touching bodies with strong hugs and kisses, contact often considered to be invasive in other cultures. Whereas in India kneeling to greet the elderly is a sign of respect, in Brazil it is seen as a demonstration of submission. What does a man convey in Western society if his movement is soft, slow, and indirect? What kind of prejudices are related to that? What types of movements are expected of women in society? Why? What are the implications? Can we change it? Do we want to change it?

I understand that too much time spent talking can make a dance class lose energy and sometimes its main goal of working in, with, and through the flow and movement of the body. Nevertheless, I believe talking is also part of dance classes as it allows us to have a different perception of our bodily experiences, not to explain them, but to let us comprehend the dance more thoroughly. I am currently working and experimenting with how we can have all these questions and conversations as part of the body creative process in our dance classes, and I have had very successful results.

REVISITING PAULO FREIRE

I was first acquainted with Paulo Freire's ideas 15 years ago when I was an education student at the University of São Paulo. I was enchanted then by the possibility of studying a Brazilian theorist who had contributed in large scale to the development of a critical theory in the field of education throughout the world. Freire's ideas are based on an emancipatory, and perhaps modern, theoretical framework that might be said to oppose

© Ringo

postmodern thought. The emancipatory educational action has been criticized by some authors (e.g., Ellsworth 1992; Lather 1991) because of its limitations concerning the right to speak for the oppressed instead of letting them speak for themselves. Even so,

> Regardless of these potential dangers critical [education] research may be used as a powerful approach; it is capable of changing people's lives and society. With dimensions of self reflexivity to keep biases and agendas in check, it may help researchers [educators] to create pedagogical and socio-political change. (Green and Stinson n.d.)

Freire, along with other critical theorists, has illuminated a different view of education that has certainly changed the way traditional education has been conceptualized. By placing students' social and cultural reality at the core of curriculum planning,[7] Freire's works (1982a, 1982b, 1983a, 1983b, among others) call for a breakdown of the boundaries between school and

---

[7] See Marques (1995) for a discussion about Freire's ideas and concepts on education and their relationship to dance education.

society, advocating a close link between the two, and a pedagogy that questions this relationship. His concepts contributed to rethinking the role of the education process, which had been isolating students within the school walls either by their banking concepts[8] or by their exclusive emphasis on the psychological and developmental characteristics of the students. I propose that Freire works in favor of a "society-centered" education (see Marques 1996) that allows us to establish room for a constant dialogue among students, teachers, and their social reality in order to embrace transformative actions (Freire 1983a).

It has always made sense to me that Freire's work was extremely relevant in a society such as Brazil's: poor, socially and economically unbalanced, unjust, and multicultural. In fact, his ideas emerged from living, experiencing, and reflecting on Brazilian society and its inequalities (Freire 1992). Later on I figured out that Freire was not only talking about, to, and for the "third world" and the socially oppressed, but he was also talking about a larger concept of validating diversity and the possibility of establishing a critical dialogue between and with the different. Today I mainly understand his vast work as a call for liberation, for diversity, for local—and yet universal—knowledge that is crucial to the development of a more engaged education approach.

More than 20 years after Freire raised concerns for a more committed educational process, I realize that following his calling has also created a heavy burden for educators. In 1991 and 1992 I worked as a dance education specialist in a major education project in the city of São Paulo under Freire's leadership (see Marques 1995). Working directly with the urban social realities of São Paulo city was sometimes as petrifying as looking at the eyes of the great Medusa. On one hand, I often felt impotent as a teacher and university consultant to make resolutions and to fight against the unfair and aggressive urban reality, which went beyond my pedagogical work. Likewise, I understood why students who lived everyday in poverty and distress were not so often willing or wishing to revisit the same problems in their school work. On the other hand, working with Freirian concepts helped me learn that to ignore our social, cultural, and political reality could lead me to an endless route of escape, of fearing the future, and feeling absolutely powerless to do something about our social situation (Marques 1996).

Now that Freire is no longer with us, I hope that in my research and practice to develop his work in the fields of dance and education I can continue contributing toward his ideals of justice and liberation. I suggest that before this "great Medusa" that Western society has become, it would be interesting to

---

[8] According to Freire, the banking education "is the act of depositing, transferring, transmitting values and knowledge" (1983a, 67), without calling for action and reflection upon the world in order to transform it (see Freire 1982a, 1983a).

like Perseu, fly to another space. It does not mean we have to escape to a dream or to an irrational world. It means we should *change our points of view, we should consider the world under a different perspective, other means of knowledge and control* [italics added]. (Calvino 1990, 19)

I understand today that Freire's theory should encompass a larger concept of reality when I look at his work from a different point of view. No longer should we only be talking about the concrete reality of class and social conflicts, the mass movements for liberation and emancipation. It is time that we also consider the imaginary world and the technological society that have changed our concepts of subject, knowledge, and social relations (Marcondes Filho 1994; Vattimo 1991). We cannot separate the "real" and the "imaginary" worlds any more; they are part of contemporary communication and the media nets that belong to our daily lives (Baudrillard 1991; Trivinho 1994). I suggest therefore that we seek to understand and extend Freire's work to include valuing students' context in a broader sense—a concrete ("real") context (i.e., hunger, the homeless, urban violence, children's prostitution, etc.) that sustains multiple and circular relations with the huge imaginary ("virtual") contemporary reality (Marques 1996).

The intersection of these realities is part of our spatial practices in society and articulates three distinct spheres: the living space, or the material practices (e.g., money, work, transportation, market); the perceived space (e.g., social, psychological, mental representations); and the imagined space (e.g., attraction/repulsion, distance/desire, science fiction, mythologies, poetry) (Harvey 1992, 203). When we apply David Harvey's proposals to the field of dance education, the lived, perceived, and imagined space can be understood as constitutive interrelated elements of what I called in my doctoral work an amplified students' context or a proposal for a context-based dance education (Marques 1996).

CONTEXT-BASED DANCE EDUCATION (IN PROCESS)

There is no separation between dance and its mundane context.
—(Kaye 1994, 100)

Based on my Laban studies, I experimented and figured out that dance has specific contents to be developed to sense, feel, understand, and connect movement structures, the creative process, and the artistic/aesthetic purposes of dance. In working with a context-based dance education, my main interest is not to disassociate these contents from who/what/how we are in society. To me dance has become a way to look at the "great Medusa" as Perseu did: through the mirror. In other words, I see dancing effectively (i.e., with direction, intention, and purpose) as a possible way for us to understand, confront, and eventually transform our petrifying reality into a horse like Pegasus: light, vibrant, strong, and wonderful.

Coming from a Freirian background, I believe education is a political act and educators should be committed to developing a more conscious and critical relationship between the school work and society. For the past five years I have been working on a *context*-based dance education (as opposed to a *discipline*-based arts education), which aims at valuing and working with meaning in the vast net of relationships and communication of Brazilian society. Most of all, I am interested in what Fritjof Capra (1982) called the "eco-action"[9]: a systemic and multiple way of connecting knowledge; people; and their social, cultural, and political realities. According to Capra this action builds cooperation and relationships instead of separation and individualism.

I proposed in my doctoral work that the student's context—the intersection of lived, perceived, and imagined realities—should be both the starting point and the continuation of what is to be understood, constructed, unveiled, transformed, problematized, and deconstructed in a transformative educational action. A very important aspect of this educational proposal is choosing the context in which to work with the students. It calls for a receptive, attentive, giving, and flexible attitude by the teacher. As a qualitative researcher, the teacher should observe, dance, examine, and discuss the students' dances, attitudes, activities, dreams, and fantasies. The chosen context should not only be interesting and motivating, but it also should be meaningful and open to ongoing development of the dance contents themselves. Some examples of contexts that have already been developed in my teaching at the university are "violence," "bodily dialogue," "communication," "relationships," "being a woman (sister, student, mother, teacher, companion)," and "religion" (see Marques 1996, 1997).

In my own proposal of a context-based dance education there is no set serial or sequential preestablished national program or curriculum to be followed; the teacher is autonomous in connecting his or her dance knowledge and competence with the multiple voices, bodies, and cultures present in the dance classroom. More than listening to and respecting students' voices and bodies, this educational standpoint considers working with multiplicity as a value and not as something to be overcome, tolerated, or ignored. As a consequence, no aim is to be achieved in the unattainable future. Instead, structures and proposals are developed and transformed according to the relationship established in the classroom among the context, the teacher, the students, and the dance contents. By adopting this dance education proposal, I intend to work with the notion of valuing the present time, the limitless space, and the unforeseeable in postmodern

---

[9]As opposed to the "ego-action" (Capra 1982).

dance and society. I also intend to propose dance lessons that allow me to connect the dance body of knowledge (choreographic studies, improvisation, composition, repertory, dance history, etc.) to contemporary society.

I see a huge dance education net being woven with different textures, colors, sizes, structures, and complexities. This dance education net does not ignore human relationships; it heightens our capacity to find new and different ways to build a world where injustice has no place.

CONCLUSION

I now return to the issue of what made me develop and start working on *dance education in/and the postmodern*: my student teachers' lack of commitment to dance education. I realize my proposal to work toward a context-based dance education also implies a different attitude toward teaching dance. It is clear to me that, as it presupposes a close link between dance as art and society, context-based dance education also connects the actions of teaching and being an artist. First, planning a lesson based on the student's context is similar to choosing where to start one's choreographic process. The context is the theme, or starting point, that enables us to connect with and to communicate our art, and with people around us in society. *Both* require attention, sensitivity, respect for the other, critical understanding, competence, some degree of structure, and specific contents and movements to convey our ideas. Second, entering the classroom or the studio to teach or to create calls for flexibility, openness, and nonpreconceived programs or movements: The experience itself tells me and my body (my teaching) where to go next. At last, instead of copying, modeling, and reproducing bodies, minds, and social structures, the unpredictable outcomes generated by the contact and the communication process allow us to *create* and therefore to contribute toward society's transformation.

Critical Reflections

Where do we look for the historical/cultural underpinnings that can tell us about the separations of "dance" and "dance education," "dancer" and "dance educator"? These separations refer to how we define and give value to each within the dance world and the larger cultural world. There can be little doubt of the higher status that is accorded to performance over the teaching of dance. The American Dance Festival, arguably one of the key events in the dance calendar, allocates no significant time to the question of dance pedagogy. Of course these hierarchical divisions are connected to the distinction we make between "dancers" and "nondancers," between "dance as performance" and "dance as a way of knowing," and between choreography and pedagogy. As Marques showed us and is echoed in many of the authors' work in this book, these separations lead to a notion of art abstracted from the often grim realities of our everyday world, where art becomes an escape into a more precious and beautiful world. Following Freire, Isabel Marques calls for a form of dance that is integrated into the everyday struggles, concerns, and needs of human beings.

Take a Moment to Reflect

You may want to answer these questions for yourself and then have a group dialogue.

1. Should we continue to separate programs for dance performance and choreography from programs for dance education?
2. What are the master-narratives that underpin our notions of ballet, modern dance, creative dance, and folk or ethnic dance?
3. In what way do these master-narratives contain assumptions about the unchanging nature of being human, being a child, or being male or female?
4. How has dance been shaped by the scientific master-narrative?
5. What does it mean to say that dance education is a political act?

REFERENCES

Banes, S. 1987. *Terpsichore in Sneakers*. Middletown, CT: Wesleyan University Press.

———. 1993a. *Democracy's Body: Judson Dance Theater, 1962-1964*. Durham, NC: Duke University Press.

———. 1993b. *Greenwich Village 1963*. Durham, NC: Duke University Press.

———. 1994. *Writing Dancing in the Age of Postmodernism*. Middletown, CT: Wesleyan University Press.

Baudrillard, J. 1991. *Simulacro e Simulações* (Simulations). Lisbon: Relógio d'Água.

Benjamin, W. 1985. "A Obra de Arte na Era da Reprodutibilidade Técnica" (The Work of Art in the Era of Technological Reproduction). In *Walter Benjamin: Obras Escolhidas* (Chosen Works), Vol. 1. São Paulo: Brasiliense.

Bordo, S. 1993. *Unbearable Weight*. Berkeley, CA: University of California Press.

Brady, J. 1982. *The Unmaking of a Dancer: An Unconventional Life*. New York: Harper & Row.

Calvino, I. 1990. *Seis Propostas para o Próximo Milênio* (Six Memos for the Next Millennium). São Paulo: Cia. da Letras.

Capra, F. 1982. *O Ponto de Mutação* (The Turning Point). São Paulo: Cultrix.

Copeland, R. 1983. Postmodern Dance and the Repudiation of Primitivism. *Partisan Review* 1 (1): 101-121.

Ellsworth, E. 1992. "Why Doesn't It Feel Empowering? Working through the Repressive Myths of Critical Pedagogy." In *Feminisms and Critical Pedagogy*, C. Luke and J. Gore (eds.). New York: Routledge.

Favaretto, C. 1985. "Arte Contemporânea: Obra, Gesto e Acontecimento" (Contemporary Art: Work, Gesture, and Happening). In *Filosofia, Linguagem e Arte* (Philosophy, Language, and Art), C. Favaretto and A. Moreno (ed.). São Paulo: EDUC.

———. 1991. "Notas sobre Arte Contemporânea" (Notes on Contemporary Art). In *Comunicação, Educação e Arte na Cultura Infanto-Juvenil* (Communication, Education, and Art in Youth Culture), E. P. Soares (ed.). São Paulo: Loyola.

Freire, P. 1982a. *Ação Cultural para Liberdade* (Cultural Action for Freedom). Rio de Janeiro: Paz e Terra.

———. 1982b. *Educação e Mudança* (Education and Change). Rio de Janeiro: Paz e Terra.

———. 1983a. *Educação como Prática da Liberdade* (Education as a Practice of Freedom). Rio de Janeiro: Paz e Terra.

———. 1983b. *Pedagogia do Oprimido* (Pedagogy of the Oppressed). Rio de Janeiro: Paz e Terra.

———. 1992. *Pedagogia da Esperança* (Pedagogy of Hope). Rio de Janeiro: Paz e Terra.

Giroux, H. 1996. "Jovens, Diferença e Educação Pós-Moderna" (Young People, Difference, and Postmodern Education). In *Novas Perspectivas Críticas em Educação* (New Critical Perspectives in Education), M. Castells et al. (eds.). Porto Alegre, Brazil: Artes Médicas.

Gordon, S. 1983. *Off Balance: The Real World of Ballet*. New York: Pantheon Books.

Green, J., and S. Stinson. n.d. "Postpositivist Research in Dance." In *Researching Dance: Evolving Modes of Inquiry*, S.H. Fraleigh and P. Hanstein (eds.). Pittsburgh: University of Pittsburgh Press (forthcoming).

Habermas, J. 1983. Modernidade versus Pós-Modernidade (Modernity versus Postmodernity). *Arte em Revista* 7: 86-96.

Harvey, D. 1992. *Condição Pós-Moderna* (Postmodern Condition). São Paulo: Loyola.

Hodgson and Preston-Dunlop. 1990. *Rudolf Laban: An Introduction to his Work and Influence*. Plymouth, UK: Northcote House Publishers.

Huyssen, A. 1990. "Mapping the Postmodern." In *Feminism/Postmodernism*, L.J. Nicholson (ed.). New York: Routledge.

Jameson, F. 1991. *Postmodernism or the Cultural Logic of Late Capitalism*. London: Verso.

Kaye, N. 1994. *Postmodernism and Performance*. London: Macmillan.

Laban, R. 1975. *A Life for Dance*. London: Macdonald and Evans.

———. 1985. *Modern Educational Dance*. Plymouth, UK: Northcote House.

Lather, P. 1991. *Getting Smart: Feminist Research and Pedagogy with/in the Postmodern*. London: Routledge.

Lebrun, G. 1983. "A mutação da Obra de Arte" (The Mutation of the Art Work). In *Arte e Filosofia* (Art and Philosophy), E. Leão (ed.). Rio de Janeiro: Funarte.

Lyotard, J.F. 1989. *A Condição Pós-Moderna* (Postmodern Condition). Lisbon: Gradiva.

———. 1990. *O Inumano: Considerações Sobre o Tempo* (The Inhuman: Considerations About Time). Lisbon: Editorial Estampa.

———. 1993. *O Pós-Moderno Explicado às Crianças* (The Postmodern Explained to Children). Lisbon: Publicações Dom Quixote.

Marcondes Filho, C. 1994. *Sociedade Tecnológica* (The Technological Society). São Paulo: Scipione.

Marques, I. 1994. Didática para o Ensino de Dança: Do Imaginário ao Pedagógico (Didactics of Dance: From the Imaginary to the Pedagogical). *Educação e Sociedade* 15(48) (August): 261-270.

———. 1995. "A Partnership Towards Art in Education: Approaching a Relationship between Theory and Practice." *Impulse* 32 (April): 102-119.

———. 1996. A Dança no Contexto: Uma Proposta para a Educação Contemporânea (Context-Based Dance Education: A Contemporary Proposal). Phd dissertation, University of São Paulo, Brazil.

———. 1997. "Context-Based Dance Education." In *Proceedings of the 7th Dance and the Child International Conference*, E. Anttila (ed.). Kuopio, Finland: daCi.

Ramsay, M.H. 1991. *The Grand Union 1970-1976*. New York: Peter Lang.

Rios, T.A. 1995. *Ética e Competência* (Ethics and Competence). São Paulo: Cortez.

Shilling, C. 1993. *The Body and Social Theory*. London: Sage Publications.

Stinson, S. 1993. "Journey Toward a Feminist Pedagogy for Dance." *Women & Performance* 61: 131-146.

Taylor (Shapiro), S. 1991. "Dance in a Time of Social Crisis: Towards a Transformational View of Dance Education." In *Proceedings of the 5th Dance and the Child International Conference*, S. Stinson (ed.). Salt Lake City, UT: daCi.

Trivinho, E. 1994. "Tendências do Ano 2000" (The Year 2000 Tendencies). *Atrator Estranho*, 8 (December).

———. 1995. "Tempo Real e Espaço Virtual" (Real Time and Virtual Space). *Atrator Estranho*, 17 (October).

Van-Dyke, J. 1992. *Modern Dance in a Postmodern World*. Reston, VA.: National Dance Association and American Alliance for Health, Physical Education, Recreation, and Dance.

Vattimo, G. 1991. *A Sociedade Transparente* (The Transparent Society). Lisbon: Edições 70.

Vincent, L.M. 1989. *Competing with the Sylph: Dancers and the Pursuit of the Ideal Body*. Kansas City, MO: Andrews & McMeel.

Yeatman, A. 1994. *Postmodern Revisionings of the Political*. New York: Routledge.

CODA

Deconstructing the theories, histories, texts, and methodologies with which we approach dance education is part of a broader move in academia toward seeing things in their historical and cultural contexts and acknowledging that the world we know is always socially constituted. For example, asking in what historical context Laban created his philosophy and movement framework can help us understand what principles and assumptions shaped the way he viewed and valued dance. Laban lived in a time when modernism was still the generally unquestioned force for understanding the world and acting in it. The scientific Truth was still being pursued at all costs, and autonomy was the overarching moral principle along with a pronounced essentialist view of human nature. Reflections of both can be found in Laban's work. He sought to find the natural, or true authentic, movements of the individual. Yet, when analyzed today from a feminist standpoint, one might question his exemption of hair as a body part. (In contrast to this, Isabel Marques has discussed elsewhere that the movement of hair was one of the major components of a dance composition by one of her female students (Marques 1994).) Feminist criticism has shown how even scientific explorations contain their silences and selectivity.

The move to postmodernism has provided us with new avenues for change. Rejecting the notion of a single Truth and asserting the inescapable nature of situational or contextual knowledge, we are presented with the dilemma of *choosing* what our truth is. We have come to see that our notions of *what is true* and *what we value* are never easily separated. Dance, like all social texts, represents to us both reality and possibility. In the field of pedagogy, Paulo Freire's work has given us powerful insight into this dialectic of "what is" and "what might be." Within this dialectic Art and Arts Education are especially important in the space they provide for "playing with" ideology; ways of thinking and being—the ground on which we represent reality and envision human possibility. The choices given to the Arts and Artists by society are always ultimately political choices. Do we choose to create art that affirms or challenges the dominant culture? Do we teach our students to question or to follow? These are political decisions. In accepting the premise of dance education as a political act, we as dance educators have the power to help students see dance as a vehicle for self- and social transformation. We must encourage our students therefore to question, reflect upon, imagine, and cocreate both themselves and the world in which they live.

We live in a time of immense economic, political, and cultural change, where life is thrown into a constant spin of shifting signs and identities and where it seems that, as phrased by Morris Berman, "all that is solid melts into air" (Berman, 1982). In this context we are faced with new and profound questions concerning issues of human meaning and commitment. Dance educators such as those in this book are working on some of these difficult questions in their classrooms. Challenging the status quo in dance, however, comes out of the vision of possibility not the anger of cynical destruction. The hope is to encourage dialogue and reflection on the purpose of why we teach dance; whom does it serve; and, most important, how dance might enable us to live lives that are more humane and compassionate. Those of us who have made a commitment to dance do so with a gut knowledge that dance is a rich and powerful experience that can give meaning to our "embodied" lives by threading together self and society, intellect and intuition, passion and compassion. The authors in this book call for a vision of dance that might bring about a more just world, one that nurtures students to be more compassionate human beings. This notion of dance education is only now taking shape in our imaginations. My hope is that you too have heard the call.

REFERENCES

Berman, Marshall. 1982. *All That Is Solid Melts Into Air*. New York: Simon & Schuster.

Marques, Isabel. 1994. Paper orally presented at the Conference of Dance and the Child International, 12-20 July, at Macquarie University, Sydney, Australia.

ABOUT THE EDITOR
AND CONTRIBUTORS

© Steve Wilson

Sherry Shapiro is a professor and coordinator of the dance education program at Meredith College, Raleigh, North Carolina. She earned her EdD from the University of North Carolina at Greensboro in 1991. Her work integrates critical theory, philosophy of education, feminist and cultural studies, and dance, and emphasizes issues relevant to the lives of young women. She has pioneered the development of a critical pedagogy of the body and has written widely on the subject. Sherry Shapiro is the author of the forthcoming *Pedagogy and the Politics of the Body: A Critical Praxis* (Bergin & Garvey 1998).

Jan Bolwell is Head of the Department of Performing Arts Education at Wellington College of Education/Te Whānau O Ako Pai Ki Te Upoko O Te Ika, Wellington, New Zealand. In the past 10 years she has worked intensively in the area of biculturalism, exploring the relationship between Maori and Pakeha (European New Zealander) cultures within both theater and education. Currently she is engaged in a new bicultural dance theater production, "He Apakura Tohora/Sing Whale!," and is also writing a book entitled *Dance Theatre and Education in Aotearoa, New Zealand.*

Sylvie Fortin has been a professor in the dance department at the University of Quebec at Montreal since 1986. She received her PhD from Ohio State University. Her research focuses on research methodology, teaching analysis, and the contribution of somatics to dance training. A certified teacher of the Feldenkrais method, she also has studied other somatic methods including Alexander Technique, Body–Mind Centering, Ideokinesis, Kinetic Awareness, and Bartenieff Fundamentals. Her scholarly work has appeared in many professional journals, and she has presented her work at several dance education conferences in Canada as well as in the United States, Australia, and Europe.

Clyde Smith is a doctoral student in Cultural Studies at Ohio State University.

Christine M. Lomas is a Senior Lecturer in Dance and Theater and serves as Coordinator of the Dance Program at University College Bretton Hall of the University of Leeds, West Yorkshire, England. Areas of special interest include philosophical issues in dance theater and community dance contexts. Since 1984 she has been working with Jabadao, a community-based dance company that prioritizes people with special needs, such as people with disabilities and the elderly.

Isabel A. Marques is a lecturer on the Faculty of Education of the University of Campinas (UNICAMP), Brazil, where she teaches undergraduate and graduate courses in dance and dance teacher preparation. She received her MA in Dance Studies from the Laban Center for Movement and Dance and her EdD from the University of São Paulo, Brazil. From 1991 to 1992 she was in charge of developing a dance education program curriculum for São Paulo City public schools under the supervision of Paulo Freire. In 1993 she was awarded the Vitae Foundation Scholarship for the Arts to conduct research and teach dance to underprivileged teenage students in the city of São Paulo. Dr. Marques is currently the Brazilian National Representative of Dance and the Child International (daCi-UNESCO). For the past five years her research has centered on the development of a context-based dance education that encompasses critical and postmodern issues.

Sondra Stamey Sluder is a dance educator and choreographer in Ashville, North Carolina. She works with a range of people from disadvantaged youth to the elderly who are seeking self-renewal and spiritual awareness. Focusing on dance as a narrative process, she hopes to instill in her students values of human dignity and social justice.

Sue W. Stinson is Professor of Dance at the University of North Carolina at Greensboro, where she serves as Department Head and teaches undergraduate courses in teacher preparation and graduate courses in research and curriculum in dance. Her scholarly work has been published in a number of journals, including *Dance Research Journal; Design for Arts in Education; Drama/Dance; Educational Theory; Impluse: The International Journal of Dance Science, Medicine, and Education; Journal of Physical Education, Recreation and Dance; Journal of Curriculum Theorizing; Women in Performance;* and *Journal of Curriculum and Supervision.* Her book on dance for young children, *Dance for Young Children,* was published in the United States in 1988 and rereleased in a Japanese translation in 1994. She was selected as the 1994 Scholar by the National Dance Association.

INDEX